Iron and Blood

Iron and Blood

Civil Wars in Sixteenth-Century France

HENRY HELLER

McGill-Queen's University Press
Montreal & Kingston • London • Buffalo

©McGill-Queen's University Press 1991
ISBN 0-7735-0816-3

Legal deposit first quarter 1991
Bibliothèque nationale du Québec

Printed in Canada on acid-free paper

This book has been published with the help of a grant
from the Social Science Federation of Canada, using
funds provided by the Social Sciences and Humanities
Research Council of Canada.

Canadian Cataloguing in Publication Data

Heller, Henry, 1938–
    Iron and Blood
    Includes bibliographical references.
    ISBN 0-7735-0816-3

    1. France – History – 16th century.
    2. Revolutions – France – History – 16th century.
    I. Title.

DCIII.H34 1991   944'.028   C90-090515-8

Typeset in 10 on 12 Janson
by Nancy Poirier Typesetting Limited, Ottawa

To Joanne

And accursed our corroded age
Age of iron all stained by murder
Wholly disordered in morals and life
An age neither of iron or bronze
But one of alluvial slime ...

Pierre de Ronsard,
Les élémens ennemis de l'Hydre (1569)

They have found the means not long since to return
to the age of gold which they maintain in their
houses with all their strength while leaving the age
of iron for the poor who day and night have
great difficulty in collecting the gold and silver
which they must supply to these fat cats and gross
pleasure seekers ...

Pierre Viret,
Le Monde à l'Empire et le Monde Demoniacle,
fait par dialogues
(Geneva, 1580)

Contents

Preface

Traditionally the history of sixteenth-century France has been seen as divided between a luminous Renaissance marking the first half of the century and a largely dark and inexplicable civil war overshadowing the second half. While doing research for *The Conquest of Poverty*, it occurred to me that I had hold of a key that could unite these two eras in a historically significant way. In that work I traced the roots of the civil wars to the social and economic discontent that was festering below the brilliant surface of the Renaissance monarchy of Francis I and Henri II. It seemed to me that this perspective offered the possibility of logically connecting the rising level of social conflict of the first part of the century to the religious and political chaos of the civil wars. In particular, such a viewpoint would make it possible to link the popular protest of the earlier decades of the century with the Calvinist Revolt, the ensuing Catholic League and the revolts of the 1590s. Thus, even before completing my research on *The Conquest of Poverty*, I began to collect materials toward the present volume.

But the present work has a broader purpose than merely offering a unified perspective on the sixteenth century. The larger aim is to connect the social movements of the sixteenth century with those that both preceded and followed it. As Jacques Solé has recently pointed out: "the Revolution in this sense and realm in no way marks a rupture ... for popular movements as a form of social contestation of public order and its political and cultural norms constitutes one of the laws of the evolution of France since at least the sixteenth century."[1] In other words, the social movements of the sixteenth century are a distant harbinger of the revolution of 1789. Indeed, one could take the roots of the 1789 revolution a step further backward to find its still more remote antecedents in the *Jacquerie* of the fourteenth century.[2] But from my point of view, the immediate task is to link up the research that has been done on late medieval revolts with that that has been done on early modern popular revolts through a study of those of the sixteenth century.

For assistance in researching this book I would like to thank the librarians of the *Bibliothèque Nationale* and the University of Manitoba. I owe a special debt of gratitude in preparing this manuscript to Joanne Inglis, Carol Adam, and Brenda Missen.

Glossary

Bailli   The principal judicial and administrative officer of the king at the local level normally drawn from the old nobility. Within a seigneurie *bailli* denoted a steward or bailiff.

Bailliage   Territorial jurisdiction of a *bailli* equivalent to a county.

Cahiers des doléances   Lists of complaints or grievances drawn up by each order at the local level, consolidated within each bailliage, and transmitted by deputies to provincial or national estates. In the estates, one cahier was drawn up by each order represented.

Cens   Money dues more important as proof of a tenant's obligation to the seigneur than as a contribution to segneurial revenue.

Cour des aides   A sovereign court that primarily heard appeals from taxpayers. Also concerned with the registration of letters of nobility.

Croquants   Literally those who have been cracked, i.e., derisive term applied to the rebellious peasants of Guyenne in 1594–5.

Crues   Direct taxes in addition to the *taille* and *taillon*.

Échevinage   Town council made up of elected *échevins* or aldermen.

Élus   The officials of a local fiscal administrative court known as an *élection*.

Gabelle   The salt tax.

Juge Mage   Municipal judge appointed by the king.

Livre tournois   The most common money of account in sixteenth-century France.

Manouvrier   Rural worker.

Métayage   Sharecropping. *Métairies* replaced the old communal type of peasant cultivation in much of France in the late sixteenth century.

Plat Pays   The countryside, including the small towns.

Politique   Those of moderate Catholic opinion who supported the monarchy, as opposed to Catholic extremists or Calvinists.

Présidiaux   The so-called *présidial* courts established in 1552 between the provincial parlements and the courts of the *bailliage*.

Prévots Officers of so-called *prévotés* or courts inferior to that of the *bailliage*. The *prévots des marechaux* were empowered to enforce the peace especially on the roads and highways.

Rebeine popular insurrections at Lyons, especially the insurrection of 1529.

Sénéchal The equivalent of a *bailli* in the south of France.

Sénéchaussée Jurisdiction in the south of France equivalent to a *bailliage*.

Taille The poll tax, the most onerous direct tax levied on the person of the unprivileged in the north and *Dauphiné* (*taille personelle*) and on non-noble land (*taille réelle*) in the south. The *taillon* was an addition to the *taille* introduced by Henri II.

Viguerie The equivalent of the *prévôté* in the south of France.

Iron and Blood

Introduction

It was Fernand Braudel who first described the sixteenth as the "beautiful century." Compared to the crisis of the late middle ages that preceded it and the depression of the seventeenth century that followed it, the sixteenth century certainly has the appearance of beauty. Furthermore, Braudel and the historians who followed in his footsteps considered the sixteenth not only as a beautiful but also as a "long" century. The sixteenth century, according to this viewpoint, saw a European-wide economic and demographic expansion that actually began in the mid-fifteenth century and continued into the opening decades of the seventeenth.

How does the Kingdom of France fit into this panorama? At first glance, it occupies an apparently prominent position. Following the expulsion of the English from French soil, a prolonged epoch of internal peace and economic growth marked the latter half of the fifteenth and the first half of the sixteenth century. The external signs of renewal are there in abundance. The monarchy was powerful as never before, its authority bolstered by an impressive and swelling bureaucracy, a reliable system of taxation, and an ecclesiastic order that was becoming more and more pliable and dependent. The new power of the Valois kings was reflected through the construction of a magnificent series of châteaux and palaces, the creation of a splendid court composed of thousands of nobles and their servants, and an unprecedented patronage of arts and letters. Endowed with a hitherto unseen degree of financial and military power, the Valois kings of the sixteenth century dreamed recurrently of conquering Italy, the richest prize in Europe. Failing that, they sought to extend the boundaries of their state at the expense of their neighbours to the north and east.

Underpinning the extravagance of the French Renaissance monarchy was the support and loyalty of the towns and, above all, of their leading citizens. This elite of wealthy merchants, office holders, and patricians provided the money and expertise that formed the sinews of the new monarchy. In control of the economic and political life of the towns and, both directly and indirectly, the administration of the countryside, this urban elite ensured an uninterrupted flow of taxes to satisfy the appetite of the expansive territorial monarchy. The members of this elite took their turn as municipal officers and councillors or served the monarchy as tax collectors, crown attorneys, barristers, magistrates, administrators, professors, cathedral canons, secretaries, and masters of request. It was members of this upper stratum of the commons who most easily acquired or usurped titles of nobility, acquired fiefs and seigneuries, and sooner or later obtained the substance of nobility itself. It was they who created the culture of humanism and later of evangelical reform.

On the one hand, the upper middle class was on the rise, but on the other hand, the nobility apparently did not decline. It emerged from the Hundred Years War with its power intact, indeed, enhanced. Just as the bourgeoisie strengthened itself by means of the state so, too, the nobility used the state to reinforce itself. Individual nobles certainly lost some of their local power, but the key institutions of the new territorial state – the army and the Church – were shaped in the image of the nobility. It was from the ranks of the nobility that the principal officers of the state – bishops, abbots, governors, lieutenants, seneschals, bailiffs, captains, and ambassadors – were chosen.[1]

To be assured that this interpretation of the French state is not merely a case of hindsight we have only to turn to the views of contemporaries. In 1558, the sieur de La Buissière, Jean du Tillet published a treatise entitled *Advertissement à la noblesse tant du parti du roy, que de rebelles*.[2] In this work, Du Tillet admonished those nobles who, in choosing to become Protestants, espoused a religion opposed to that of the king. According to Du Tillet, this was treason,

when one considers that the whole substance and opulence of the Kingdom, the whole of its grandeur and commodities find their way to the nobility, that the whole of the revenues of the King are such that the maintenance and payment of the great establishments and pensions of the officers of the Crown, the marshalls, governors, captains, lieutenants and men-at-arms, that all benefices of any value are given to their relatives. In brief, if investigation of the means of the Prince and the people were made one would find that the surplus and revenue of both are distributed and divided between them (the nobility).[3]

In DuTillet's view, not only did the nobility occupy the most powerful positions in the state, but the state's very mechanisms were designed to ensure income to the nobles in the form of a centralized system of rent.

It was the monarchy that made possible for the nobles the great adventure of the Italian Wars. Moreover, the luster of this ruling class was by no means diminished by the end of these wars. The Wars of Religion that followed, fratricidal though they may have been, ensured that the nobility remained at the forefront of military and political events. The Wars of Religion closed with the aristocracy more than ever in the ascendant. The monarchy of Henri IV, like that of Charles VII a century and a half earlier, was designed above all to safeguard the social and political pre-eminence of the aristocracy.

The sixteenth century witnessed the rise of many notables and bourgeoisie into the nobility.[4] While some noblemen regarded this penetration of their ranks as a threat,[5] this was nothing new; it had been going on for centuries. In retrospect, it is plain that the nobility were strengthened rather than weakened by the new blood being added to their ranks.[6] These newcomers sought mainly to obliterate the memory of their humble origin and to gain acceptance from established noble families as quickly as possible.

Economic trends likewise favoured the nobility. The sixteenth century was a period of increasing population, stagnant productivity, and rising rents, which could only favour landlords in the long run. Undoubtedly certain nobles became impoverished as a result of imprudent expenditure. Indeed, the outbreak and prolongation of the religious wars were attributed even then, as they are now, to a crisis of noble incomes.[7] On the other hand, the opportunities for pillaging, extortion, rack-renting, and expropriation during these wars had the overall effect of strengthening the position of the nobles.[8]

Mention of the religious wars brings us back to our point of departure: "the beautiful sixteenth century." If it was beautiful, the sixteenth century in France also terminated more quickly than anywhere else in Europe. The outbreak of the Wars of Religion abruptly tarnished the brilliant face of French Renaissance society. Indeed, the outbreak of the wars in mid-century must lead us to challenge the concept of a beautiful century altogether. A beautiful sixteenth century, to be sure. But beautiful for whom? Beautiful for the monarchy, for courtiers, nobles, notables, and great merchants without question. Beautiful in the sense of art, scholarship, display, and magnificence undoubtedly. Beautiful, too, perhaps in the sense of "beaux jours," that is, apparently unassailable elite power and popular acquiescence. But not beautiful for the commons.

It is evident that it was the commons who had to pay the price of enlarged powers of royal taxation, noble pretention, and bourgeois ambition. Craftsmen and lesser merchants appear to have shared in the general prosperity of the kingdom until about 1500 or even 1520. Population, trade and manufacture, agricultural output all made gains. But even before the 1520s, the failure to find new sources of productivity and the growing load of rent, taxes and merchant exploitation began to weigh on the commoners. Modern scholars have now established that from the 1520s onward the majority of craftsmen, peasants, and workers struggled and ultimately floundered under the burden of taxation, rising rents, and the economic monopolies of the urban rich. Indeed, as the century moved on, the splendours of Renaissance culture – courtly extravagance and royal patronage, *hôtels* in town and *châteaux* in the country, investment in arts and letters – seem to be concommitant with this growing impoverishment of the commoners. So tenuous and fragile was the economic renewal among the commoners during this period that one student of the period has been led to question the concept of a Renaissance altogether. For Guy Bois, the so-called Renaissance is an interlude of uncertain light between two periods of darkness. The sixteenth century proper is an age of little growth and high prices at best. As for the peasantry, their golden age came to an end in 1500 rather than in 1550.[9] At an international colloquium held at Tours in 1983, Philippe Contamine likewise painted the sixteenth century in sombre tones. For Contamine, the economic zenith of the peasant and artisan is likewise situated at the end of the fifteenth and beginning of the sixteenth century.[10]

Of popular protest little or nothing has been recorded. Certainly the first half of the sixteenth century seems far removed from the *jacqueries* and urban rebellions of the fourteenth century or the great cycle of insurrections that mark the seventeenth century. And yet, one day in the 1540s, Jean de Vasses, seigneur de la Richardière, payed Clermont-Ferrand a visit to purchase some silk. But the merchant with whom he dealt, Come Laboureur, complained that de Vasses had paid in debased coin. A fight broke out, during which Laboureur's wife and son stole de Vasses's sword and dagger. Aided by several passers-by, the family beat up de Vasses and threw him out of their shop.

A few days later de Vasses returned to Clermont-Ferrand accompanied by three or four of his friends. His initial plan of attack was simple: he intended to stab Come Laboureur. His noble companions more prudently counselled him to take a stick to Laboureur, who, after all, was a commoner. When the group entered the shop, however, they found not Laboureur but his wife behind the counter. Not being able to confront the merchant they proceeded to abuse his wife with a flood of insults.

Having spent their anger in this way, De Vasses and his companions returned to their lodgings at the Inn of the Crescent. In the midst of their dinner, the inn-keeper suddenly rushed up to their table. "Messieurs," he exclaimed, "I don't know what you have done in the city but it must have been something, for the whole town has risen and is headed this way. I hear the tocsin ringing, messieurs, so I advise you to save yourselves." De Vasses and his friends fled into the street where they were immediately confronted by the whole community armed with pistols and clubs. Miraculously they were able to fight their way on foot to the nearby town gate before it could be closed, escaping with their lives while abandoning their horses and livery.[11]

The simplicity of this drama strikes at the imagination. It is a good story worth the retelling – insolent nobility confounded by an aroused and hostile bourgeoisie. But it is more than a colourful tale. It is one of hundreds of such incidents that reflected opposition between commoners and nobles in the first part of the sixteenth century all over France.[12] It is simply not the case that the commons bowed their heads in the face of noble pretension, fiscal oppression, social domination, and economic exploitation. To be sure, historians have recognized the existence of popular protests at the end of the sixteenth century. The revolts of the *Gautiers*, *Bonnet-Rouges*, and *Tard-Avisés* have been recognized as a belated and desperate reaction to the Wars of Religion. As such, these upheavals are seen – and properly so – as a prelude to the profound and widespread unrest of the following century.

What must be underlined is that these peasant uprisings at the end of the sixteenth century were part of a larger pattern of conflict that marked the whole of the century – a pattern that has largely eluded historians. It is not just a question of acknowledging the existence of a prolonged if at first largely subterranean history of popular resistance; rather it is a matter of recognizing a history of ongoing, bitter, and complicated social conflict in which more often than not the upper class took the initiative. Viewed in this perspective, the magnificence of the court, the martial exploits of the nobility and the religious conflicts of the age take on a distinctly self-serving character. Rather than dealing with just a record of popular protest we are dealing with a history of both resistance and domination.

The study of conflicts of class in the *Ancien Regime* began with the work of Boris Porchnev on the revolts of the seventeenth century.[13] His research has been enlarged upon in a distinctive way by Roland Mousnier and his students.[14] At the same time, interest in the history of late medieval urban and peasant revolts has grown.[15] Finally, the upheavals of the eighteenth century have attracted an increasing amount of attention.[16] The present work on the sixteenth century is among other things, designed, to bridge the gap between the history of the revolts of the late middle ages and those of the last two centuries of the *Ancien Regime*.

In embarking on this enterprise, I recognize the importance of distinguishing the theoretical basis of my approach from that of Mousnier.[17] Mousnier argues that the society of the *Ancien Regime* was a society of orders organized on the basis of a hierarchy of clergy, nobility, and commoners. In this society, the place of each group was recognized by the other groups as necessary to the proper functioning of the community as a whole. Commoners accepted this order of things as much as the privileged. In contrast to a society of classes characteristic of modern history, the society of the *Ancien Regime* was not split horizontally into economically opposed classes. Rather it was vertically integrated, the orders differentiated according to status, but mutually dependent on one another. Of course conflict existed within the system but not such as to put the latter itself into question. Popular revolts occurred; indeed, it is important to study them. But they themselves were safety valves, helping the system find a new equilibrium, rather in the way that present-day labour strikes supposedly function in capitalist society. Indeed, according to Mousnier, far from being class conflicts between peasant and aristocrat, the revolts of the seventeenth century were most often directed against the growing power and oppressiveness of the absolutist state; in fact the nobility often assumed the leading role in these revolts.

Although the notion of French society as a society of orders was current in the *Ancien Regime*, it should be pointed out that it was a conception most often articulated by magistrates, clergymen, and noblemen closely linked to the monarchy. Mousnier assumes that this ideology of domination was more or less accepted by peasants, craftsmen, and merchants. But in the absence of proof, this cannot be assumed to have been the case. The confrontation of de Vasses and Laboureur would seem to invite a certain skepticism in assuming that the lower orders shared the social and political outlook of their betters.[18]

Contemporaries themselves were certainly not as naive as Mousnier appears to be. For example, Claude de Seyssel's *La Monarchie de la France* (1513), a work cited by Mousnier himself, gives a much more sophisticated view.[19] Seyssel's treatise is at one and the same time a description of and an apology on behalf of the new monarchy under the Valois.

Seyssel, the jurist and ecclesiastic, was convinced that the hierarchy of orders was the proper structure of society.[20] But, unlike Roland Mousnier, he was under no illusion that the commoners shared this point of view or accepted their inferior status; on the contrary, he warned that, given the means, the commoners would rebel against the nobility and "le peuple gras," overwhelming them, as had happened at various times in different parts of the kingdom and in other kingdoms.[21] He cautioned that the commoners ought not to be given too much liberty or allowed to become too wealthy or too experienced in the bearing of arms, because of their multitude and their natural desire to attain the highest reaches of society.

Marxists have been accused by Mousnier among others of imposing anachronistic concepts on the past. It is because Mousnier believed that the concept of class was an anachronism when applied to the *Ancien Regime* that he substituted the idea of a society of orders in its place. However, even this idea is anachronistic. As Armand Arriaza has demonstrated, Mousnier's society of orders is based on a reading back of contemporary American structural-functional sociology onto seventeenth-century French society, and a particularly rigid and regressive interpretation of this modern social theory at that.[22]

The test of a concept for the historian ought to be not its origin in time but the degree to which it helps one to understand a particular epoch of the past. The *Ancien Regime* should be considered as much a society of classes as is our own. Ninety per cent of the population lived in the countryside, and the fundamental antagonism in this society lay between the mass of peasant producers who worked the land and the landlords who took away part of the surplus from them in the form of rent. The dominance of the aristocracy over the rest of society was based on the maintenance of this relationship.

The notion of a society of orders – elaborated on by ecclesiastics, lawyers, and magistrates – rested on this aristocratic power and simultaneously helped keep it in place. When he discusses ideology, Mousnier explains the hegemony of the aristocracy not as arising from their control over land and people but rather as flowing somehow from the fact that some or all of the people had the notion of a society of orders in their minds. This is to put the cart before the horse. The concept of a society of orders had meaning to sixteenth century elites because of aristocratic domination over land and people. The idea of a society of orders both reflected and confirmed that domination.

Ideology is not something that is merely accepted from one age to the next. It has to be restated and reaffirmed in each generation in order to maintain itself. Moreover, a ruling ideology has to do battle with those who, tacitly or explicitly, by word or by deed, seek to modify, transform, or undermine it. Ideology is as much a part of class struggle as is the level of rent or incidence of taxation. It ought to be considered not as inert and static but as a weapon used to affirm one form of social order while excluding the crystallization of alternative and rival conceptions of social organization.

It can be said, then, that French society in the sixteenth century was dominated by a society of orders. But this society of orders included only the clergy, nobility, and urban bourgeoisie. It excluded the urban craftsmen and poor, as well as the peasantry and rural bourgeoisie. The fundamental conflict of the period was thus between the excluded majority and the existing society of orders.

This study will try to document the degree to which the commoners of the sixteenth century opposed themselves both to the wealthy merchants and notables who controlled the towns and to the nobles who were masters of the land. Often this hostility was visceral and barely articulate, expressing itself through organization and language that were pitifully inadequate. At other points, lacking the political and social strength to challenge the existing hierarchy of orders, commoners sought at least to gain some recognition within it. Such behaviour may be taken as evidence of political and social weakness, but it signifies realism not acquiescence. Moreover, the society of orders itself came under attack on both religious and political grounds as the century wore on.

Having argued for an approach to early modern social conflict based on the concept of class, I must acknowledge the complexity of such antagonism. It is certainly true that horizontal social conflict was initially based on the antagonism between lords and peasant. But this antagonism was made more complicated by increasing social differentiation in the countryside. The struggle over rent between peasant and lord was coupled with an incipient conflict over profit and wages between agricultural entrepreneurs and labourers. Conflicts might take the form of a division between town and countryside in which the peasants and small-town bourgeoisie would find themselves at loggerheads with the patricians and great merchants of a regional metropolis. Antagonism was likewise endemic between these urban elites, and the plebians of the towns. Through a judicious combination of political power, taxation, and monopoly, the urban elites extracted a surplus from urban as well as rural producers. Urban notables were in some ways the lesser partners of the aristocracy in ruling over sixteenth-century France. But at times even the interests of these two ruling groups came into conflict. Rent conflicted with profit. Power over land collided with power in the market. Rule by the sword found itself opposed by the rule of ideas and the law. Conspicuous consumption as an ideal clashed with that of capitalist accumulation.

In short, while the main axis of class conflict seems clear, it was inflected by other antagonisms of great complexity that must be borne in mind. Moreover, there were factors operating in sixteenth-century French society that clearly mitigated against class conflict. The persistence of relationships of personal dependency and clientage inhibited the development of horizontal social conflicts. In addition, the religious divisions of the period tended to reinforce ties between widely different social strata. The threat of external invasion or the prospect of foreign wars likewise strengthened vertical alliances in town and countryside. In part born as a way of moderating the conflict between the aristocracy and commoners, the early modern state, continued to play that role for much of the sixteenth century. However, the intrusion of the state sometimes caused the inhabitants of certain provinces and regions to regard the state rather than the local elites as their principal enemy. All of these factors tended to blunt or inhibit the social polarization of the population.

History is complex, and the history of the sixteenth century – a century divided between feudalism and capitalism and torn apart by religious conflict – is supremely so. Serious study of the society of the French sixteenth century must be based on an awareness of this complexity. The starting point of the present study lies in earlier archival research into the history of French Protestantism. I have extended these investigations through work in the *Archives Nationales* as well as in the archives of the *Haute-Loire*, *Ardèche*, and the *Gard*. Likewise I have exploited the published journals and treatises of the period. I have made extensive use of the huge monographic literature on French urban history, as reflected in the bibliography of Philippe Dollinger and Philippe Wolff,[23] as well as of the up-to-date bibliography of French history in the *Bibliothèque Nationale*.

A great deal of the monographic literature in these bibliographies is not up to the standard of the present time, from my point of view devoting far too little attention to the history of class conflict. Many of the archivists and historians who wrote local histories in the nineteenth and early twentieth centuries ignored or suppressed the existence of such conflicts as an embarrassment. On the other hand, given the enormous quantity of this monographic material, enough has been recorded to be able to reconstruct a fair picture of these struggles. I have not been able to take into account every instance of class conflict or popular contestation that marked the sixteenth century; however, I believe I have uncovered enough to provide a sense of the nature and extent of such antagonism.

CHAPTER ONE

The Golden Age Turns to Iron: The Small Producers' Revolt

... the third estate of labour ...
being the one most charged

the commons of Velay

The great watershed in sixteenth-century French history was the outbreak of the religious wars at the beginning of the 1560s. This upheaval was caused by a variety of factors, including religious hostility, inter-elite conflict, and fiscal, economic, and dynastic crisis. However, the outbreak of these wars had certain characteristics of a class conflict. The Calvinist party launched attacks against the Church, one of the pillars of the monarchic and aristocratic order. In many towns the Catholic notables came under fire, and in certain places the nobility itself was assaulted. These attacks occurred because the base of Calvinist strength lay among craftsmen and lesser merchants who were vehemently hostile to these elites. Moreover, the ideology of Calvinism called for the annihilation of the medieval Church and the establishment of a new religious order in which the middle class would definitely have established its cultural hegemony.

Traditional narratives of the French Calvinist revolt begin by examining its roots in the intellectual and personal experience of its leader. Such accounts then carry on with the history of the clandestine dissemination of heretical books and pamphlets, the growth of persecutions, which is taken as a measure of Calvinism's increasing appeal, the organization of evangelical sympathizers into Calvinist churches, and finally the accumulation of signs of open Calvinist resistance. The revolts of the 1560s that followed are then seen as the climax of this process.

On this occasion, however, I propose an entirely different approach. The Calvinist revolt was a religious outburst but one sustained by strong currents of popular economic and social discontent. Accordingly, I will seek the roots of this violent upheaval in sixty years of accumulating social unrest. Admittedly, popular social tumults and religious dissent were quite different phenomena, which for many years pursued quite separate trajectories. At a certain moment, however, the paths of religious dissidence and popular protest crossed one another. At a given stage Calvinism turned itself into a mass movement by mobilizing and channeling as much as possible of this social and economic discontent behind it. Calvinism in turn provided the ideology, organization, and leadership that helped transform much of this discontent into a national movement. Accordingly, it would be worthwhile to document the development of such popular contestation in the first half of the sixteenth century while trying to measure its point of intersection with Calvinism.

The forms of popular resistance in the first half of the sixteenth century varied from the disorderly subsistence riot of the poor and unemployed to the ongoing and premeditated suits and litigations of the bourgs and villages. In between came the riots and rebellions of the urban plebians against their betters, the strikes of the employed against their employers, the peasant revolt, and the religious protest. Motivation ranged from hunger and exploitation to economic crisis, class oppression, political and social exclusion, oppressive taxation both direct and indirect, social discrimination and religious protest.

Invariably the targets of such protest were urban oligarchs, nobles, royal officials, and the Church, depending on the circumstances. It would be a mistake to see these groups as mutually exclusive targets. The period was marked by both urban and rural unrest. In certain instances rural upheaval sparked urban protest. Indeed, study of popular contestation in this period leads one to question a too simplistic division of commoners into plebians living in the towns and peasants in the countryside. The principal towns were surrounded by smaller towns and villages. So-called peasants were to be found not only in the villages but also in the small and larger towns. In many villages, the sixteenth century saw the implantation of industry based on the putting-out system. Even where this was not the case, villages normally had at least some inhabitants – blacksmiths, wheelwrights, millers – who carried on skilled work. What we normally consider urban economic activity penetrated deeply into the countryside. It is therefore difficult to separate clearly rural from urban protest. The countryside was made up of more than isolated petty producers who were incapable of organizing themselves. On the contrary, although far less so than in the towns, it is evident that a capacity for organized and sustained contestation existed. In any case we are far from Marx's characterization of the nineteenth-century French countryside as "a sack of potatoes."

SERFDOM HAD VIRTUALLY disappeared in France as a result of the late medieval crisis. Tenants in most places still owed rents in kind, cash, or even labour to their landlords but personal bondage had more or less vanished. The only exceptions lay in Burgundy and parts of Champagne. Even in these regions, however, the impetus toward personal freedom intensified in the sixteenth century, undoubtedly in part because of the growing strength of commercial influences in the countryside.

In Champagne at the beginning of the century, the centre of this movement toward personal liberty was located at Attichy, a bourg not far from Châlons, where, in a veritable free town, serfs from nearby villages in flight from their masters could find refuge.[1] It was the policy of the bourg to protect the runaways as much as possible. Once arrived, fugitives were immediately given new names signifying their new condition. A peasant militia made up largely of ex-serfs assumed the responsibility of protecting the freedom of the newcomers. The militia, organized into companies under a captain, was especially on the lookout for bounty hunters who were sent to track down runaway peasants.

Armed resistance met the efforts of the agents of the abbey of Saint-Pierre-aux-Monts (Châlons) and the lord of Arzillières (near Vitry) to recover such fugitives. The enterprise of the sergeant of the bailiff of Senlis met a similar rebuff. On his arrival at Attichy, he and his men were confronted by forty of the militia equipped with bows, crossbows, pikes, javelins, and other arms. The sergeant's attempt to read his warrant was received with curses and death threats, and he and his retinue were forced to flee for their lives. Resistance appears to have sharpened in following years. A witness testified in 1527 that the appearance of bounty hunters immediately set off the tocsin in the bourg. Immediately, at least one hundred or more of the inhabitants would turn out ready to confront any would-be intruder.[2]

Violence thus commonly marked the struggle for personal freedom. But we ought not to forget that such episodes took place in the context of a continuing non-violent movement, whose progress may be followed in the hundreds of court proceedings, transactions, and agreements that date from the first half of the sixteenth century. Typical is a legal arrangement concluded between the seigneur and the inhabitants of Talmay in Burgundy in 1533. In a document drawn up in June of that year, Claude de Pontaillier, seigneur of Talmay, recognized that although the inhabitants of Talmay performed many corvées on a daily basis for him they did so not out of any obligation of servitude but because of their love for him. It is doubtful that this new arrangement was the result of a spontaneous act of generosity by Pontaillier. More likely it was the outcome of a prolonged process of litigation and negotiation out of which the inhabitants of Talmay were able to acquire their freedom in principle.[3]

Evidence of success in the struggle for personal manumission in Burgundy and Champagne might lead us to expect that commoners were faring well generally in the first half of the sixteenth century. Such was not the case. It was the force of the market that facilitated the decline of personal servitude. But these same commercial pressures, which led to higher food costs and increases in rent, undermined the economic position of the majority of commoners. By 1500 and certainly by 1520 the boom times for commoners – peasants, craftsmen, journeymen, apprentices and day labourers – were already in the past. Between 1450 and 1500, when labour was relatively expensive and land and food relatively cheap, the work of all producers had been well rewarded. Cheap food and low rents bouyed up the market for industrial products. After 1500 this changed noticeably for the worse. Population increased while rents and food prices moved sharply upward. Wages fell behind prices while industrial prices lagged behind the cost of food. From the beginning of the reign of Francis I, the war against the Hapsburgs became the occasion for a sharp increase in taxation. Moreover, the wars themselves posed an increasing threat to the population. Although no prolonged occupations of French soil had to be endured, the repeated incursions of the Spanish, English, and Germans into Gascony, Provence, Picardy, and Champagne prompted the monarchy to enlarge the size of the army and increasingly to garrison cavalry and infantry at the expense of the population. The passage of these troops through the countryside caused continuing anxiety. Companies of gendarmerie or infantry, regularly paid or not, often turned into brigands who wantonly attacked both hamlets and towns. By the 1530s and 1540s, the quartering of troops, the furnishing of supplies, and the imposition of royal *corvées* were commonplace not only along the frontiers but even in the central provinces of the kingdom.[4]

With rent increases, a decline in real wages, a gradual constriction of the internal market for manufactures, and increased taxation, both direct and indirect, the economic position of most producers declined through the first half of the sixteenth century. The good years of the first half of the sixteenth century were good only for a minority – a minority that became ever smaller as the century wore on. Thus, the brilliance of French Renaissance elite culture must be understood against the counterpoint of rising population, stagnant productivity, and increasing misery. The prosperity – indeed, the profligacy – of the courtiers, aristocrats, upper clergy, urban notables, and great merchants came at the expense of the larger working population.

But it is a mistake to believe that all the commoners retreated into sullen acquiescence. Hundreds of lawsuits were brought before the courts of the *bailliages*, *sénéschaussés*, *présidaux* and *parlements* on their behalf. Often the population resorted to direct action – riot and sedition – against their oppressors.

The kinds of collective action that commoners engaged in during the first half of the century varied greatly. Some had a directly anti-noble cast. Others were aimed against the army – perceived to be an instrument of both aristocratic and monarchical oppression. The most common kind of conflict occurred between the inhabitants of the towns. The commoners rose frequently against the economic exploitation, political exclusion, and social discrimination imposed upon them by urban oligarchies. Such conflicts were the more feasible because it was in the towns that the population was most detached from and able to challenge the seigneurial order. The narrow streets and byways of the towns were an ideal setting in which the mass of artisans and journeymen could confront their masters and governors. Moreover, the gilds and corporations, which helped to control and divide the working population, were weaker in the sixteenth century than in the middle ages.[5]

These struggles in the towns found an echo in the countryside. The urban oligarchies extended their control over the surrounding regions, provoking a spirited resistance from the inhabitants of the small towns and surrounding rural areas. Increasingly hard times fed a growing resentment against royal taxation everywhere and in the 1540s in Guyenne brought on a revolt of major proportions. Gradually, these acts of dissidence became also religious in nature, taking the form of iconoclasm, smuggling of evangelical literature, and underground prayer meetings. These acts are significant in that they provide the transition between popular dissidence and organized religious opposition that came together eventually in the form of subterranean churches directed by elements of the bourgeoisie.

Some historians are still prepared to gloss over the antagonistic relationship between nobles and commoners. But as Jean-Marie Constant points out, the violence of the nobility against the peasantry was a fact of life in the countryside.[6] Chasselas in Burgundy was the site of a more or less typical encounter. One Sunday in March 1532, the seigneur Bellecombe, Baron of Vinzelles, accompanied by the seigneur of Estours, left the chateau of Estours in order, Bellecombe later claimed, to go to mass. As the two gentlemen were setting out, they heard the ringing of the tocsin in the nearby village of Chasselas. Their curiosity aroused, the two nobles decided to make a detour in order to see what was afoot. As a precaution, according to his own testimony, Bellecombe donned a suit of armour on top of which he wore a peasant's smock. He also provided himself with a javelin, while his companion equipped himself with a lance. Thus armed, they set out for Chasselas accompanied by two servants. On arrival they found themselves in the midst of a crowd of peasants who were at the point of subduing a gang of brigands. After the latter had been captured, the prosecutor of Mâcon told the two nobles to leave immediately. Bellecombe turned his horse about at once and tried to make his way across the bridge of Chasselas, asking the crowd to make way for him. The villagers obeyed, except for one, Benoît Pierre, who stood in his path with an arrow at the ready in his crossbow. Bellecombe ordered him out of the way but Pierre refused, threatening to discharge his arrow if Bellecombe advanced. As Bellecombe tells it, out of fear and rage he charged and could not prevent his javelin from stabbing Pierre. The latter was wounded in the stomach and died three days later.[7]

Antagonism between noble and non-noble lay just under the surface and could burst out spontaneously on the most trivial of occasions. The feast of St John on 23 June 1527 at Dijon provides a good illustration. That night, as was customary, festivities took place at which nobles and commoners mingled indiscriminately. At the dance, Guillaume de Mothe, a fuller by trade, began dancing with a girl who was the fiancée of another man. Apparently this caused eyebrows to be raised and sparked a certain excitement in the crowd. The couple attracted the attention of Charles de Baissey, seigneur de Beaumont-sur-Vingeanne. The noblemen tried to cut in on the couple, asking to dance with the girl. But the fuller de Mothe refused to allow Beaumont to have his way. Beaumont remarked that de Mothe was lowering himself by behaving in this manner. De Mothe responded that he wanted to dance just as much as Beaumont did. Moreover, he added, he was as much an "homme de bien" as Beaumont, fit to be the dancing partner of the girl. Beaumont responded with his fists, and a general mêlée broke out between nobles and non-nobles. The way in which sexual rivalry suddenly transformed itself into class antagonism between these young hotheads throws the nature of relations in this society into sharp relief. In this case the lowering of social barriers at the dance was enough to ignite the fire of sexual jealousy and class hatred between noble and non-noble.

The rest of the story is no less revealing. A bourgeois notable, Pierre Fourneret, decided to intervene to appease the quarrel before it got out of hand. He tried to calm de Mothe by reassuring him that he was indeed an "homme de bien," that is to say, "homme de bien," in his estate. As for Beaumont, he went on, he was of course of another quality than the fuller, because he was a gentleman of noble birth. De Mothe's response to this intercession was to knock Fourneret off his feet. So much for the society of orders as far as De Mothe the craftsman was concerned. Fourneret having been flattened to the ground, the conflict became even more menacing. Beaumont and the other noblemen drew their swords while the mass of plebians swarmed about them. Only the intervention of the popular mayor Jean Noël made it possible to calm the commotion.[8]

The town, with its relatively large population concentrated into a small area, was a micro-society in which people of different quality or class could easily come into conflict. Personal quarrels became inexplicably confused with class conflict. Trivial differences could become enlarged into full-scale social war. It is in this light that one must view the "war of the fish" that shook Le Puy-en-Velay in the 1550s. By established rule in Le Puy, fresh fish was sold in the *rue des Tables* and in the *place du Forn du Poisson*. The fish markets were thus located close to the residences of the nobility and upper clergy, who lived in the "cloister" or upper town near the cathedral. But in the course of the first half of the sixteenth century, the established rule was more and more violated. The residents of the cloister became vexed that increasing numbers of fish were being sold in the lower town where the merchants and artisans were concentrated. The servants of the noblemen and cathedral canons found themselves inconvenienced and often forced to accept fish of less than first choice. Acting as a body, the powerful inhabitants of the cloister tried to pressure the fishermen and peasants of the Velay to bring their fish to the established markets. The commoners interpreted this action as both a slap in the face and as an attack on the free market. Indeed, by the early 1550s the bourgeoisie of the lower town had broken the monopoly imposed by the cloister on the sale of fresh fish. Fish were once again on sale in the markets of the lower town. The merchants of the *rue des Tables* whose monopoly was threatened brought suit with the support of the aristocratic inhabitants of the cloister. The case was ultimately heard by the Parlement of Toulouse. The court handed down a decision that not only restored the monopoly of the *rue des Tables* and *place du Forn* over fresh fish but also conceded to them a monopoly over the sale of salted fish. The commoners of the lower town were incensed. A series of popular commotions followed. Alarmed at the possibility of a mass sedition against the government of the town, the judge of the common court of Le Puy arranged a compromise by negotiating with the leaders of the contending factions.[9]

The war of the fish at Le Puy affords the modern historian a window onto the spectacle of urban conflict in sixteenth-century France. But the drama of this feud had already struck the imagination of Etienne Médicis, who recorded it in his chronicle "The Book of Le Puy."[9] One of the great town chronicles of the sixteenth century Médicis's work was designed to establish a coherent record of the history and traditions of the town from the perspective of its aspiring bourgeois elite. Médicis himself was a member of that stratum of wholesale merchants and bourgeois notables who led the commons against the old elite of the cloister.

Médicis's chronicle makes it clear how much those in control of the town prided themselves on their ability to maintain a sense of order, place, and rank. Médicis and his fellow great merchants and notables were as fervent believers in the society of orders as were the nobles and clergy. But this was not a concept that was taken for granted. The bourgeois elite attempted to reaffirm its sense of order as frequently as it could through religious and civic processions that restated on each occasion for all to see the appropriate religious and social order of the community. These were thoroughly stage-managed affairs with each detail, particularly the ranking of the citizens according to status and craft, carefully arranged. Médicis describes these events almost lovingly in his chronicle. But such ceremonies, designed to promote and inculcate an illusion of timeless and inevitable order, ironically could themselves become occasions for riotous outbursts, exposing in a dramatic way the intense conflicts smouldering beneath the apparently smooth surface of an officially imposed order. An earlier feud between the canons of the cathedral of Notre Dame of Le Puy and the monks of St Pierre Le Monastier, which broke out toward the close of the fifteenth century, helps demonstrate that the war of the fish of the 1550s arose out of a deep and long-standing animosity.

It was the custom of the canons of the cathedral of Le Puy to carry the holy sacrament in procession on Corpus Christi Day through the upper town. Likewise on that day, the prior and monks of St Pierre Le Monastier organized a procession through the parishes in the lower town served by their church. The canons took it into their heads to extend their procession to include the parishes served by St Pierre Le Monastier. As a result, the two processions confronted one another in the narrow streets in what became an annual quarrel dividing not only the clergy but also their lay supporters. The canons of Notre Dame could rely on the support of noble and clerical inhabitants of the cloister, as well as on their dependants. St Pierre Le Monastier was the parish church of many of the rich merchants and well-to-do artisans who sided with the monks. According to Médicis, it was as a result of the involvement of some of the laity that the quarrel became a feud not simply between the clergy but between the residents of the upper and lower town – between the old elite and the aspiring merchants and artisans. The annual confrontation between the two processions became a carnival of disorder involving mutual insults, commotions, and physical assaults. The nobles organized themselves under the cover of theatre. They staged histories of St Michael that became a part of the procession of the canons. Some of the actors disguised themselves as devils, under their costumes hiding iron clubs to use as weapons during the inevitable mêlée.

Under the guise of a religious dispute between two ecclesiastical bodies thus developed what amounted to a social war revolving around control of the Corpus Christi Day. In defiance of the monks and their supporters, the canons decided to interrupt their annual procession with a sermon on the Place Martouret immediately adjacent to St Pierre Le Monastier. In reaction to this provocation, the monks and their followers took to exiting St Pierre Le Monastier while loudly ringing its bells in order to disrupt the sermon. The canons were able to suppress the ringing of the bells of St Pierre for a few years, but after a time, the monks of St Pierre and their supporters declared that they would not only sound the bells as their procession left St Pierre Le Monastier but that they would invade the cloister in the upper town to hear a sermon of their own presented on "enemy territory."

The canons appealed to their bishop. He agreed to reside each year at Corpus Christi so as to suppress the procession of St Pierre Le Monastier. Involvement of the bishop, far from resolving the argument, escalated the quarrel. The consuls now took sides with the supporters of St Pierre Le Monastier. In reaction, the bishop excluded them from their traditional place in the cathedral's Corpus Christi procession. Only the intervention of the Parlement of Paris put an end to the feud by imposing a compromise.

A scandal of such proportions, which went on for so many years, could only have happened in an unreformed Church. Indeed, Médicis himself was at pains to point out that the problem arose in the first place owing to the non-residence of the bishops of Le Puy. Nonetheless, such as it was, the struggle between canons and monks illuminates the degree of anger that lay cloaked beneath the veneer of decorum and formality in this small but highly stratified society. The appearance of devils equipped with iron clubs in a religious procession reflects a degree of imaginative malevolence possible only in a small community that based itself normally on a tightly controlled social order. Late medieval religion served as a cloak for a classic confrontation between nobles and upper clergy on the one hand and the clergy and commoners of the lower town on the other.[10] It is clear that the "war of the fish" was but one more episode in an unending dispute.

DISPUTES BETWEEN NOBLES and non-nobles were more commonly based on what was tangible rather than on what was intangible and symbolical. Above all, such conflicts revolved around entitlements to land. The inhabitants of Vorilhes in the county of Foix, for example, had long claimed the right for their animals to graze and forage in the woods of Vals nearby. In 1535 they were at law with the seigneur de Marseilles over the matter. One day in mid-February the syndic Francis Clavière and the vice-consul Pierre Bayard, along with three other men, spent the day working in a vineyard that belonged to one of them. On their way back to Vorilhes they passed the garden of the seigneur de Marseilles. At that point they met the seigneur's son, the Cadet Bezian de Loubens, and his companion, the Bastard of Méserville, both armed with swords. As they passed, the townsmen saluted the young nobles. But instead of acknowledging the salutation, the Cadet answered, "You want to prevent me from warming myself from my wood." He threatened the syndic, who responded, "You will do nothing, Cadet, we are at law." A mêlée ensued in which the syndic was mortally wounded and the other townsmen forced to take flight.[11]

Noble violence could assume the proportions of a reign of terror. A spectacular instance was the career of Guy, baron of Montpezat (1490–1526), in the Agenais. He arbitrarily increased seigneurial dues and *corvées* on his tenants. He changed measures of grain so as to augment the portion due to him and diminished the customary land measures so as to increase rents owed to him. Illegally, he instituted fines for the use of trees on the public thoroughfares. As an amusement he took potshots at those at work on roofs, walls, or in trees. His favourite targets were carpenters. Followed by five trusty servants, he abused, beat, mutilated, and killed those of his subjects who crossed him, including the consuls and inhabitants of the town of Montpezat. Those who resisted the baron saw their livestock confiscated, were put into prison, and sometimes starved to death.

The baron pastured his flocks where he pleased, knocking down fences and enclosures put in his way. In 1519 he murdered two of his tenants who tried to protest. At Agen, when a priest began to preach against him, Guy and his retinue at once made their way to the town. On their arrival, hearing that the priest was saying mass at the Cathedral, they hurried there and stabbed him to death at the foot of the altar. The consuls and inhabitants of the town were too paralyzed by terror to react.

The Crown was apparently powerless against Guy. In 1511 the Parlement of Bordeaux declared that the seigneuries of Saint-Sardos, Saint-Damien de Granges, and Cours held by Guy actually belonged to the Crown. When the court sent its sergeants to dispossess him, Guy resisted, forcing them to flee. He was still in possession of these lands at the time of his death fifteen years later.

The inhabitants of Montpezat did try to put up a resistance in the courts. Over one hundred of Montpezat's citizens bought suit against Guy in the Parlement of Bordeaux. But he so intimidated them that they withdrew their suit *en masse*. He likewise terrified the inhabitants of Saint-Damien de Granges and Saint-Sardos into dropping their cases against him.[12]

The anarchic violence of the nobility is once again demonstrated in the private war of the seigneur de Ribiers against the peasants of Le Noyer on the border of Provence and Dauphiné. The struggle began as a trivial conflict over rights of pasture between the villagers of Le Noyer and those of Ribiers. At issue was the grazing land on the so-called "Pierre Impie" or Mountain of Brisons. By 1516, a range war had broken out between the two communities. The Parlement of Provence charged Rostain de Vesc, captain of the royal court of Sisteron, to arbitrate the dispute. No sooner had he arrived at Brisons than the lord of Ribiers appeared on horseback with a troop of followers that included twenty of the principal inhabitants of Ribiers, who, it later turned out, had been forced to accompany him. The lord of Ribiers attacked the villagers of Le Noyer, putting them to flight. Three of them were captured, along with the captain de Vesc. Following this minor triumph, the lord of Ribiers organized a full-scale attack on Le Noyer involving some twelve hundred vassals and dependants, a few equipped with arquebuses and even a small train of artillery. Although the stout resistance of the villagers prevented him from taking Le Noyer, the lord of Ribiers definitively established the grazing rights of his dependants to the mountain of Brisons.[13]

Peasants, as we have seen, were prepared to defend themselves against lords by both direct and indirect action. At Saint-Romain in the Mâconnais peasants resisted what they regarded as unjust seigneurial dues by refusing to plant crops.[14] In the Roannais in 1517, the inhabitants of Renaison were accused of breaking the sluices on a ditch feeding water to the pond of the chateau of Boisy.[15] In 1521 the syndic of the abbey of St Chaffroi sued twenty-one tenants – men and women – from the dependent village of Lantriac in the Velay for acts of armed rebellion.[16] More often, tenants went to law against their landlords. Thus at Faugères in the Haut-Biterrois, the syndics appealed to the *Grands Jours* of Toulouse in 1550 against their lord, the Baron Claude de Narbonne. Their complaint was that the Baron was imposing new and oppressive seigneurial dues on them. Moreover, the syndics complained "that the said de Narbonne and his predecessors have been terrible men of war who have made themselves feared and redoubted by their subjects so much so that the poor inhabitants who are laymen, rustics, and labourers burdened with wives and children, do not dare contradict them in or for anything."[17] In the end, the Parlement of Toulouse was able to impose a compromise that at least in part forced the Baron to reduce the burden of seigneurial claims on the peasantry of Faugères.

This kind of compromise was relatively rare; more often than not the courts reinforced rather than weakened seigneurial power. A striking demonstration comes from the Velay, admittedly among the most feudal and ecclesiastically dominated regions of the kingdom. Owing to the civic-mindedness of a mayor of Le Puy in the mid-nineteenth century, the municipal library of the city contains a remarkable record of the litigation in the Velay before the Parlement of Toulouse for the late fifteenth and sixteenth centuries.[18] This document is striking for the number of lawsuits brought by peasants against their seigneurial and ecclesiastical overlords in this period over seigneurial dues. No less remarkable is the fact that in none of these instances did the commoners win their cases.

The nobility in Languedoc, in contrast to other places, were at least subject to some taxation. Nobles were required to pay the *taille réele* on the *roturier* land that they held or acquired. This did not mean that controversy over the taille between nobles and non-nobles did not exist. But it did mean that commoners were in a position to look for redress from the courts.

An illuminating example of the mediating function of the royal courts is provided by the struggle in the bourg of Aimargues in the 1540s between its noble and non-noble inhabitants. Aimargues was one of the most important localities of the Nîmes region. It was the site of an archpresbytery of the diocese of Nîmes, the seat of a *viguerie*, and a seigneurie of the diocese of Uzès. A small community of some two thousand inhabitants, it was located in the midst of the best land of the plain of Languedoc. Ninety-five percent of the land was devoted to the cultivation of grain, with the grazing of sheep complementing agriculture. In summer the flocks were accommodated in the nearby marsh and in winter they were brought into the arable. Although the majority of the population were artisans, a large minority were peasants. The government of the town was divided between the *viguier* and the town consuls, the latter elected by indirect election based on property. The first scale was established on the basis of property worth twenty *livres tournois* or more. Those who owned property worth ten *livres tournois* or more were in the second scale. All other electors were lumped together in the third scale. Each scale chose electors who in turn elected the consuls and other municipal officers. The government of the town, dominated by the nominees of the larger property owners, was thus in the hands of a narrow oligarchy.

It is evident that the sixteenth century witnessed a massive redistribution of property in favour of the wealthy. In the second half of the century already fifty-nine percent of the population was in the third scale. By the mid-seventeenth century 86.5 per cent were in this category. Given these tendencies at work at Aimargues, the question of exemption from the taille was a burning issue in the second half of the fifteenth and the first half of the sixteenth century.[19]

A dozen or more families claiming nobility held land at Aimargues. Of the 2,386 hectacres of land in the land survey of 1544, twenty-three percent was recorded to be in the hands of five noble families.[20] Of these families, only one could trace its origins at Aimargues back to the end of the fifteenth century;[21] nevertheless they all claimed that their land was exempt from the taille by virtue of their personal nobility. In 1542, after years of feuds, at times violent and bloody, a lawsuit was argued before the *Cours des Aides* of Montpellier. At the end of the lawsuit, in 1544, the commoners had their way, with the nobles forced to pay the taille on their landholdings. This judicial process, expensive and long drawn out though it was, had a peaceful outcome. It proved a wholesome alternative to the murderous violence that marked the early stages of this dispute back in the fifteenth century.

THE REVENUES OF THE FRENCH state multiplied several times in the course of the first half of the sixteenth century. It has nevertheless commonly been argued that increases in the taille were no greater than the rate of inflation. It should be pointed out, however, that they were felt the more acutely by a population the greater part of which was suffering from the effects of inflation and a deteriorating standard of living. Moreover, in the Dauphiné at least, the absolute increase of the burden of the taille on the commons has been proved.[22] In addition, while the taille may not have increased disproportionately to inflation elsewhere, it is by no means certain that the *crues, taillons,* and forced loans did not. Furthermore, any study of taxation must take into account the cost of quartering, provisioning, and supporting the growing military establishment of the Valois. This burden greatly multiplied under Francis I and Henri II. It was a weight that was unequally divided and largely unpredictable. In the records of many towns of the first half of the century, the loudest and most continuing complaint is directed against the burden of the military.

This isn't surprising, given that war was the most important preoccupation of sixteenth-century society. As far as the monarchy and nobility were concerned, this was the natural order of things, justifying their own supremacy over the rest of society. It is only in this light that we can appreciate the subversive character of the pacificism of Erasmus or of the Anabaptists. To be against war was to attack the very roots of aristocratic power. Pacificism was accordingly an unpopular idea in the French kingdom.

The French army was a profoundly aristocratic institution, and the nobility did all that they could to keep it that way. Predictably, two attempts made to create a national infantry based on the peasantry failed. The first attempt was the formation of the *franc-archers* under Charles VII. The second was the creation by Francis I of the so-called *légions* designed to rival the *tercios* of Charles of Hapsburg. That both experiments ended in failure is no doubt in part because of the ineptitude of those who tried to implement them. But there is no question that they were unsuccessful chiefly because of the opposition of the nobility, who were hostile to the idea of putting arms into the hands of the people for fear of losing their control over them.[23] According to Guiccardini, writing at the beginning of the sixteenth century, the nobility sought to keep the people of France disarmed and deprived of military training for fear of the latter's impetuosity. The Venetian Ambassador Francesco Giustiniani elaborated on Guicciardini's observation *à propos* the *légions*. The *légions*, he concluded, had failed because they were made up of peasants brought up in servitude without experience in the handling of arms. Passing suddenly from a state of subjugation to the liberty and licence of war, they no longer wished to obey their masters. Accordingly, the nobility complained on repeated occasions that by putting arms into the hands of the peasants and freeing them from long established charges the king had made them stubborn and disobedient. The nobility added that they themselves had been deprived of their privileges, with the result that before long the peasants would become noble and the nobles villains. Brantôme, always the spokesmen of the nobility, denounced those who wanted to make the peasants upstarts by giving them arms. Not only was supplying arms to the peasants illegal, he argued, but it distracted them from their labour on which both they and others depended.[24]

The core of the French army was the cavalry. Captained by noblemen its ranks were filled with the sons of the nobility or would-be nobility. Indeed, the presence of even some *bourgeois gentilshommes* was intolerable to the nobles. Thus, in 1537, when the seigneur de Vieilleville was named *liéutenant* of the company of the maréchal de St André, he expressed his disgust to find so many of the sons of hotel and inn keepers, domestic servants, *concierges*, and peasants in the ranks. All those who did not appear to be gentlemen he got rid of.[25]

The nobility feared the notion of the people in arms for good reason. The idea of warfare as foreign to the commoners of France is a myth. The merchants and craftsmen of the French towns were no more pacifist than the nobility was. The Hundred Years War had made it necessary for every town to be able to defend itself. The fortified walls and the armouries full of weapons, armour, and artillery were a part of the civic privileges of every self-respecting French Renaissance town. The towns, especially "les bonnes villes" with their trained bands, were proud to recall that they had played a key role in the consolidation of royal power under Charles VII and Louis XI.[26]

The martial traditions of the towns continued to thrive in the first part of the century. Along the frontiers, urban fortification and militias provided an important element of the defence of the kingdom against invasion. But the martial fervour of the citizens could also be aroused against what was considered the outrageous behaviour of the King's soldiers. A striking example is provided by the town of Caen. In the 1580s a notable of that town, Charles de Bourgueville, wrote a history entitled *Les Recherches et Antiquitez de la province de Neustrie*.[27] Among the most noteworthy events of the century he recalled "the day of the lansquenets." In 1513, six thousand German mercenary soldiers passed through the town on the way to guard the Norman coast from English invasion. The reaction of the citizens of Caen was one of apprehension rather than relief. The people turned out in arms to insure that the lansquenets made their way through the community in good order. But once the citizens had dispersed, the soldiers invaded pell-mell to enjoy the pleasures of the town. They lodged themselves wherever they pleased and engaged in the usual drunken and riotous behaviour. After several days, their commanders finally recalled them to the ranks. Some lansquenets, abandoning their lodgings, refused to pay their hosts. Fights broke out between soldiers and artisans, which turned into a full-scale mêlée. But it was the citizens rather than the lansquenets who were the better prepared for battle; the latter were defeated, with between two to three hundred massacred. On the other side, only one citizen was killed, a metal founder named Vaillant. Bourgueville recounted how the wife of Vaillant joined the battle on the death of her husband, purportedly killing several lansquenets herself to avenge her husband's death.[28] This day of the lanquesnets was the single most famous date in the history of Caen in the sixteenth century. Bourgueville records that even in his own time people still dated events from before or after this triumph.

Attacks on the military were not confined to those by townsmen. In 1525, peasants, emboldened by the defeat of the French nobility in Italy, set upon one such retreating company of gendarmerie, led by the seigneur d'Alègre, as they passed through Languedoc. The peasants were from a wide area of the dioceses of Uzès and Vivarais, including the villages of Robiac, Chambonas, Gravières, Les Salelles, Pontelet, Bonne, Saint-Ambroix, and Saint-Jean de Valeriscle. Most of the company was unhorsed, pillaged, killed, or put to flight. The king's regent, the queen-mother, Louise of Savoy, ordered the *sénéschal* of Nîmes and Beaucaire to investigate. The latter sent a commission of noblemen into the area to set things in order.[29]

Tension between aristocratic soldiers and commoners increased in the following decades. The growing animosity was the indirect result of the increasing burden of the wars on the population. Le Puy affords a striking illustration of such hostility. On the last day of September 1536, the captain Tournon rode into town with his suite and took lodgings at the Falcon, one of the best inns in the city. He presented the consuls of the town with letters-patent, which ordered the diocese of Velay to furnish provisions for his men-at-arms in the course of their passage through the region. His troop consisted of between fifteen and sixteen hundred men located some five or six leagues from Le Puy.

At that time, the estates of Velay were in session. Informed by the consuls of the content of Tournon's commission, the estates agreed to grant him sixty *écus*, provided his company passed through the Velay without delay. Meanwhile the commons of Le Puy received word of this agreement. The war had already cost them dearly. That very year the whole of Languedoc had been put on a state of alert because of the invasion of Provence by the Emperor Charles V. The taille had been drastically increased, the ordinary revenues of the town seized, and the inhabitants forced to perform *corvées*, furnish provisions, and strengthen the towns defences in support of the army.[30]

Four days after Tournon's arrival, the plebians revolted. Defying the consuls and the estates they surrounded the Falcon, demanding that Tournon immediately return the monies voted by the estates, on pain of death if he refused. At the same time, another group of plebians besieged the *hôtel de ville*, warning the consuls that if Tournon left without returning the money it would be the consuls and not the people who would pay. Thoroughly shaken, the consuls nonetheless left the *hôtel de ville* and made their way to the Common Court to join forces with the officers of that body. Not without difficulty the consuls and magistrates threaded their way to the Falcon and ordered the people massed there to disperse. Far from intimidating the population, this command made them even more furious. The notables were required to beat a disorderly retreat.

Fortunately for them, the Vicomte of Polignac, the most powerful noble in the Velay, happened to be in town for the meeting of the estates, and he was persuaded to intervene. He and his retinue hurried to the Falcon, where he conferred with Tournon, urging him to return the money before he and his entourage were killed. Tournon handed over his purse, and the Vicomte of Polignac was able to show it to the people assembled before the inn. "Let him go, my lords," he cried. "He has given me the money – look, here it is." Pacified, the commoners dispersed.[31]

It was not only the commons who were prone to outbursts of violence. The very next year the younger brother of Blaise de Montluc Joachim unleashed a reign of terror in the Albigeois. Montluc and his retinue had already got into trouble by murdering the curé of the village of Gimbrède in the course of a quarrel. They devastated part of the village in a first assault and were beaten off in a second at the cost of the lives of several of the peasants. By October 1537, Montluc had raised a company of several hundred men for the war in Provence, including over one hundred nobles. On 4 October, Montluc led his company in an attack on Lisle in the Albigeois. Not only did they rape and loot in the town but went on to invade the *hôtel de ville*, systematically destroying the charters and records of the municipal government.

The band moved on to attack Gaillac, which was spared only by paying two hundred *écus* in blackmail. Montluc then ordered an assault on Albi and the villages nearby. The citizens and rustics of the area broke the charge of Montluc's company, crushing it at the ferry crossing of Saix. One hundred and twenty drowned in the Agout river and fifty-two were captured and later punished.[32]

A MAJOR CAUSE OF PROTEST in the first half of the sixteenth century was a shortage of food. By the first decade of the century, the absence of any real gains in rural productivity manifested itself in the first of many subsistence crises. Riots motivated by hunger and instigated by the commoners broke out in many towns. The focal point of the conflict was the town. This was not because peasants were not affected, but because townspeople, by their sheer geographical concentration could more easily organize protests. In 1505, for example, the Languedoc was badly hurt by a grain shortage. At Nîmes a gardener, Jacques Vire, led a mass of the poor to impose a *tribut populaire* on those hoarding grain. The keys of the Dominican convent were seized and the granary was stormed. "Honest" citizens tried to intervene but were repelled by the swords, clubs, and rocks of the hungry rioters. Eventually Vire and other instigators were punished by the *sénéchaussée* of Nîmes.[33]

Despite the fact that the disorganized nature of the riot points to hunger and not political or social concerns as a motivating force, subsistence riots were rarely simply motivated by hunger. As the upheaval at Nîmes or that classic food riot, the "Rebeine" of Lyons, demonstrate, the rioters, however unpolitical they may have been, certainly knew who to blame for their plight. In both cases the notables and clergy were the target of their anger. Usually the causes and motivations behind such a tumult were more complicated, having at their root a larger political and social malaise, at the source of which often lay the ravages of war.

Rouen in 1542 affords a useful example. In September of that year, part of the populace attacked a ship being loaded with grain for export.[34] At first sight, this appears to be an instance of a subsistence riot, pure and simple. Those who took part, however, were far from being all from the poorest stratum of the population. Moreover, the year 1542 was not a year of particular grain shortage. The economic crisis that existed was brought on not by strictly economic factors but by war with the Hapsburgs, which interrupted the town's normal commerce with the Low Countries. The war was greatly resented by merchants and craftsmen, many of whom found themselves unemployed as a result of the conflict. Attacking the ship, then, was both an economic and a political act.

Three years later, in Rouen again, there can be no doubt that the crafts-men were at the heart of the popular tumult. Subsistence was certainly on their minds, but social and political factors were also in play. A decade earlier, a *Bureau des Pauvres* had been established by the lay elite of the city. Its resources were severely strained by the economic crisis that paralyzed the industries of the town between 1542 and 1545. The *Bureau des Pauvres* devoted its resources mainly to the upkeep of unemployed artisans, the so-called "pauvres-valides." At the end of July 1545, the funds of the *Bureau des Pauvres* were exhausted, and when the treasurer found himself unable to make the expected distribution of relief, a riot broke out. A mob of four or five hundred largely composed of craftsmen, surrounded the treasurer's house insulting and threatening him.[35]

The situation was much the same at Tours, where a popular movement involving craftsmen and master artisans became visible as early as 1542. The upheaval was sparked by a paralysis of the silk industry brought on by the outbreak of war.[36] At Troyes a popular upheaval in 1529 appears in part to have been economically inspired. Like the rest of northern France in the 1520s, Champagne had been troubled by subsistence crises. But the immediate occasion for the rebellion at Troyes in 1529 was an outbreak of disease, which itself had been stimulated by the difficult times. Because of the plague, the town council was forced to curtail the importation of linen and wool. The paper and drapery manufacturers were brought to a standstill. Thousands of workers found themselves without employment and reduced to begging. The result was a popular revolt that prompted the council hastily to cancel the embargo it had imposed.[37]

The subsistence riot *per se* was not particularly dangerous, but it terrified the great merchants and notables because it could lead to something more terrible, namely, a revolt by the craftsmen and lesser merchants. Thus, at Meaux in 1522 a grain shortage that was linked with unemployment turned into a plebian revolt.[38] Likewise, at Agen in 1528, a popular movement broke out, which began as a grain riot among the poor. This upheaval became the catalyst for a revolt leading to the displacement of the ruling oligarchy and the establishment of a democratic commune.[39] Even the "Rebeine" of Lyons posed that threat. Conflict between plebians and patricians had been intense at Lyons in the first two decades of the 1500s. As it happened, when the "Rebeine" swept the city in 1529 the plebians ultimately took sides with the patricians. But not without hesitation; it took several days before the artisan train bands decided that they were prepared to come out against the rioting poor.[40]

The food riot represented a form of popular protest that was familiar from the past. In that sense it reflects continuity between the sixteenth century and the middle ages. The strike as a means of protest involved an entirely new form of social confrontation. The first industrial strike in French history took place in Lyons, ten years after the *Rebeine*. Printing had become one of the most important industries in the city by the 1530s. The industry was organized on a more or less completely capitalist basis, employing some six hundred *compagnons*. These were grouped in a powerful syndicate known as the Company of Griffarins. The strike, which began in the spring of 1539, involved a dispute over salaries, working conditions, and the maintenance of the open or closed shop. The strikers defied not only the master-printers but the consuls and even the officers of the king. Violence punctuated the work stoppage, which dragged on for two years. A similar conflict raged in the printing industry at Paris between 1539 and 1541. In the short run the workers were defeated.[41]

The towns of the late medieval period were hardly democracies. But many French towns in the late middle ages did provide for a limited degree of democratic participation in politics. The urban elites of the sixteenth century did away with these vestiges of popular government, often with the help of the monarchy. But in many cases these attacks on popular rights inspired protest and upheaval. In some French towns democratic elections were held up to the time of the Religious Wars – the city of Dijon being an outstanding instance. But democratic elections were accepted only grudgingly by an increasingly powerful oligarchy. Indeed, the St John's eve riot of 1527, which we have already examined in part, was an outgrowth of the increasing tension between the patricians and the plebians. A few days prior to the feast of John the Baptist, Jean Noël had been elected with massive support to his second term as mayor. With the exception of a single dissenting vote, the election had been unanimous in the popular assembly. But this near acclamation concealed bitter divisions in the community. Noël, himself a notable, was the favourite of the vine-dresser and craftsmen majority. His popularity was resented by most of the notables led by Pierre Sayve, seigneur de Flavignerat, who had been mayor in 1514–8 and again in 1523–5. Indeed, Sayve and certain others had tried to undermine Noël at the time of his first election as mayor in June 1526 by trying to discredit him with the governor of Burgundy, the admiral Chabot. They claimed that Noël had packed the election with artisans and vinedressers. Chabot, nevertheless, was induced to confirm the election.

Noël's second election had been followed almost immediately by the St John's Eve riot between the notables and nobles and the plebians. Indeed, it is plain that the conflict between notables and plebians formed the background to this confrontation. Thus, while Noël was trying to appease the tumult Jean Sayve, a young notable, had run up to the mayor and demanded the arrest of those who were seditious, meaning the ring-leaders of the popular party. Noël answered that Sayve was trying to make things worse rather than better. Intimidated, Sayve tried to retract his words, babbling that "there were different kinds of revolt like those in debate, those in speech and those of a town against its prince." Nonetheless, Sayve could not avoid the wrath of the plebians. Only the level-headedness of Noël made it possible to avoid bloodshed.

But these events were not forgotten. At the next mayoral election, the Admiral Chabot sent a message that was read to the popular assembly, recommending Jean's father, the *avocat* Pierre Sayve, to them as the preferred candidate of the king. Following this declaration the notables proceeded to elect

Sayve while the mass of plebians clamoured for the re-election of Noël. Indeed, the latter refused to allow the election ordered by the king to be formalized. Despite this, two days later the new mayor and council went in procession to the church of Saint-Philibert while they were hooted through the streets by the plebians.[42]

Democracy at Dijon obviously had clear limits. The plebians did not participate in the government but merely elected those who did. They favoured Noël because, as one of those subsequently arrested put it, "he treated them well." In addition, the approbation of the governor was necessary to any election. Chabot had at first approved of Noël, calling him a loyal servant of the king and a dependable client. When he lost confidence in him he was easily able to name a rival candidate. Despite the continuing opposition of the majority, the candidate who embodied the principle of orders was imposed from above. By no means does this allow us to conclude that the plebians welcomed this result. On the contrary, as we have seen, it was forced on them.

Intervention from above could lead to the suspension or abolition of representative government altogether. A striking instance is provided by La Rochelle where the suspension of elections was the consequence of an alliance of the governor and the estranged plebians.

In contrast to Dijon, the plebians of La Rochelle had long been excluded from the electoral process and thus completely estranged from the ruling oligarchy, which tightly controlled the government of the city. In 1521 the oligarchy imposed an excise tax on wine. Troubles began when elements of the bourgeoisie who were excluded from the oligarchy began to ally themselves with the plebians. With the support of the populace, the dissident bourgeoisie brought a suit in the Parlement of Bordeaux against the new tax. The judicial process soon led to popular commotions and riots against the oligarchy.

The dispute between the oligarchy and the estranged plebians intensified in 1525 when the former imposed an additional tax of ten thousand *livres* on the town in response to the urgent appeals of the government then under the regency of Louise of Savoy. Charles Chabot, seigneur of Jarnac, was appointed governor of the city the same year. Determined to restore order he planned an attack on the government of the oligarchy, his strategy designed to appease the plebians and the alienated elements of the bourgeoisie. In the first place, Chabot insisted on taking the place of the mayor as head of the urban militia and introducing his own men-at-arms into the town. In addition, his influence at court induced the king to suppress the constitution of the town in July 1535. The new government was made up of an appointed mayor, Chabot himself, and twenty elected aldermen. This regime, although less independent than the former municipal government, was based on the support of the hitherto excluded bourgeoisie and plebians. It survived until the monarchy chose to attack the privileges of the Rochelais by the introduction of the gabelle in 1541.[43] Notables, bourgeoisie, and commons at once rallied together in opposition to the king.

In most places the tendency was to exclude the plebians from political life altogether. At Carcassonne as early as 1506, the notables attempted to bar the plebians from municipal elections. The latter marched on the *hôtel de ville*, arms in hand, forcing the notables assembled there to flee. The plebians then proceeded to elect four consuls. The Parlement of Toulouse thereupon restored the government of the oligarchy.[44] At Nevers the elections of 1507 gave rise to confrontations between notables and plebians. The next year the local seigneur installed the consuls without elections, and this arrangement was thereafter confirmed by the monarchy.[45]

By now most of the world is aware of the drama of the Carnival of Romans. The roots of this conflict lay in the struggle between patricians and plebians for control of the municipal government. But it is important to stress that the seeds of the tragedy of 1579–80 at Romans had been sown at least two generations earlier. From the mid 1520s, the town was bitterly divided by the exclusion of the plebians from the government. The notables secured exclusive control of the office of first consul and were able to dominate over the deliberation of the town assembly. During the next two decades, however, there is evidence of an ongoing series of commotions, riots, and seditions. This led to an attempt definitively to establish the oligarchic government of the city in 1542 by the Parlement of Grenoble. The new constitution preserved a veneer of popular participation, but it once and for all excluded "the most ignorant and incapable" from the government.[46] These events were a kind of prologue to the revolt of 1579–80.

Fiscal conflict often provided the motive for popular revolt. The upheaval of 1514 at Agen began as a protest against a new tax.[47] Similarly, popular opposition to the oligarchy at Rodez flared up over the issue of finance. Troubles there began in 1506 with the dismissal of the town clerk, who then took the title of syndic of the *Basse Commune*. A parallel movement emerged in December of the next year at the time of the consular elections in the *Cité*, when, again, a syndic of the plebians emerged. At that time, the upsurge was strong enough to force the oligarchy into allowing the commons a part in the auditing of the town accounts. Thirty years later the situation of the artisans had deteriorated still further. As a result, a new and stronger popular movement emerged in both the *Cité* and *Bourg*. The essential demand on this occasion was popular participation in the consulate. In the *Cité* the popular party was strong enough to form a syndicate against the oligarchy.[48]

The history of Vitry-le-François affords yet another insight into the nature of the urban conflict between plebians and patricians that marked the first half of the sixteenth century. Vitry-le-François is well known as an outstanding example of Renaissance military architecture. Not so well known is the fact that the town got its start as a grand real estate speculation. In 1544, the old town, Vitry-le-Perthois, was burned down by the Imperial army invading Champagne. Following the retreat of the Imperial forces, many of the poor and the plebians returned to the devastated town and began to rebuild their homes. But the notables, led by Antoine Lignage the *liéutenant général du bailliage*, had another plan in mind. Under the leadership of Lignage they bought properties at a site away from the old town and subsequently induced the king to establish an ostensibly more defensible town at the new location. They literally forced the plebians to remove themselves to the new town, the real estate of which they completely controlled. Between 1545 and 1547, this process was accompanied by bitter litigation, popular riots, and the jailing of those who protested too vehemently.[49]

This story has an interesting sequel. Two generations later, the grandson of Antoine Lignage was likewise *liéutenant-général du bailliage* and head of the local oligarchy. At the end of the century, the popular party tried to reform the *échevinage* to try to break the power of the traditional elite headed by the younger Lignage. Once again the popular party went down to crashing defeat.[50] As the earlier discussion of Le Puy and Romans has already suggested, urban conflicts were long-lived, playing themselves out over several generations.

IN HIS LAST, POSTHUMOUS work Fernand Braudel has left us with a keen insight into the structure of the French society. Seeking to define the place of the town under the *Ancien Regime*, he observed that it was above all to be understood as a system of domination over the bourgs and villages that surrounded it.[51] Throughout France, the town was encircled by a ring of dependent bourgs and subordinated villages. From at least the sixteenth century the urban oligarchies dominated not only the urban population but also the smaller towns and villages in the surrounding area. Such control took the form of economic as well as political and administrative subordination.

Such rights of dominion were maintained by direct coercion. In 1512, for example, the citizens of Pamiers attacked the inhabitants of the smaller town of Montaut to reestablish their control over the territory of La Boulbonne. Montaut had taken advantage of the Franco–Hispanic war to seize these disputed lands. In reaction, eight hundred armed citizens of Pamiers marched on La Boulbonne. A pitched battle took place, which resulted in at least one death. The citizens of Pamiers drove off their rivals, destroyed their *metairies*, and seized their grain.[52]

Urban control over the countryside was more often exercised indirectly. A particularly clear example is provided by Bordeaux in the first half of the century. Bordeaux was the administrative and economic centre to which the other towns and the countryside of Guyenne were subordinated. The oligarchy of Bordeaux already held possession of the best land in the Bordelais. Through the parlement it was possible for the oligarchy to dominate administratively the entire region beyond. Because of its control of the estuary of the Garonne, for instance, the elite of Bordeaux were able to force Agen and its region to serve its economic needs. The Bordelais specialized in the production of good wine for export. On this account the parlement gave short shrift to the wines of the Agenais, compelling the latter to supply Bordeaux largely as a granary.

Partly in compensation, the oligarchy of Agen itself was given extensive control over the countryside of the Agenais. The peasants in the surrounding area were subjected to taxes in money and kind. Meanwhile Agen exercised dominion over the other towns in the Agenais through its control of the local estates. Using its dominant position in the estates, the oligarchy of Agen was able to shift the weight of taxation onto the shoulders of the smaller towns and the peasants in the countryside.[53]

This system of exploitation extended even further downward. Thus the smaller towns of the Agenais tried to dominate their peasantries in turn. The peasants around Villeneuve d'Agenais, for example, were forced to do *corvée* labour for the town. In 1502, when they attempted to resist, their land was seized for their trouble.[54]

Resistance to the hegemony of the oligarchy of Agen assumed different shapes. In the 1520s the peasants under Agen's government began to organize an association under the leadership of their own syndic. It was the formation of this peasant league in defiance of the consuls that actually set off the democratic revolt in the town. Moreover, following the defeat of this commune, the artisans looked to the syndic of the peasants for leadership in the continuing struggle against oligarchical control.[55] In 1555 the consuls of the other towns brought suit against Agen for imposing excessive taxation on them. Three years later they challenged Agen's control over the local estates by electing their own syndics.[55]

Undoubtedly the conflict between Agen and the bourgs and villages of the countryside represents an urban–rural struggle. But at a deeper level it represents a conflict of craftsmen, peasants, and lesser merchants against an oligarchy of great merchants and *officiers*. It demonstrates that the split between patricians and plebians that we have seen to be characteristic of the towns extended to the commoners in the countryside as well.

This conflict emerges in its full light if we examine the case of the Velay. Isolated by the mountains of the Vivarais, Cevennes, and Auvergne, the Velay was the most backward area of Languedoc. Its hilly terrain and isolated towns could not compare with the fertile plains and teeming cities of the plain of Languedoc. No where else in France, save only the Auvergne, was the nobility so strong or the Church so powerful. Indeed, the bishop of Le Puy was the principal lord of the Velay. As seigneur he controlled over forty per cent of the land of the region. Notwithstanding its backwardness, the Velay possessed a surprising economic vigour at the end of the Middle Ages. Despite its high altitude, the region became a major producer and exporter of wheat. Cut off from the Rhône, the Velay nevertheless managed to establish busy trading routes with the Auvergne and the lower Languedoc. A revival of interest in the pilgrimage of the Black Madonna in the meantime helped to reinforce the commercial and manufacturing development of Le Puy.

Politically, the Velay formed part of the Languedoc, subject to the decisions of the Parlement of Toulouse, the *Cours des Aides* of Montpellier, and the Estates of Languedoc. Like the Agenais, the Velay had a local estates, but unlike it, the nobility rather than the third estate, controlled its proceedings. Presided over by the bishop of Le Puy, the membership of the local estates was limited to the sixteen major nobles of the region. Its principal function by the end of the fifteenth century was the establishment of the assessment of the taille for the Velay.

The critical date in the history of the estates of Velay was 1493, when representatives of Le Puy were allowed to sit in the estates. Until then, relations between the elite of Le Puy and the nobility were continually strained. The ongoing feud between the lower and upper town over the Corpus Christi procession toward the close of the fifteenth century was an expression of this tension. So, too, were direct clashes over taxation. Thus, for example, in 1487 the Parlement of Toulouse had to order an enquiry into a conflict between the consuls and inhabitants of Le Puy and the estates over the taille.[56]

The entry of representatives of Le Puy into the estates marked a turning point. Increasingly, one notes a tendency toward the integration of the nobility of the region and the notables of Le Puy. Whereas up to the last decade of the fifteenth century the land holdings of the latter were relatively sparse, the new century was to see a massive infusion of urban capital into the countryside, particularly in the region around Le Puy. The greater part of this investment came from the notables and great merchants. Some of these were able to acquire fiefs and titles of nobility. Their sons even came to dominate the college of canons of the cathedral of Le Puy.

While the notables and big merchants of Le Puy prospered, evidence in the form of the expropriation of property and the rising number of poor suggests a deterioration in the economic circumstances of the majority of the rural and urban population. While most of the population regressed under the weight of rising numbers, stagnant productivity, and inflation, the elite grew prosperous through their acquisition of land, monopoly of government, and control of trade. By the mid-sixteenth century the chronicler of the town noted wistfully that while a minority of the population appeared to be prospering the majority was increasingly impoverished.[57]

In the countryside, growing difficulties provoked ongoing agitation on the part of the peasantry for relief from seigneurial and ecclesiastical dues.[58] At the same time, there was increasing resentment against payment of the tax on livestock imposed on those who sought to market their animals in Le Puy.

But above all there were complaints from the bourgs and villages of the Velay at their exclusion from the estates – in 1513 the nobles and consuls of Velay had agreed to exclude representatives of the bourgs or villages from the estates so as to assure, so they said, the appropriate assessment of the taille.[59]

These conflicts came to a head over the plan to reform the assessment of the taille, launched in the 1540s. The motivation behind this proposal seems clear. The Velay was divided between the region around Le Puy, known as "the region on this side of the woods," and the area to the east and north, known as "the region on the other side of the woods." In the latter region were to be found Yssingeux, Monistrol, Montdidier, Tence, St Didier, and the other principal bourgs of the Velay. By mid-century the merchants and notables of Le Puy had acquired substantial holdings in the "region on this side of the woods." The revision of the assessment was designed, as they themselves admitted, to shift the burden of the taille onto the shoulders of the "region on the other side of the woods."

These disputes came to a climax at the time of the *Grands Jours* of Le Puy in 1548. The bourgs of the "region on the other side of the woods" were represented by a group of complainants led by the so-called syndic of the *plat pays*, Master Amblard Bruissol. The other side was headed by the syndic of the consuls of Le Puy as well as of Boussols, Espaly, Vals, and Polignac. The latter communities were entirely under the control of Le Puy. Apparently to counter the other side, some forty-five to fifty peasants from these villages were brought along to demand a revision of the assessments.

At the first hearing on 15 October, Bruissol, representing the *plats pays*, complained about the tax on livestock that Le Puy had imposed on the people of the countryside. He remonstrated that for the last fifty years Le Puy had resisted by every means possible payment of a fair share of taxation. He denounced the proposed revision of the assessment as yet another way Le Puy was attempting to maintain the system of inequality.

At a second hearing a week later, Bruissol returned to the charge. He introduced himself as "the syndic of the poor inhabitants of the *plat pays* of the Velay comprising the third estate." It was not for nothing, according to Bruissol, that the practice had developed of calling representatives of the third estate to meetings of the estates both local and general. This practice had particularly been instituted with respect to "the third estate of labour as being the one most charged." Here we have an attempt to distinguish a third estate that laboured from one that did not, that is, the notables and bourgeoisie of Le Puy.

Bruissol described the way in which the estates of Velay were used to oppress the inhabitants of the *plat pays*. At one time, the nobles and clergy tried to control the assessment of the taille as well as other charges. In the 1480s the commons of the Velay challenged this practice before the Parlement of Toulouse. At that time, claimed the syndic of the *plat pays*, the parlement ordered the estates not to confuse the royal taille with the collection of taxes for local purposes. More to the point, it ordered that taxes ought to be collected only after obtaining the consent of the greater and saner part of the population. Again in 1509 the parlement commanded that syndics or representatives of all of the seigneurial jurisdictions of the Velay be called to the estates at the time of the assessment of the taille. The reason for this decision of the court, according to Bruissol, was to prevent the nobles and ecclesiastics who did not pay taxes from imposing them. Such taxes, he went on, ought not to be imposed except by the estates-general of France and then only with the consent of the poor inhabitants who bear all the weight and charge. But, according to Bruissol, the representatives of the *plat pays* had never been able to implement the judgment of 1509. Each time they had tried to enter the estates of Velay they had been denied entrance. Above all they singled out the syndic of the estates Gabriel de St Marcel as obstructing their entry with various reasons and excuses. St Marcel is known to have been one of the most powerful notables of Le Puy. He was a doctor of laws and, as Bruissol noted, the magistrate of many of the courts maintained by the seigneurs sitting in the estates. Not only, claimed Bruissol, were the estates imposing the taille on the commoners without their consent, they were imposing additional extraordinary charges to the benefit of those nobles in attendance. There was no possibility of sustaining an objection to what the nobles decided in the meeting, Bruissol complained, because they allowed no written record of its proceedings.

To cover themselves, concluded Bruissol, the nobles and clergy had allowed the consuls of Le Puy to attend as the representatives of the third estate. But since the extraordinary taxes were not assessed on Le Puy the consuls never objected.[60]

I have paraphrased Bruissol's speech at length because it is a truly extraordinary a document from the first half of the sixteenth century. The actual voice of the *plat pays* in this period is virtually never heard. Its survival in the Velay in the words of Bruissol is truly exceptional. It enables one to achieve an unusual insight into the system of domination current in the Velay but also over much of the rest of the Midi as well. Bruissol's speech makes it clear that it was the nobles and ecclesiastics who controlled the countryside. But it also illuminates the way in which Le Puy's notables had been co-opted by the ruling classes. Together they were able to rule over the petty producers and workers in both town and country.

Tantalizing is Bruissol's reference to "the third estate of labour." Are we going too far to suggest that contained in the expression of Bruissol we have reference to a primitive theory of the value of labour? If not we catch a glimpse – all too brief – of a current of opinion among small-scale producers that is rarely visible in the archival sources of sixteenth-century French history. It bespeaks a democratic view of society that was markedly different from that of the privileged orders.

Did the third estate for which Bruissol spoke accept the society of orders? Clearly not, since as it was constituted in the estates of Velay the society of orders refused any recognition to the "third estate of those who laboured," whose consent to taxation was legally required. The actions of the society of orders were, therefore, illegitimate. Only in so far as "the third estate of those who laboured" was included would it become legitimate. The demand of the rural bourgeoisie thus was to become part of a reconstituted society of orders. Given the actual limited strength of the rural bourgeoisie of the Velay, such a program was realistic rather than acquiescent. It certainly does not allow the conclusion that the commoners did not have another way of looking at society. The *Grands Jours* of Le Puy decided that in future the estates should call representatives from the principal towns of the *plat pays* to attend its meetings. Not surprisingly, the latter stubbornly refused to do so.

It is no wonder then that when the religious wars broke out in the Velay they began as a massive rising of the towns and villages of the "region beyond the woods" against Le Puy. The occasion of this uprising was, of course, religion. But this repudiation of the old faith by the people of the eastern Velay was rooted in a refusal of a whole system of domination whose locus was the city of the "Black Madonna." They had attacked Le Puy to get rich was the interpretation given by the chronicler of Le Puy to the Calvinist assault on the city.[61] Such a view of the Huguenots was at best a crude simplification. And yet like many such simplifications, it contained a kernel of truth. Above all, Médicis's observation reflects the sense of imperilled dominion felt by the notables at the time of the outbreak of the Reformation crisis in 1562.

Unrest in the countryside against elite rule was not confined to the Agenais and the Velay. In the Comminges in 1545, peasant associations began to crystallize in opposition to the threat of heavier taxation. Over one hundred communities there leagued themselves together, electing syndics to represent them against both the nobility and the bourgeoisie, who sought to pass the burden of the taille onto their shoulders. By 1560 the bourgeoisie began to throw in their lot with the peasantry, taking up their grievances in return for their support in opposing the nobility's attempts to escape the *taille réelle*.[62]

A similar evolution is notable in the lower Auvergne. There the estates were dominated by the city of Clermont, whose representatives controlled the deliberations of the assembly of the thirteen "goodly towns" (*bonnes villes*) of the province. The first challenge to this order came in 1537 when the royal *élus* protested that the nobles and clergy of the province ought to have the right to oversee the expenditure of local subsidies hitherto controlled by the third estate alone. Conflict between the different orders was soon followed by a challenge to the third estate by the inhabitants of the *plat pays*.

In September 1554, the estates of Lower Auvergne met together at Clermont to consider the approval and distribution in the countryside of the *taillon* imposed by Henri II. On 6 September, an extraordinary assembly of towns, bourgs, and villages excluded from the estates took place to discuss this new tax. Some forty-seven localities sent representatives to this assembly of the *plat pays* at Clermont. Faced with this unprecedented meeting, the third estate decided on a conciliatory posture. The president of the estates, the consul of Clermont, declared that the estates made up of Clermont and the thirteen "good towns" alone had the authority to decide on matters affecting the commoners of the province. The *plat pays*, he affirmed, had no such right. On the other hand, faced with the assembly of the latter, he allowed that on this one occasion the third estate was prepared to allow the *plat pays* in on the deliberation.

The essential problem faced by Clermont and "the good towns" was to get the *plat pays* to agree to the imposition of the *taillon* on the whole province when the king had restricted its imposition to the "good towns." The estates succeeded in getting the *plat pays* to go along by associating the latter in a suit of all the commoners against the nobility and clergy to force them to pay the *taille réelle*.[63] For the moment the matter of representation in the estates was resolved. But it was to arise anew in the course of the struggles of the religious wars.

Virtually at the same moment, the peasantry in Dauphiné began also to raise their heads. Excluded from the estates and subjected to the *taille personelle*, the peasants increasingly felt the burden of the direct and indirect taxation on their shoulders. At last in 1547 they began to protest, complaining in particular about the tax exemption of townsmen who were buying up peasant holdings. The cancellation of these exemptions by Henri II the next year set in motion the *procès des tailles* between nobles and commoners in the Dauphiné.[64]

The countryside in rebellion against the towns is an important feature of the most celebrated revolt of the first half of the sixteenth century, the revolt of the gabelle in Guyenne. Most students of the subject rightly stress the degree to which this upheaval represented a reaction to the abolition of local privileges by an encroaching central power. Likewise important to the uprising was the establishment of new taxes at a time when the condition of most petty producers was increasingly precarious as a result of previous tax increases, rising rents, and the garrisoning of troops on the population.[65]

In 1541 a royal ordinance had abolished the exemption of the provinces of the west of France with respect to the gabelle, placing them under the regime common to the rest of the kingdom. Immediately the price of salt – a commodity critical to the economy of La Rochelle and its region – rose by one-third. This imposition led to an abrupt rapprochement of the patricians with the plebians of La Rochelle. Faced with the prospect of an uprising, Chabot, the mayor and governor, decided to reinforce the garrison. On 26 August 1542, he ordered two or three hundred men-at-arms into the city. The population met the troops head on upon their entry. The soldiers were scattered and hunted down from street-to-street and from house-to-house. Some were killed, others were wounded and taken prisoner. Chabot and his remaining forces were obliged to quit the town. The rebellion at La Rochelle found echo in parallel upheavals on the islands of Ré and Oléron, and at Marennes.[66]

The institution of the gabelle involved the establishment of a whole network of commissioners and officers who operated out of the *greniers à sel* established throughout Aquitaine. In the spring of 1545, we hear of disorders and illicit assemblies at St Foy and Duras.[67] In April a popular rising at Périgueux forced the *gabelleurs* to flee the town.[68] We learn likewise of a popular upheaval at Sarlat the same year.[69] In 1546 eight *officiers* of the gabelle at Conse were assassinated by the inhabitants.[70]

At last, in the spring of 1548, came the general rebellion of Guyenne. It was an uprising of the small-scale producers in town and country who reinforced one another. Thus, at Libourne, the rebellion started as a protest of the craftsmen and sailors against the gabelle. They were joined by the peasants, who were mobilized in the countryside.[71] At Limoges the plebians seized the keys of the town and opened the gates to the country-folk. At Bordeaux the insurgent townsmen reinforced their numbers by opening the city to thousands of peasants from the surrounding country. The *gabelleurs* were the immediate object of attack.

Ideologically, the rebels based their cause on resistance against the encroachment of the crown on the liberties of Guyenne. On the other hand, it is clear that the revolt overflowed these limits into an attack on the urban rich. At Bordeaux the homes of many of the wealthy were put to the sack.[72] Rural protest against the urban elite was nowhere more evident than at Libourne. There the initial wave of unrest was suppressed by the bourgeois militia. One of the leaders of the peasant insurgents, Piron, was captured. The authorities refused the peasants' demands for his freedom. Between four and five hundred rustics invaded the city once again. Seizing the mayor and holding him by the beard, the peasants demanded the release of Piron. They broke into the prison, liberated Piron, and locked up the mayor in his place. The *hôtel de ville* was attacked and a bonfire made of certain of the town archives. Some of the rich citizens were rounded up and held to ransom before the peasants retired from the city.[73] Rural protest against the town was thus as much an aspect of this revolt as was protest against royal fiscalism.

But in a revolt of these dimensions it was not only tax officials and the urban rich who came under attack. Nobles, too, became targets. The rebels in the Angoumois and Saintonge burned the chateaux of the Seigneur Daubteuile on the pretext that he was a *gabelleur*. Insurgents around Cognac put the chateau of Godemoulin to the torch, accusing the seigneur of concealing *gabelleurs*. Chateaux were burned at Anqueville and Saint-Même as well.[74] Thus, while there can be no doubt that the gabelle revolt was above all a protest against the encroachment of the state and the oppressive urban bourgeoisie, it overflowed these limits in various places into a revolt against all authority, including that of the nobility.

The mood of rebellion in Guyenne found expression in the work of the young Etienne de la Boétie. La Boétie was no more than eighteen years old when he penned *Le Discours de la Servitude Volontaire*.[75] A native of Sarlat the young scholar must have been attuned to the mood of rebelliousness that pervaded his own city and the surrounding countryside at the time he wrote. The still adolescent La Boétie offers a critique of political and social obedience that has more to do with the psychology of youth than with a full, articulated theory of politics. Nevertheless, La Boétie's description of the violence, oppression, and suffering caused by monarchy reflected not only the point of view of patrician youth in revolt but that of a whole generation of commoners. The unformed and rhetorical nature of this treatise corresponds in a way to a movement of popular protest that had not fully matured. That maturity was to come only in the course of the religious wars, in the writings of the champions of Calvinist resistance. On the other hand, it should be underlined that La Boétie's fiery defence of individual liberty, even of social equality, was in total opposition to the notion of a society of orders.

THE LAST CATEGORY of popular revolt that marked the first half of the sixteenth century was based on religion. Overwhelmingly, this kind of popular resistance took the form of individual or isolated acts of refusal and disobedience by religious dissidents. Such defiance must be understood to have been directed against the established Church and so necessarily, albeit indirectly, against the existing political, legal, and social order. It was so interpreted by the authorities of the time. While members of the urban elite were involved in it from its inception, their practice of heresy was for the most part private or clandestine. More commonly it was the plebians who were prepared to risk their faith through acts of iconoclasm. It was they, in any case, who were most often punished for the crime of heresy in the period up to the religious wars. Despite the scattered nature of these acts of religious dissidence, what strikes one from the first is their ubiquity. Certain places in the kingdom – the Brie, Normandy, Languedoc – were more touched than others and from an earlier date. On the other hand, by the 1530s hardly a place in France had not been affected. Heresy was the least overt or spectacular but the most generalized and persistent form of popular protest in the first half of the sixteenth century. It proved to be the kind of resistance under which many other forms of popular discontent could be organized into a more or less coherent protest movement at the outbreak of the religious wars.

From the beginning, religious contestation was mixed up with other forms of political and social conflict. The resistance of the Vaudois of Provence and the Comtat-Venaissin is perhaps the best example. The history of this movement in the sixteenth century has been analyzed exhaustively in the magisterial work of Gabriel Audisio.[76] Such is the profundity and density of Audisio's treatment that the history of Vaudois resistance runs the risk of being buried in this great volume.

The persecution of the Vaudois began in the early 1530s. Its inception coincides with the turn in the economic conjuncture that marked the late 1520s and the 1530s in the south of France. Under such circumstances the Vaudois – despite or because of their relative poverty – became the object of attack, not only by the Church, state, and nobility but by the population of Provence as a whole.

Increasingly isolated and under assault, the Vaudois responded by taking to arms. The inquisition of the Dominican Jean de Roma in the early 1530s provoked the first opposition. In March, 1533 a riot took place at Cabrières-d'Aigues. The inhabitants assembled in large numbers armed with arquebuses and other weapons. They assaulted the agents of the inquisitor as well as the seigneur of Cental, crying "Kill! Kill! Finish them off!" Further, they menaced the inhabitants of the bourg of Apt for helping the inquisitor.[77] Another armed assembly took place in 1535.[78]

Five years later, in July 1540, the Vaudois attacked the prison at Apt in an unsuccessful bid to liberate their brethren being held under arrest there.[79] One of these prisoners, Colin Pellenc, was subsequently burned alive at Aix. Following an auction, a new owner tried to take possession of Pellenc's mill at Plan d'Apt. A riot by the Vaudois made it impossible for him to take over the property.[80]

The massacre of the Vaudois was the climactic event of their history as a sect. Ranged against them in 1545 were not only the Church and the Parlement of Provence but all the forces of order. The *ban* and *arrière-ban* as well as the *gendarmerie* of Provence were called out. But the spearhead of the army sent against them was made up of the seasoned troops of the army of Piedmont. It is a mistake to believe that the Vaudois did nothing but patiently submit to this onslaught. Faced with the overwhelming forces sent against them, they abandoned their villages, sent their wives and children to the safety of the mountains, and took up arms to defend themselves. They threw themselves into fortified places, especially Merindol and Cabrières d'Avignon in which they put up a heroic if unsuccessful resistance.[81]

The will of the Vaudois to resist was far from broken by the massacre of 1545. In 1553, the Vaudois of Mérindol blocked the transfer of their property to new owners by force of arms. In September 1555, they attacked and sacked the fortress built by one of these new owners. Seven months later they laid siege to the same fortress once again.[82] In September 1560, many of the Vaudois who had been driven from Cabrières d'Avignon launched an attack on that town. They had been living as exiles in the bastides and villages around

Gordes, as well as elsewhere in Provence. Heavily armed, they approached the town under cover of night. When setting fire to the gate of the chateau failed to gain them entry, they attacked a bourgade located outside the walls and put it to the sack, warning the inhabitants "to depart because the property belonged to them and not to those who occupied it nor to the seigneur."[83] At this date, Vaudois violence throughout the region was general.

The relationship between religion and politics in the towns is evident at Meaux from the inception of the Reformation. A democratic upheaval coincided with the initial stages of the Fabrist reform. The radicalization of the reform in 1524 represented the seizure of the initiative in the process of reform by the more plebian elements within the community.

Likewise, in the 1540s at St Maixent in Poitou we can see clearly how political and economic discontent helped to influence religious dissidence, the one reinforcing the other. Thus, by 1544, it was reported that taxation and the garrisoning of troops on the town during the third Imperial-Valois war had exasperated the people. These impositions gave rise in the first place to a popular movement against the clergy led by a friar named Jerome. The preaching of Jerome and other radicals soon turned against the civil as well as the religious authorities in the town as well as in the surrounding countryside.[84]

THE RHYTHM OF POPULAR disorder closely follows that of the economic crises of the first half of the sixteenth century. Looking across the decades between 1500 and 1560, it seems plain that the 1520s and 1540s were particularly disturbed.

Popular Contestation: 1500–1560

Region/Town	Year	Method of Protest	Reason for Protest
Nîmes	1505	riot	subsistence
Carcassonne	1506	riot	political exclusion
Rodez	1506	democratic movement	political exclusion
Nevers	1507	riot	political exclusion
Caen	1513	day of the lansquenets	popular revolt against soldiers
Agen	1514	revolt	taxation, political exclusion
Le Noyer	1516	range war	land rights
Laval	1516	riot	ecclesiastical dispute between people and seigneur

Popular Contestation: 1500–1560 *(Continued)*

Region/Town	Year	Method of Protest	Reason for Protest
Attichy	1518–27	peasant violence	resistance to serfdom
Libourne	1519	revolt	plebian exclusion from politics
Lantriac, Velay	1521	peasant revolt	rents
Aix, Marseilles, Tarascon	1521	riots	grain shortage
Meaux	1522	revolt	plebian exclusion from politics
Beauvais	1522	riot	grain shortage
Tours	1522	riot	grain shortage
Ile-de-France	1523	brigandage, insurrection	revolt of Captain Montélon
Romans	1525 +	riots	plebian exclusion from politics
Dijon	1526	riots	political rights of plebians attacked
Sarladais	1526–7	riot	peasant unrest
Bordeaux	1528	revolt	excise tax on wine: patricians vs plebians
Lyons	1529	"rebeine"	grain shortage
Dijon	1529	riot	grain shortage
Troyes	1529	riot	unemployment
Vorilhes, Foix	1535	riot	nobles vs commons over woodlands
Le Puy	1536	riot	taxation, provisioning military
Provence	1536	peasant risings	war, foreign invasion
Rodez	1537	democratic movement	taxation
Albi & Albigeois	1537	attacks on villages	war between gendarmerie and commons
Marseille	1539	revolt	gabelle
Ramieville? (Vermandois)	1539	riot	taxes
Lyons, Paris	1539–42	strikes	printers' wages
Rouen	1542	riot	subsistence
Tours	1542	riot	economic crisis

Popular Contestation: 1500–1560 (Concluded)			
Region/Town	Year	Method of Protest	Reason for Protest
La Rochelle & Les Iles	1542	revolt	gabelle
St Maixent	1544	revolt	taxation, religion
Sarlat	1545	revolt	taxation
Niort, Saintes, Périgueux, St Foy, Duras	1545	revolt	gabelle
Rouen	1545	riot	subsistence
Comminges	1545	peasant league	taxation
Luberon	1545	attack and resistance of Vaudois	religion
Meaux, Senlis, Orleans Soissons, Langres, Saint-Menehould, Tours, Saintes, La Rochefoucauld, Agen, Iles de Ré, Oléron, Bayonne, Nîmes, Lyons, Uzès, Alès	1545–6		religious agitation
Vitry	1545–7	riots	real estate speculation
Guyenne	1548	revolt	gabelle
Dauphiné, Auvergne, Velay Agenais	1548–51	leagues of peasants and bourgs	taxation, political exclusion
Nay	1552	revolt	political exclusion
Le Puy	1553	riots	noble provocation
Normandy	1554	peasant revolt: eighteen villages	disputes in forests around Alençon

These two decades seem to foreshadow the fiscal and economic crisis that accompanied the outbreak of the religious wars themselves. The 1520s marked the first wave of major unrest that shook the kingdom,[85] with serious outbreaks of urban strife at Meaux, Troyes, Paris, Agen, Lyons, Tours, La Rochelle, Romans, and Dijon. But evidence also exists of widespread rural disorder, for example the attacks already noted on men-at-arms in Vivarais and Gevaudan in the mid 1520s. In the Sarladais, the end of 1526 and beginning of 1527 saw an uprising of the peasantry who called for the death of both the nobility and the magistrates.[86] Throughout the centre and north of the kingdom the chronicles of that decade are filled with accounts of a wave of brigandage, which followed in the wake of the movements of conscript infantry in the early 1520s. The most spectacular of these bands was that of the captain de Montélon operating in the Ile-de-France. It attracted a wide following and assumed a proto-political form before it was suppressed.[87]

The 1540s were even more agitated. The frequent incidence of civil disturbance coincided for the first time with widespread popular religious unrest.[88] Indeed, it is in the 1540s that we can speak of the large-scale conjuncture of religious non-conformity and popular protest. It is the same decade that witnessed the extension of disorders on a broad basis into the countryside. The appearance of leagues of peasants and bourgs, to say nothing of the revolt of the gabelle, bespeak the regionalization of popular movements on a scale not seen before. War, taxation, quartering of troops, subsistence, and economic crisis underlay these further upheavals. The popular contestation of the 1520s and 1540s, then, ought to be viewed as stepping stones to the outbreak of general revolt at the beginning of the 1560s.

No less striking than the agitation of the 1520s and 1540s is its relative absence in the early 1550s. This is to be accounted for on the one hand by the massive apparatus of repression deployed by the monarchy under Henri II, and on the other hand, by the widespread process of Calvinist church formation, which during the 1550s, contained unruly plebian elements. But the religious disorders of the late 1550s indicate the limitations of such ecclesiastical discipline.

The forms of popular resistance varied greatly, particularly in the towns. New taxes, economic crisis, and political exclusion were the most frequent causes of urban seditions. One of the most striking features of popular protest in this period was the growing mobilization of the countryside against the town elites. Far from accepting the increasing control of the urban elites, the rural population showed an increasing capacity for organized resistance. Royal officials, urban notables, clergy, and nobles became targets of popular anger. Increasingly, the rural population was able to concert their protests with those of the urban plebians.

Noteworthy in conclusion is the rarity of conflict between the urban bourgeoisie and the crown. It is only in the 1550s, under the weight of growing economic difficulties and unrelenting royal fiscal pressure, that part of this stratum became estranged from the monarchy. Their hostility led them to a growing sympathy toward Calvinism. Indeed, it was their leadership that made it possible to transform Calvinism into a national movement of political as well as religious opposition. On the other hand, their control also tended to limit the degree to which peasants, journeymen, and the majority of craftsmen were prepared to lend their support to the movement.

CHAPTER TWO

Bourgeois Calvinism and Aristocratic Reaction

... aussi gens de bien que toi!

the compagnons of Autun

The upheavals and revolts of the 1560s were the product of two generations of accumulating social, political, and religious grievances. The mass of discontent then exploded into popular violence during the 1560s. During this tumultous decade, scarcely a region of the kingdom was spared by the wave of revolt against the local ecclesiastical establishments, the oligarchies who controlled the towns, and the representatives of the monarchy. Here and there, this broad horizontal current turned into a movement against the nobility itself.

The revolts of the 1560s were the outgrowth of the popular protest that had marked earlier decades, notably the 1520s and 1540s. The rank-and-file of the movement was drawn from the mass of urban artisans who allowed themselves to be led by Calvinist merchants and notables. The leadership of this Calvinist bourgeoisie gave the movement a cohesiveness that earlier waves of protest had lacked and turned it into a political and religious movement embracing the whole kingdom.

The temporal and religious grievances of the Calvinists were inextricably mixed. For example, the Duke d'Etampes, writing from Brittany in August 1562, urged the monarchy not to impose new taxes because the levies already made had provoked the Protestants in the Breton towns once again to hurl down crosses and attack images.[1] In Brittany, fresh taxes led directly to renewed attacks on the Church.

On the other hand, the discontent of the early 1560s was not confined to the Calvinist minority. Urban and even rural Catholics voiced many of the complaints common to the Calvinists. Typical were the *cahiers des doléances* drawn up by the third estate of Comminges. These grievances were composed in 1560 for the Estates-General of Orleans. Article one denied that there were any Protestants in the Comminges. A succession of following articles then detailed the principal abuses among the clergy: non-residence, ignorance, immorality, ostentation, excessive tithes, failure to maintain the Church fabric, and outrageous mortuary and wedding fees. Following these came the usual roster of complaints against the officers of the king, the administration of justice, and the weight of taxation. Also typical were the grievances of the third estate against the nobility: refusal to pay taxes, excessive rents in labour and kind, and the unlawful imposition of all manner of seigneurial dues and charges.[2] The Huguenot revolt must thus be understood as the most visible aspect of a broad movement of protest among the bourgeoisie and commoners, Catholic as well as Protestant.

As noted earlier, French society in 1560 was in a state of crisis that in many respects resembled the revolution two hundred years later. It was divided by class hostility, beset by growing poverty and economic crisis, and menaced by the spectre of royal bankruptcy. In 1560, as in 1789, the established Church was under attack from a rival ideology and alarmed at the threat of a secularization of its properties. Like the eighteenth century, the sixteenth century had created a class of merchants and craftsmen who were prepared to challenge the religious as well as the political and social foundations of the existing order.[3]

While the above sketch does capture the outlines of the crisis of the early 1560s, it is important to note that there were many exceptions. The Calvinist revolts of the 1560s were popular movements, but only in a few places did they win over a majority of the population of the towns, to say nothing about the peasants in the country. In some communities, the ties between the Catholic establishment and the mass of the population proved stronger than the coalition of Protestant notables, merchants, and artisans. At Sens in 1561, for example, the Catholic party incited a popular fury to forestall the Protestants. The canons of the cathedral of Sens even went so far as to call in their tenants from the countryside to help the urban mob to carry out the pillaging and massacre of the Protestants.[4]

In Provence, Protestantism enjoyed popular support only in areas of Vaudois strength. Elsewhere, a Catholic revival evident from the 1550s consolidated the loyalty of peasants and artisans. The attraction of the mass of the populace to Catholicism was assured by the proliferation of a great variety of popular observances and celebrations.[5] Particularly notable was the spread of companies of penitents, who attracted a base of mass support but whose leadership came from the urban elites.[6] In the popular mind, Protestantism became identified with marginals such as the Vaudois or with oppressive urban elites of bourgeois and notables. The outbreak of the religious conflict at the beginning of the 1560s in Provence accordingly became the occasion for popular revenge against the rich – or at least some of the rich.

At Salon, the rank-and-file of the Catholic party was to be found in the mass of agricultural labourers who lived both inside and outside the town. On the other hand, by 1560 the government of the town was firmly in the hands of a patrician elite that was more and more openly Calvinist. Nonetheless, the day labourers of the town still clung to the right to participate in municipal elections. Louis Villemerin (alias Currier), himself a bourgeois notable, was the tribune of this popular and Catholic faction at the beginning of the 1560s.

May Day 1562 became the occasion for a popular uprising incited by what was regarded as a Huguenot provocation. The Calvinist elite sent their children as a body to sing evangelical hymns out in the street. Urged on by Currier, the agricultural labourers in the city rebelled, joining forces with fellow rural workers and peasants in the countryside. Together they overthrew the oligarchy and instituted a reign of terror on the Protestant elite. Aside from immediate social vengeance, the objective of the rebels appears to have been to defend their traditional faith against those among the elite who were trying to undermine it, evidenced by the fact that those among the bourgeoisie and notables who championed the traditional beliefs of the rural and urban folk were not molested. Indeed, Currier and his allies among the Catholic notables were looked to for leadership. Once the plebians had finished with the Protestants, the Catholic notables had little trouble restoring order and re-establishing elite control.

It was the Protestant notables who were not prepared to let bygones be bygones. They had been threatened, manhandled, and arrested, but their power had not been eliminated. By the beginning of July the balance of forces in Salon had shifted again in their favour, many of the agricultural labourers having gone off to distant parts to participate in the harvest. Currier was assassinated and an attempted Catholic uprising on his behalf suppressed. The victory of the Protestant elite entailed the abolition of the democratic franchise.[7] Thereafter, extremist politics and militant Catholicism at Salon were closely mixed together in a way that anticipates the outlook of the radical wing of the Catholic League. Indeed, the League revolt at Salon assumed the characteristics of a democratic movement that directly echoed the struggles of the 1560s.[8]

At Aix, too, a Protestant elite appears to have acquired inordinate influence at the beginning of the 1560s. Overreaching themselves, they provoked a popular reaction that destroyed their power. The populace was already incensed at reports of outrages against the Catholic clergy and attacks on holy places and monuments throughout Provence by the Protestants. An anti-Catholic provocation itself immediately set off an insurrection. It had long been the custom at Aix for the common people to make a procession in barefeet from the gates of the town to the shrine of St Mark located in a chapel about a league from the town. But on the eve of the annual procession, the Huguenots spread thorns on the pilgrims' route. The next day some Protestants assembled at the gates of the town to mock the pilgrims as they made their way painfully to the sanctuary.

The peasants and artisans who had been humiliated by this trick resolved on revenge. But far from acting on their own they appealed for help to a

Catholic noble, the sire de Flassans, who was the underground leader of the
Catholic party in Aix. Flassans set in motion a plot designed not only to gain
vengeance but to liberate the city from the grip of the Calvinist notables.
At the prompting of Flassans, the rector of the Company of Black Penitents
initiated a campaign to collect stones, ostensibly to pave the confraternity's
chapel. When enough stones had been gathered, the rector announced that
the company would make a procession to the shrine of Notre Dame de Grace
in the countryside at Pentecost. As they would be gone for more than a day
he asked each of the brothers to bring a sack for provisions.

When the Black Penitents had assembled in the chapel, Flassans, himself
a member of the company, disclosed his plan to seize the town from the Protestants. The stones in the chapel were to become the needed weapons. The
brothers filled their sacks with stones and marched out of the chapel followed
by a throng of peasants and artisans. Together they were easily able to over-
come the Protestant resistance, despite the fact that the latter had a fifteen-
hundred-man garrison to back them up.[9]

For most of the craftsmen, workers, and peasants of Provence there was
no question of challenging the principle of oligarchy itself. They sought to
protect their way of life, as well as their right, in however limited a form,
to participate in civic life. They were deferential to those among the elite
who put themselves forward as champions of popular tradition. Their enemies
were those who sought to exclude the plebians from politics while putting
popular religious belief and practice into question. In plebian eyes, Protestant
religious hegemony entailed unlimited elite political and ideological domination.

The Catholic "mob" attached to Church if not to king was not confined
to Provence. Its presence was felt virtually everywhere in the kingdom in
the course of the religious wars. The Catholic popular party appears less affluent
and literate than its Protestant counterpart. As such, it ordinarily outnumbered
the Calvinist rank-and-file in any community. Increasingly organized, the
Catholic crowd became a force to be reckoned with at the massacre of
St Bartholomew's Day and at the time of the Catholic League. In so far as
it became a threat, it was subject to manipulation by Catholic notables,
ecclesiastics, or aristrocrats.[10]

But in the first years of the civil wars, it was not the Catholic "mob" that
maintained the offensive; rather it was the Protestant notables and merchants
allied with the evangelical craftsmen. Seldom a majority of the population,
the Protestant artisans provided popular support for the Calvinist cause, while
the merchants and notables supplied it with financial and moral leadership.

The national aims of the Calvinists at the beginning of the civil wars were
spelled out in a directive prepared by the Huguenot leaders for the estates-
general of Pontoise. It called for the establishment of a regency council named
by the estates-general. It demanded that no offensive war be initiated or new
taxes imposed without the consent of the estates. It insisted on a reduction

in the taille while proposing to meet the state deficit by confiscating part of the revenue of the Church. Finally, it appealed for the granting of religious liberty and an end to local ecclesiastical jurisdiction.[11]

While these constitutionally radical proposals were being voiced at the national level, grassroots coalitions of Calvinists were springing into action. In many instances, revolt against ecclesiastical domination entailed a popular uprising against seigneurial jurisdiction. At Aubenas, for example, the Calvinists revolted against their seigneurial overlord and the Church at one and the same time.[12] At Brioude, the reformation revolt offered the population the occasion to liquidate an uncompromising seigneurial regime maintained by the Church.[13]

The Protestant revolt at Millau is a prime example of an urban revolt against ecclesiastical domination. The town was both a spiritual and temporal dependency of the bishop of Rodez. At Millau, as in so many other places, the *collège* – itself a symbol of municipal independence of the Church – was turned into the headquarters of the Reformation. One evening in mid-October 1560, the *lieutenant du bailliage* walked into the auditorium of the *collège* and found to his astonishment four or five hundred townsfolk attentively listening to a sermon by a Calvinist minister, Jacques Duval of Rouen.

By 1563 the Calvinists had achieved an overwhelming ascendancy in Millau, largely as a result of making their cause synonymous with urban independence. On 3 June, the consuls, followed by three quarters of the population, presented themselves before the judge of the *bailliage* asking that they be permitted to petition the king to allow the establishment of Calvinist churches in the town. This having been accorded, the consuls then asked the *bailli* to allow a survey of the eight hundred assembled citizens to see whether any wanted the mass restored. The resulting on-the-spot survey could find no one among the crowd in favour of such a restoration. At this point, the syndic of the town, Dominique Casson, apparently a Catholic holdover, pointed out that at least a quarter of the population was absent and that, to be fair, only a house-to-house census could establish the real sentiments of the population. Two days later, following this further investigation, it was reported that not a single citizen wanted the mass brought back.

How can one explain such unanimity? It may be that many Catholics had already fled Millau. It may be, too, that the pressure of public opinion forced many to keep their true feelings to themselves. But the main explanation for this overwhelming tide of Calvinist sentiment lies in the identification of the Calvinist cause with municipal independence. The establishment of Calvinism meant the liberation of the town from the tutelage of ecclesiastical–seigneurial domination founded on Rodez. Indeed, Millau was to become a bastion of the Huguenot urban federation in the Midi.[14]

We have already seen that the Protestant rising in the Velay amounted to an insurgency against the Church as the mainstay of a whole system of seigneurial and oligarchical domination. In the case of the Velay, it is noteworthy that the Protestant attack on Le Puy in 1562 was accompanied by a revolt within the town walls that had the support of at least a third of the population.[15] The Calvinist revolt was, as it were, a revolt of the external and internal petty producers against the local elite.

One of the clearest examples of the anti-oligarchical element in the initial Protestant revolts can be found at St Maixent nearby to Poitiers. St Maixent has an excellent chronicle of its history in the sixteenth century in the form of the journal of Guillaume and Michel Le Riche, who were *avocats du roi* there for over fifty years.[16] In 1580, Michel Le Riche made note of the death of Master Jehan de Launoy, who had been one of a multitude of Catholic clergy won to the side of the Reformation. In noting Launoy's death, Le Riche recollected the history of the attempted Protestant *coup de main* in Saint Maixent of 9 July 1562, which Launoy had led. From the time of his conversion in the mid 1550s, Launoy had spent his time organizing the Calvinist congregation in St Maixent, and once the reformed church was constituted, he became its minister. His influence in the town became enormous and omnipresent. He was nicknamed "Bon-Vouloir," and, as Michel Le Riche informs us, he was honoured by the Protestants and feared by everyone. Using the pretext that his life was in jeopardy, he staged a revolt against the principal citizens of the town. According to Le Riche, his followers consisted of between three and four hundred "workers." This enterprise missed its mark and as a result, Le Riche concludes, Launoy's credibility suddenly collapsed.[17]

Le Riche's reference to "workers" sounds at first strange. The archetypical Protestant was the urban artisan or small-scale, skilled producer who might indeed be referred to as a worker. But the term "worker" might also include the journeyman printer of Lyons or the so-called "carder" of Valence, both of whom were attracted to Protestant ideas and who were "workers" in the modern sense, that is, proletarianized or semi-proletarianized producers. The importance of this kind of "worker" to the Protestant cause can be seen from the case of Dijon. The repression of the Protestant movement there was carried out in 1562 by Saulx-Tavannes, who called for the arrest of the ringleaders and the disarming of the rank-and-file followers of the Huguenot party. Saulx-Tavannes then ordered a public review of all of the employees of the merchants and artisans of the city. The great majority of the workers were Swiss and Germans who were unemployed at the time. Saulx-Tavannes ordered their expulsion from the town as trouble-makers.[18] Recalling this event in his memoirs, Saulx-Tavannes claims that he rid Dijon of fifteen hundred "valets huguenots."[19] This example confirms the fact that the Calvinist element in many towns included a large number of migrant and mobile newcomers.[20] It ought to caution us against using tax-roles as an infallible guide to the study of urban Protestantism.[21]

The majority of urban insurrections of this period were carried out by coalitions of Huguenot craftsmen, merchants, and notables, which more often than not attacked an entrenched Catholic oligarchy as well as the Church.

In 1561 at Gap, for instance, a crisis in the town's finances created intense popular dissatisfaction with the ruling oligarchy. The Protestant leaders – largely from the secondary elite of merchants and lesser officials – were thus able to mobilize popular support behind them for an attack on the establishment.[22]

As we have seen, the Protestant revolts of the 1560s occurred in the throes of an economic crisis – a crisis that had been in the making through the first half of the century. The 1520s and 1540s were already marked by grave social disorders. The Protestant upheaval marked the third and culminating stage of these difficulties. The root of these problems was to be found in French agriculture. Rising population with no increase in agricultural productivity cut into the profit margins and the markets of manufacturers, threatening the livelihood of craftsmen and the enterprises of merchants.

In an earlier work, *The Conquest of Poverty* I pointed out how on the eve of the civil wars it was the Huguenot potter from Saintes Bernard, Palissy, who put his finger on the sources of the problem.[23] Palissy stressed the need to capitalize and improve the efficiency of agriculture. He even encouraged the monarchy to reward those who invented mechanical devices that would improve agricultural output. At the time of writing that work, I emphasized the utopian quality of Palissy's proposals. However practical and insightful they were, I nevertheless insisted that in view of the political and social realities of French society it would have been difficult if not impossible to apply these ideas. The resistance to such notions, I concluded, goes far to explain why Palissy cast his treatise in utopian rather than practical terms.

I believe this analysis still holds water. However, I perhaps exaggerated the degree of hostility that existed to ideas such as Palissy's. In doing so I was too influenced by the neo-Malthusian pessimism of Le Roy Ladurie, who admittedly portrayed the Calvinists as a skilled, literate and relatively well-off minority, but also tended rather wistfully to view them as implicated in the crisis rather than bent on overcoming it.

On the other hand, it is Le Roy Ladurie who has instructed us on the existence of a sixteenth-century agrarian capitalism. It is Le Roy Ladurie who spoke of this period as the time of "the offensive of profit" as against the time of the "offensive of rent" to come.[24] However regressive this capitalism was, its existence nonetheless left room for some experimentation. Despite the outbreak of the religious wars, or perhaps because of it, an effort was made to put Palissy's ideas or similar notions into practice. Thus, in 1566 Charles IX issued a patent for seven years to Henri Rambault of Marseilles for a new plow. As the text of the patent explains, Rambault "had invented a form of agricultural machine or tool by which the land can be much more quickly, cheaply and easily cultivated and worked than by the plow or other device presently used in the Kingdom."[25]

But it was at Nîmes, long since passed into Huguenot hands by 1566, that an attempt was made actually to put Rambault's invention into use. Like other French towns Nîmes was already experiencing economic difficulties in the 1550s. The town council, under Protestant influence, tried even then to counter the growing economic malaise with a program of incentives. In 1552 the municipality established a weekly livestock market.[26] In 1554 it subsidized the establishment of the workshop of a pinmaker from Le Puy in the city.[27] In 1557 it supported the establishment of a manufacturer of velvets,[28] and in 1558 a manufacturer of silks.[29] Thus, when the town councillors decided in 1567 to promote the use of Rambault's invention, the initiative represented a continuation of past policy. The town agreed to pay the inventor sixty *livres tournois* for the right to use his device in the faubourgs of the town and in the surrounding countryside.[30]

It is possible that the initiative of the town fathers was related directly to Palissy's work. More likely, however, the city's sponsorship of agricultural inventions such as Rambault's reflects a common perception among those involved in manufacturing that the decline of the secondary sector was not unrelated to the failure of agriculture. How successful this initiative was in the midst of the calamities of the religious wars is questionable. But what has to be borne in mind was that there was a certain awareness of the problem of agricultural stagnation among the Calvinists and an attempt to remedy the situation. Contrast this perspective with the view of Le Roy Ladurie who envisions the Languedoc as caught in an inexorable Malthusian cycle from which it was to be rescued from the outside a century and a half later.

One of the most enigmatic aspects of the Protestant–Catholic cleavage is that of generational conflict. In 1573, the governor of Narbonne, the baron Raymond de Fourquevaux, reported to Charles IX on the state of Languedoc in the wake of the massacre of St Bartholomew's Day. He assured the king of the loyalty of nine-tenths of the people of Languedoc. According to Fourquevaux, most of the people were Catholic and devout, wishing to live and die in obedience to the king. On the other hand, he noted that those who were notables but still commoners were exceptions tending toward Calvinism. Likewise, the merchants favoured the Calvinists. Also sympathetic to the Protestant cause, Fourquevaux claimed, were "those among the youth who are educated as well as those among them who are friends of liberty."[31]

According to Fourquevaux, then, those among the young who had been exposed to an education were favourable to Calvinism. We can assume that Fourquevaux was referring to the kind of humanist education that would be available to the sons of the bourgeoisie in a municipal *collège* or at the University of Valence or Poitiers.

Even more interesting is the fact that Fourquevaux singles out among this rebellious youth those who are friends of liberty. In the sixteenth century, the word "liberty" had at least two distinct meanings. One, which harked back to the Middle Ages, referred to the franchises and privileges enjoyed by a community. The second sense of the word was that of personal and individual freedom, recalling its meaning in Antiquity. Fourquevaux's use of the term entails both senses of the word but the sense of personal and individual freedom predominates.

Fourquevaux thus evokes a youth that is humanistically educated, attracted to the idea of personal freedom, and consequently drawn to Calvinism. What is perhaps a surprise is the way Fourquevaux associates those who are drawn to Calvinism with those who are friends of liberty. We, on the contrary, are accustomed to thinking of Calvinism in terms of discipline and a surrender of the will rather than in terms of individual liberty. But perhaps the concepts of discipline and liberty were not so far apart in the minds of Calvinist youth in the revolutionary 1560s. As is frequently the case, the quest for freedom from existing oppression led the young to embrace the fetters of a new kind of discipline.

Rebelliousness among the sons and daughters of the bourgeoisie plagued even the most zealous Catholics. Louis Cosset was long the head of the Catholic party at Meaux, and, as *procureur du roi*, he had himself led the civic militia in the attack on the evangelical artisans of the *Marché* of Meaux in 1546.[32] In 1560 we find him forcing his son and future daughter-in-law to sign a marriage contract in which they promised "to preserve the law of their mother and father ... living and dying in it while renouncing all other sects and heresies presently reigning."[33]

At nearby Melun in 1562, the *procureur du roi*, Christophe Rossignol, deprived his son Jean of his inheritance as a result of his religious defiance. Jean had become notorious in the city as an evangelical agitator. One day he encountered a group of peasants from the village of Corbeil in pilgrimage to the abbey of Mont Saint-Père in the faubourg Saint-Barthélemy. He reproached them, remarking that in kissing the relics there they were in fact kissing the head of a sheep. In disinheriting his son Jean Christophe Rossignol stressed that his son had not only repeatedly refused to go to Church and shown contempt for its ceremonies but "had disobeyed [his father's] commandments and remonstrances."[34] Young Rossignol was punished because he had challenged his father's authority, as well as the authority of the Church.

At Bar-sur-Seine the religious revolt of the early 1560s produced a dramatic instance of conflict between generations. The Protestants briefly seized both the town and the chateau. They were led by a young *avocat*, Ralet, who was the son of the *procureur du roi*. The Catholics were quickly able to re-establish control, capturing and imprisoning some of the Huguenots involved in the uprising, including Ralet. It was Ralet's father, the *procureur du roi*, who pronounced the bill of indictment against him and demanded the imposition of the death penalty.[35]

Fourquevaux, reporting to the king, emphasized the strongly Protestant sympathies found among the artisans, as well as among the merchants and notables. These elements, he noted, constituted the core of the Protestant party. The artisans tended to Protestantism, according to Fourquevaux, owing to their "rogue nature."[36] But this spirit itself may have been the product of their relative youth. Thus, in 1559, the official of the cathedral of Mâcon, Jean Ligeret, noted with dismay the spread of Protestantism in the town especially among the young. He complained of the reading of illicit literature, the holding of clandestine meetings, the mocking of the clergy and the sacraments, and the growing refusal to celebrate the holy days. Craftsmen were keeping their shops open on such days. In the rue Franche, he reported, he had even discovered a crowd of young men in a shoemaker's shop who were singing the psalms of David in French in the fashion of Geneva.[37]

Autun provides a striking instance of the youthful and popular spirit that infused the Protestant revolt of these years. By the spring of 1561, evangelical agitation in the town was intense. During Lent, the tradition of the canons of the Cathedral of Autun was customarily to chant the mass in one or another of the parochial churches in the city. The winding of the procession of the canons through the streets of the town was one of the spectacles of the traditional Lenten season. On 21 March, the canons were proceeding down the rue Chaulchien enroute from the cathedral to a neighbourhood parish. According to the registers of the chapter, the canons ran into a group of between twenty and thirty compagnons. The young men, employees in the shops of shoemakers and other craftsmen in that thoroughfare, had apparently waited in ambush for the procession. As the canons tried to make their way down the rue Chaulchien, the compagnons formed a counter-procession going in the opposite direction. The young artisans invaded and broke up the ecclesiastical procession, making a show of their swords and daggers and deliberately mocking the clergy and their estate. One of the canons tried to rebuke the young bravos, remarking that they were behaving badly and that in acting so they were not "gens de bien." This rebuke infuriated the compagnons, who threatened the canons, while shouting "aussi gens de bien que toi!"[38]

Conflict between the generations is obvious in this instance. But so, too, is a conflict, if not of classes, then of orders. Indeed, the egalitarian posturing of these young workers in the face of the first estate is what stands out in this encounter. The more-than-usual intolerance of these aspiring craftsmen was fueled by their new faith, as well as by a sense of declining opportunities for themselves. The latter fact helps to explain in part the attraction of Protestantism for the younger generation.

Is it possible to quantify the number of young adherents to the Calvinist party? Janine Garrison has estimated their numbers at between 7.2 and 12 per cent of the total number of Protestants based on her lists of urban Protestants from the Midi.[39] These figures should likely be taken as a minimum.

The urban and bourgeois character of the Protestantism of the 1560s is confirmed if we look at the armies it fielded. Although ordinarily commanded by noblemen, the Calvinist forces were largely bourgeois in character, comprising mainly artisans and merchants. Infantry in these armies largely outnumbered cavalry. Such cavalry as there was consisted mainly of German mercenary troops employing pistols rather than men-of-war using the lance. In contrast, the bulk of the royal army consisted of foot soldiers recruited outside the kingdom, the nobles fearing a popular army. Its leading arm remained the noble *gendarmerie*.[40]

By the 1570s, in the aftermath of St Bartholomew, Catholic observers noted that the Protestant side refused to fight in open battle, preferring to base their strategy on the defence of fortified towns. According to Pierre Brisson, "the reason for their failure in open combat and pitched battle was the consequence of their lack of good horses and cavalry in so far as their main strength lay in masses of men such as merchants and artisans."[41] Thus, at the outbreak of the third religious war in 1568, the Admiral Coligny and the Prince of Condé called for the raising of an army of ten thousand men in Guyenne. Volunteers were recruited from all over the Midi and even in Beaujolais. The aristocratic commanders were taken aback when more than thirty thousand Calvinists turned up. Among the mass of commoners who volunteered were old men, some of them over seventy, and children of ten or twelve years, as well as the lame and others likewise unfit.[42]

The town of Die in Dauphiné showed itself to be particularly zealous. The Huguenot revolt there had been a clear case of a rising of the merchants and artisans against the clergy and nobles.[43] The total population at the time was no more than four thousand, yet more than seven hundred men, constituting the overwhelming majority of the males, turned out to serve in the army of Guyenne. In the end, only two hundred of the volunteers returned from the war.[44]

It is sometimes asserted that rural Protestantism was essentially noble. Put another way, it is claimed that the peasants were predisposed to Catholicism and hostile to the new faith. Where Calvinism did implant itself in the countryside, so this argument runs, it was able to do so at the behest of Calvinist nobles who imposed it on their tenants. Emile Segui's elegant little study of Faugères en Biterrois addresses this question directly.[45] Faugères was a village of some four hundred inhabitants. Two-thirds of the population became Huguenot. Was their Calvinism due to the fact that their seigneur, the Baron of Faugères, was himself a Calvinist? Segui observes that the Baron of Faugères was also seigneur of Lunes four kilometres away and that in Lunes there were very few Protestants. In Faugères, it was the richer, more commercially active peasants and artisans who were attracted to Protestantism. Rather than their ties to the Baron of Faugères being the decisive factor, it seems that it was their links to the nearby bourg of Bedarieux, a manufacturing centre with a strongly Huguenot population, that counted most. Indeed, Segui points out that in the immediate past the Baron and the inhabitants of Faugères had been feuding with one another. Segui does allow that the conversion of the Baron to Calvinism may have provided the inhabitants of Faugères with an additional degree of protection and a sense of security. But the faith of the Baron was not determinative. This study allows us to affirm the essentially horizontal division of society at the heart of the initial wave of Protestant revolt.

Our discussion of rural Protestantism raises the question of the validity of the model of artisan as Calvinist and peasant as Catholic found in the work of Le Roy Ladurie and elaborated on by other scholars, including myself. In my opinion it is still essentially valid. It is also commonly believed that Protestantism was more an urban than a rural phenomenon. It is dangerous, however, to insist too much on a religious split between urban and rural populations. Le Roy Ladurie himself recognized this with respect to the Cevennes. He attributed the strength of Calvinism there to the presence of large numbers of rural craftsmen.[46] However, if we survey France at the outbreak of the civil wars, we find rural Protestantism to have been far more widespread than is commonly thought. Thus, we note its presence in Normandy, Brie, Orleannais, Poitou, Angoumois, Champagne, Burgundy, Cevennes, Agenais, Valentinois, Velay, Vivarais, Perthois, and Vermandois. Protestant influence in these areas was likely the result of the presence of rural industry.[47] To put it another way, rural Protestantism was the consequence of relatively strong links between the wealthier artisans and peasants in the bourgs and villages and the markets of the larger towns. The existence of a rural Protestantism is in fact an indirect albeit significant indication of the proto- or quasi-industrialized character of much of the French countryside in the sixteenth century.

The impact of the Calvinist revolt in the countryside, however, extended beyond the limits of religion itself. In the 1560s the peasantry over a large part of the kingdom refused to pay the tithe. Catholic as well as Protestant peasants took part in this boycott, which threatened both the upper and lower clergy. Le Roy Ladurie discusses the development of this movement in a masterful way in the *Histoire économique et sociale de la France*.[48] He points to the roots of this movement in the Middle Ages, evidence that resistance to the tithe was in existence long before the Reformation. After 1525, however, it seems plain that the Reformation and the Peasants War, particularly in Alsace had a major impact. Le Roy Ladurie takes note of signs of resistance in the archdioceses of Lyons and Sens in the 1520s. From the 1520s, on, if not before, there is evidence of growing resistance in the Velay and Vivarais.[49] From 1540 onwards, Nîmes and the Cevennes were affected. A royal edict makes reference to a refusal of the tithe among the peasantry of the Beauce in 1545.

With the outbreak of the civil war, the refusal of the tithe became general in the south of France. The catalyst for it was the Calvinist offensive in the towns. But the withholding of the tithe manifested itself among the Catholic peasantry of the Biterrois and Narbonnaise, as among the Calvinist peasantry of the Cevennes and Agenais.

In the north, the great open fields around Paris, especially south of the capital, were heavily affected. But even the valley of the Loire and the bocage of Sarthe and Maine were touched. According to Le Roy Ladurie, the tithe revolt of the 1560s represented the most important movement of resistance of the peasantry of the open fields of the north of the kingdom between the Jacquerie of 1358 and the Grain War of 1775.[50]

The spirit of revolt that manifested itself in resistance to the tithe was nowhere more in evidence than at Cordes-Tolosannes near Montauban, where the inhabitants refused to pay the tithe to the *fermier* of the abbey of Belleperche. The local seigneur, François d'Hébard, intervened on the side of the clergy, threatening the peasants with the anger of the king. "What king!" they responded, "We are the kings: the one about whom you speak is a little king of shit and we will teach him a trade so that he can earn a living like everyone else."[51]

The rebellion against the Church and the king here and there turned into a challenge of the seigneurial regime itself. Rural uprisings occurred at Châlons-sur-Saône,[52] in the Agenais, Gers, Velay, and Entre-deux-Mers,[53] and among the Vaudois of Provence and Dauphiné,[54] all of which were marked by anti-noble sentiment. The *cahiers de doléances* drawn up for the estates-general of Orleans for the Comminges as well as those for Vitry-le-François,[55] Avallon[56] and Provins[57] are full of complaints about the behaviour of the aristocracy.

The spirit of rebellion was thus widespread among the commoners at the beginning of the religious wars. It began as a horizontal movement of rebellion, directed against the established Church to be sure, but also against urban oligarchies and even here and there against the nobility in the countryside. But it was a movement that was still-born. If it was broadly spread it was not deeply rooted enough. In only a few regions, mainly in the Midi, did Calvinism become a movement of the majority. Elsewhere, the bulk of the peasantry, indeed, even craftsmen, remained indifferent or even hostile. What began as a movement of class from below turned into a class war from above. We are thus talking about a popular revolution that, having failed, turned into a civil war in that the leadership on both sides came from the noble class which dominated France – Catholic or Protestant. Moreover not only did this class dominate the religious wars, it turned them in its favour, using the conflicts of the second half of the century as an opportunity to restore or to consolidate itself vis-à-vis the rest of society. Across the divide of religion, the aristocratic members of this class cooperated with one another in order to exploit and suppress the commons – to put them in their place in a manner of speaking. The commoners continued to oppose the nobility where they could, as they had before. But from being on the offensive they were forced on the defensive. The French Civil Wars were a revolutionary movement that was transformed into a counter-revolutionary one.

We have already put our finger on the principal reason for this transformation. The commoners as a whole and the middle class in particular were too weak and divided to carry through a successful revolution. Economically, the middle class was still not fully formed with a sufficiently developed economic base of its own. Its weakness was manifest in the very immaturity of the state itself. A full-fledged revolution entails the overthrow of one class by another. The only way such a process can occur is through the seizure of the political institutions of the nation. But such a political apparatus itself had only begun to emerge in France and was as yet indistinguishable from the personal power of the monarchy or, indeed, the personal property of the office holder. In short, there was literally little or nothing to take over. This in itself was a symptom of the weakness of the middle class, whose progress must be measured by the parallel if contradictory growth of the early modern state. As a result of its weakness, the Calvinist party led by its middle class ministers was driven into seeking an alliance with a minority of the nobility in the late 1550s.

Historians even in the sixteenth century connected the outbreak of the civil wars to the end of the Italian campaigns. Contemporaries noted the fact that the end of the wars in Italy led the nobility almost immediately to take sides in the religious struggle at home. Such an analysis obviously continues to make a certain amount of sense. It is often coupled with the view that the nobility was losing ground economically and that the civil wars represented a golden opportunity for them to redress their fortunes. The classic expression of this view can be found in Brantôme, who saw the outbreak of the civil war as transforming the situation of the nobility. The Italian wars had forced the nobles who participated to mortgage or sell their property to the point where they were at their wit's end. Such was their plight that they could not even afford the kindling to keep themselves warm in winter. This was because the usurpers, that is, the money-lending middle class, had taken everything. But times had changed, declared Brantôme. Whereas before the outbreak of the war, he had seen a certain gentleman of quality travelling with only two horses and a servant he now espied him with six or seven horses at his disposition. As a result of the civil war, the nobles had been able to hold onto and even to buy back their property. In particular they had redeemed their fortunes by the heavy ransoms they had forced "milord usurers" to pay. "Behold then how the brave noblemen of France will restore themselves by the grace (or should I say the grease) of this good civil war!"[58] Brantôme was not in the least apologetic, particularly because he felt the nobility was at last getting back its own against the upstart bourgeoisie.

Brantôme's view was not isolated. It was reflected and expanded in an anonymous pamphlet entitled *Lettre missive d'un gentilhomme à un sien compagnon contenant les causes du mescontentement de la noblesse de France*.[59] The author laments that upstarts are usurping places in the *gendarmerie*. Some of these parvenus are the children of presidents of the Paris parlement. Some have never travelled outside the confines of Paris and its environs. Still others have commanded only their servants, who are as much gentlemen as are their masters. Others are tailors, stone masons, painters, embroiders, and so on.

The court is no less filled with upstarts. The first gentleman of the King's Chamber is the son of a banker, his mother having made her living as a prostitute. The wealth of the nobility is being drained by the expense of justice, which is equivalent to the burden of the taille. Indeed, "they" are even thinking about imposing taxes on the nobility. "They," according to this anonymous pamphleteer, wish to make us all villains. "The lesser magistrates have us by the feet, head and hands, while the parlement holds us by the neck, ready to slit our throats, the tax-gatherers standing by meanwhile to collect our blood." The author concludes that the nobility know what must be done to take vengeance and to re-establish a government under which "gens de bien et virtue" will be rightfully honoured and revered.

The author of the above missive was answered in turn by a letter, dated the same year, 1567, from a friend likewise noble and anonymous. According to the respondent, villains are being used to do service in place of the nobility. If the nobility continue to be excluded in this way over a long period, the consequence can only be a cruel war. The Florentines, atheists, homosexuals, and immoral exercise too much influence. The employment of Swiss mercenaries is a means to ruin the nobility. "You know how they have dealt with the nobility in their country?" he notes rhetorically. "The king has become so powerful that he has elevated himself above the nobility and thinks he no longer needs it. The nobility must make clear what it wants. The king will then be disposed to restore things to their former state and render the nobility its due." In doing so, the king "will not abandon the accustomed distinction in this Kingdom between villain and gentleman."[60]

From the content of these letters, it is impossible to tell whether their authors were Protestant or Catholic. Indeed, the distinction between the one or the other faction is irrelevant. Religion is beside the point. What we have instead is the authentic voice of noble reaction.[61]

Baron de Fourquevaux's report to the king likewise explains the perpetuation of the civil war in Languedoc as a result of the hostility of the nobility against the third estate. The nobles, according to Fourquevaux, find themselves continually at law with the untitled notables, merchants, bourgeoisie, or other inhabitants of the towns, especially over the payment of *censives* and other rights that the townsmen have acquired in the countryside. The townsmen provoke the peasantry to quarrel with their seigneurs. The ensuing conflicts are sustained by the townsmen in order to provoke the seigneur to some rash act that will cause him to lose his fief, seigneurie and even his life. The third estate is favoured in the courts of the *sénéchaussées*, *presidaux*, and parlement, given that most of the judges are in league against the nobility. When there are interludes of peace the courts are full of disputes between the nobility and their tenants. The most minor disagreements become subjects for litigation. In reality they are only occasions to form unions and leagues to harm the nobility. Were it not for the fact that some of the judges are themselves noble or profess to be men of honour, the nobility would be ground underfoot by its own subjects and vassals. On account of this, the nobility is pleased to see their peasants humiliated and "are not at all upset by their problems and show it by not undertaking their defence."[62]

Fourquevaux's analysis of the roots of conflicts in Languedoc is almost "vintage Marxism." The nobility is confronted by an increasingly agressive middle class. The essential arena of conflict is a struggle over control of the land in which the peasantry is drawn in on the side of the middle class. The nobility's reaction is to abandon the peasantry to the violence of the civil wars.

According to Fourquevaux, the traditional nobility is being threatened by an upstart bourgeoisie. That such a threat existed would appear to be evident, judging from the social literature of the period. Scores of treatises were written that attempted to define or redefine what a noblemen might be.[63] Many contemporaries believed that the old nobility was being attacked and was in danger of being destroyed by the bourgeoisie. Writers of this school tried to defend the old nobility by harping on its exclusiveness.

Most historians today regard the notion of a crisis of the nobility with skepticism.[64] Pointing to the renewed economic strength or the ongoing demographic vitality of the nobility, they consider the idea of a crisis of the old nobility as an exaggeration at best. Even the emergence of the *bourgeois gentilhomme* can be assimilated to this point of view. In so far as the appearance of new nobles was a novelty – and it is by no means clear that it was – the new nobles, however *parvenu*, added vigour to rather than detracted from the strength of the nobility.

Several points ought to be made in response to this optimistic view of the nobility's position. In the first place, there is no denying that the old nobility perceived itself to be threatened, and this perception, however distorted, became historically important. Thus, it is all very well to regard the phenomenon of the *bourgeois gentilhomme* as invigorating rather than weakening the nobility, but it is understandable that those who spoke for the old nobility would look askance at it – all the more so as it was part of a deeper process of a bourgeois advance, which Fourquevaux alludes to in the form of land acquisition, the usurpation of offices, and constant litigation, which challenged the position of the nobility. Furthermore, it is not very convincing to point to the increase in rents in the sixteenth century as a sign of aristocratic strength. The question of rent must be assessed in relationship to profits and wages. Le Roy Ladurie alone has approached the problem in this global way. Personifying these entities as he does, Le Roy Ladurie characterizes the sixteenth century, or at least the sixteenth century until 1580, as the "offensive of profit" relative to wages and rents.[65] Clearly rents increased during this period, but profits increased much more. Hence, the nobility, while not losing ground absolutely, may have relatively been giving up ground to the middle class.

For the next thirty-five years, the French nobility made war on the rest of society. That such was the case was well understood by contemporaries. Fourquevaux, for example, reported to the king that the common people believed that the wars were at bottom founded on a conspiracy between the Catholic and Protestant nobility. According to Fourquevaux, the general view is that the wars can be ended quickly in Languedoc if the nobility that called itself Catholic really wishes to fight the rebels. The people believe that the dissimulation of the nobility is all too evident. The trouble, according to the commoners, stems from the fact that on the rebel side are nobles who are the relatives, allies, and friends of the Catholic nobles. The latter would be disappointed if the Protestant side were defeated. The Catholic and Protestant gentlemen intervene actively on each other's behalf, the one, as it were, holding onto the lamb, while the other skins it. The Protestant nobles rob and the Catholic nobles find customers for the Protestants, or they exchange with one another horses, pistols, muskets, powder, lead, and all kinds of other merchandise. They act for one another on matters concerning ransoms and compositions without losing anything on the market as a result.[66]

Fourquevaux's observations are amplified by Pierre de la Coste, *juge mage* of Montpellier and a loyal Catholic. According to de la Coste, it is easy to see that the main reason the wars continue is the common connivance of the Catholic and Protestant nobles. They have so combined that they do no harm to each other but fall on everyone else, the clergy and common people, as if their goods were given as prey to them. The Catholic nobles step aside so as to allow those of the new religion to sack, pillage, and ransom the places inhabited by Catholics. In like manner, the Protestant nobles allow the Catholics to do the same in the places inhabited by Protestants. So much is this the case that it appears they conspire together to pillage and appropriate the goods of the clergy and of the third estate of the people. It seems that it is with these aims in mind that the nobles keep the civil war going, like a fair in a public market.[67]

Another Catholic notable, Barthélemy Balisten of Narbonne, embellished the complaints of de la Coste. He observed that the majority of the nobles in his diocese are tyrannizing the other estates using the pretext of the military commands they are vested with on account of the war. The result is that one never dares to speak of those extraordinary extortions, pillages, and ransoms made by the men-at-arms and those who lead or command them. Like his contemporaries, Balisten understood that the army was an institution controlled by the nobility.

According to Balisten, part of the nobility, especially the lesser and poorer of the nobles, no longer have any respect for justice, but do as they please, making that serve as both right and fact. They refuse to pay taxes on the commoner lands they hold or are now in the process of acquiring, and they beat, strike and murder those who dare to call them to justice or who displease them in anyway. The result is that the people are so badly disposed toward the nobility that it is to be feared that they will soon rise against them.[68]

Nicolas Fromenteau, a Protestant sympathizer, claimed that it is the new nobles rather than the old who are primarily responsible for the oppression of the commons. When the old nobles are asked why they are powerless to do something, they shrug their shoulders, replying that the ecclesiastics use the new nobles in order to enforce the collection of tithes as well as rents.[69] Another Protestant, writing around 1580 likewise pointed to the oppression of what he called the new "petty and beggar nobles."[70] But he accounted for the tyranny of these upstarts as the result of the refusal of the old nobility to protect the common people.

The idea of a conspiracy between Catholic and Protestant nobles was spread widely among commoners. On May Day 1575, a proclamation to that effect was attached to a tree planted before the quarters of the lieutenant governor in Poitiers. According to this manifesto, the wars that have brought ruin to the people of Poitou for the last thirteen years, have been caused by those who call themselves gentlemen. The object of the nobles has been the ruination of both merchants and peasants. By mutual arrangement, nobles on one side or the other have assured themselves of their own security. Based upon the behaviour of the nobility it is easy to see that religion is not an issue. Unable to support this oppression, twenty thousand Catholics as well as Protestants are ready to rise to annhilate those who abuse them in this fashion. The text is signed "Trust nothing."[71]

Another contemporary claimed that the Catholic and Protestant nobles not only arranged things between themselves to their mutual benefit but even based the religious choice of members of their family on expediency. A Catholic noblemen who has two sons will commonly encourage one to adopt the new religion while prompting the other to remain Catholic. A Protestant noble will do likewise, taking a Catholic woman in marriage, thus mutually and jointly ensuring the salvation of their children in terms of their own temporal interest. In this way the nobility assures itself that it will benefit from the civil wars, come what may.[72]

There are innumerable examples of noble families that were divided in this way during the wars. There are also many cases of aristocratic individuals who conveniently changed their religion to suit their personal circumstances. Thus, in 1562 we find the seigneur Jacques de Voisins of Salvagnac battling in the Calvinist camp against his father, the Catholic Baron d'Ambès. In 1585 Voisins himself led the Catholic forces against Montmorency in the Albigeois. The next year he was once again a Protestant.[73] We likewise find the Baron de Faugères to be a Protestant in 1562, a Catholic in 1568, and a Protestant once again in 1569.[74]

Champagne provides us with an excellent illustration of the disingenuousness of some of the nobility. In 1561, the countryside was plagued by a large company of marauders led by a colonel Beaulieu, said to be the son of an inn-keeper from Nogent. The seigneurs de la Motte-Tilly and d'Esternay led the nobility and commoners of the region against the invaders. Beaulieu and his company were hunted down and a large number of the raiders taken to Provins as prisoners. Beaulieu and his band, however, were able to buy their freedom from the seigneurs. The nobility shared the booty taken by the marauders without regard to the commoners who had been the victims of their depredations or those who had turned out to police the countryside alongside the nobility.

In the meantime, two other companies of freebooters had thrown themselves into the chateau of Eligny. When an appeal for volunteers was made once more at Provins and in the other towns of the region, not a soul responded. Nonetheless, Olivier de Soissons, *bailli* of Provins, assembled all the nobles and cannon he was able to muster and, forcing the peasants to follow him, proceeded to besiege the chateau. The besieged once again were able to gain their freedom by offering the *bailli* and the nobility large sums of money. As the marauders defiled from the chateau to the beat of the drums, the *bailli* airily explained to the assembled ranks of the peasants that the besieged had acted by order of the king and that their papers were in order.[75]

At the estates-general of 1576, the third estate accused the nobility of directly and indirectly arranging for men-at-arms to be garrisoned in their villages and seigneuries. They sought to use these troops to intimidate those of their tenants who would free themselves from seigneurial jurisdiction and dominion. Against those who sought to gain such freedom, the nobles were prepared to use direct coercion, as well as legal proceedings. Through violence, the nobility was preventing both tenants and those who wished to lease their land from enjoying the peaceable use of it.[76]

J.M. Constant has analyzed some fifty *cahiers des doléances* from the bailliage of Chartres, prepared for the estates of 1576. Twenty-seven of the fifty *cahiers* voiced various complaints about the nobility. The tyranny of the noblemen and the fear they inspired was protested in fourteen *cahiers*. Noble violence was dwelt upon in thirteen; economic conflict between nobles and commoners was evoked in twelve; the fact that the nobles refused to pay taxes was complained about in four. One *cahier* went so far as to contest the existence of the nobility itself, viewing it as wealthy, useless, and the cause of the civil wars.[77] (The authors of this last *cahier* were apparently not impressed by the notion of a society of orders.)

The *cahiers* for the estates of 1576 thus suggest that the civil wars were a species of noble reaction. This viewpoint is reinforced by the *cahiers des doléances* from the Agenais. The *cahier* of the third estate of 1583 complained that the nobles not having access to the *taillon* were forced to live off the population instead. They were increasing feudal and seigneurial dues while refusing to pay the *taille réele*.[78] The *cahier* of the third estate of 1588 in the Agenais amplified the same complaints while remonstrating as well about the beating and maltreatment of the peasants and the destruction of their crops.[79]

The records of the *Grands Jours* of Poitiers of 1579 strengthen the impression of a noble reaction. The cases heard from Poitou and Touraine voice numerous complaints of illegal enclosures, refusal to allow the collection of the tithe, violence, unlawful exactions, or defiance of royal justice on the part of noblemen.[80] The year 1580 may well be, as Leroy Ladurie suggests, the beginning of the "offensive of rent," but it is doubtful this was the result of purely economic factors. The civil wars were evidently themselves an important means by which the nobility assured their own future well-being.

Commoners, we have seen, were well aware of the way the nobles were using the religious wars to serve their ends at the expense of the rest of society. But they were more or less powerless to do anything about it. Indeed, the towns became caught up in the conflicts of the nobility in spite of themselves. In the Auvergne, division among the members of the third estate helped keep the feuds between the nobility alive. In particular, the long-standing rivalry between Clermont-Ferrand and Riom for economic and administrative supremacy in the province blocked the possibility of a common front of the third estate. A chronicler from Issoire described the effects of this vendetta on the towns of Auvergne.

If the division between the great lords of the province was great, it was no less great among the "good towns" of the province, especially because of the long standing conflict between Clermont and Riom which, in order to revenge themselves on one another, summon the nobles and great lords into their towns, taking pleasure in ruining themselves rather than keeping themselves closed and shuttered, allowing the nobles to fight one another in the countryside without involving themselves in the differences among the nobility.[81]

It was thus the quarrels among the third estate that made it difficult in this case to form a united front in the face of the nobles. But even where the towns were united, it was not easy over the long term to sustain themselves in the face of the nobility. More often than not they were too weak and too dependent on the local lords to do more than become a part of the nobility's system of clientage. There are noteworthy exceptions to this rule, but over the more than thirty years of the civil wars, the hegemony of the nobility over a divided commons remained the predominant reality. When this stopped being true the wars abruptly came to an end.

Issoire in the Auvergne provides a perfect illustration. In the 1580s, the town was racked by a ferocious social war between the oligarchy and the plebians. A democratic movement led by the Aulteroche family won the support of the craftsmen and labourers. But in order to sustain themselves, the popular party had to seek the protection of the powerful local lord, the marquis d'Alègre. Presumably he supported them because in their weakness they were prepared to be more amenable to him than the oligarchy of notables. In the event the oligarchy was driven to assassinate the marquis in order to put an end to the popular threat. The democratic movement in Issoire was undoubtedly a genuine one, but it was entirely circumscribed and limited by the seigneurial power that surrounded it.[82]

The religious issue helped the nobility to control and manipulate the commoners. Protestants were deeply hated by the majority of commoners in Provence. Among the commoners, only the despised Vaudois appear to have been attracted to the new religion. Protestantism was otherwise associated with elite oppression or noble violence. In Fréjus, in 1568, the Marquis des Arcs and certain other Catholic seigneurs were able to take advantage of such feelings to turn the overwhelmingly Catholic population of Fréjus against the Protestant Baron de Cipières, who, on his way home from a meeting with the Duke of Savoy at Nice, had stopped at Fréjus with a party of forty men-at-arms for refreshment. The seigneurs wanted to have him captured or killed. Accordingly, they went from house to house, encouraging the populace to take up arms against this Protestant lord who had suddenly invaded their town with an escort of forty men-at-arms. The marquis and his friends succeeded only too well. The whole town assembled around the inn where the baron and his men were lodged. Despite the efforts of the consuls to intervene, the townspeople proceeded to butcher the baron and his escort.[83] The citizens of Fréjus had their own reasons for killing the Baron de Cipières, but it was the incitement of the nobles that gave them the courage to do so.

Noble control likewise is evident in the assassination of the governor of Beaucaire, Pierre de Baudon, seigneur of Parrabère in 1578. Parrabère's government had made itself odious in the eyes of the inhabitants of the city. Montmorency decided that Parrabère would have to be removed. He put the matter into the hands of three noblemen and a Franciscan, who organized the affair.[84] On 7 September Parrabère and his wife went to church as was their custom. No sooner was the Mass under way than the tocsin began to sound and the population rallied. Parrabère and sixty followers tried to fight their way to the safety of the chateau, but they were confronted by a great mass of commoners led by the three nobles. Parrabère and many of his followers were killed. Parrabère's wife took refuge at the foot of the altar of the church of the Franciscans. She was butchered, stripped, and dragged through the streets to lie beside the body of her husband.

The nobility were thus able to dominate and shape the direction of the civil wars. Many commoners, unable to carry on their normal occupations owing to the disruption of the wars, became soldiers, adopting the way of life of the nobles. At the estates-general of 1576, the third estate complained of the "great numbers of His Majesty's subjects in Poitou, Languedoc and Dauphiné who, seeing their manufacturers cease, have taken up arms."[85] According to Barthélemy Balisten, the Catholic notable of Narbonne, the leaders of the Huguenot forces in his region were three lesser nobles and six others, all commoners, including three peasants, a locksmith, a blacksmith, and a renegade priest.[86] Under the exigencies of wars, which they controlled and kept going, the nobility were even prepared to overlook, when it suited them, the social origins of their companions in arms. As Montbrun put it: "In time of war, if somebody can hold onto his weapon and keep his ass in the saddle, call him comrade."[87]

The domination of the nobility transcended politics, war, and religion. It penetrated the very consciousness of the bourgeoisie. The entry of the Grand Prior Henri d'Angoulême to Carcassonne affords a striking example. In 1579 this august personage, a bastard son of Henri II, decided to visit the town as part of a tour of the Midi by the queen-mother Catherine de Médicis. In order to mark the Prior's entry into the city, the consuls decided to create an elite company of young notables. One hundred and twenty young men "from among the most handsome and well-born" were thus selected and enrolled in this so-called Company of the Consuls. They were all uniformly dressed, accoutred, and mounted on horses of the same colour. Bernard de Rech, bourgeois and treasurer of the town bourse, was named their captain and given the honour of accompanying the Grand Prior as he made his way between Narbonne and Carcassonne.

While the town awaited the arrival of the Grand Prior, the rest of the young men of the town excluded from the company became more and more jealous. Two hundred of them assembled and constituted themselves into a rival company, taking the name "the gallant band." What was the social base of this company? Judging from the fact that we are told that they were able to equip, mount, and dress themselves as finely as the Company of the Consuls, these young men must have come from merchant and the richest artisan families. In any event, led by their captain, Pierre Quot, the Company of Gallants began to parade through the town in rivalry to the Company of the Consuls; in fact they began to skirmish with the latter, making it clear that they intended to greet the Grand Prior alongside of or in competition with the Company of the Consuls.

Clearly this dispute had ceased to be a quarrel among the young and had become a feud between families – a kind of inter-class conflict between the notables and the rest of the bourgeosie. The consuls thus tried to proscribe the Company of Gallants. The mothers and fathers of the Gallants would not tolerate the prohibition. They insisted that their sons would greet the Grand Prior along with the young men of the Company of the Consuls. While the bourgeois families argued back and forth, pitched battles broke out between the Company of the Consuls and the Company of the Gallants. A war for control of the town was in the making. Several people were wounded and the consuls were unable to bring the situation under control.

In reality this was just a continuation in new form of a battle of long standing between the older elite of Carcassonne and the merchants of the bourg who sought recognition or predominance.[88] The only thing that temporarily quieted the crisis was the decision of the Company of Gallants to take themselves to Narbonne to assure themselves a place beside the Grand Prior on his journey to Carcassonne. The Grand Prior, placed in a quandry and fearing that his entry would set off a social explosion, simply left Narbonne by night several days ahead of schedule and entered Carcassonne unannounced and unescorted.[89]

What is interesting about this incident, in itself trivial, is the mental landscape it reflects. In it we discover a bourgeoisie whose aspiration for its sons if not for itself is to be taken for noble. Indeed in this case a dispute between the affluent unfolds in terms of who will or will not be included in this pseudo-nobility. It seems evident that the bourgeoisie cannot conceive of its advancement in terms other than those of ennoblement. Yet there is a converse to this picture that has to be noted as well. In the first place, one must note the mentality that believes if one dresses up one's son as a nobleman and presents him as such in a royal entry then in some sense he becomes noble. But what then can be said of the Company of Gallants who refused to be excluded from this nobility? In constituting themselves as rivals to the Company of the Consuls, they were not only challenging the claims of nobility of the latter but in effect burlesquing the very notion of nobility itself. In the sixteenth century the attitude of the bourgeoisie toward the nobility oscilated between awe and emulation on the one hand, and hatred and contempt on the other.

The feud among the bourgeoisie of Carcassonne reflects just how distracted the middle class became as a result of the ongoing civil wars. Unable to make productive investments, its obsession with status intensified. Wealth that otherwise might have been productively invested was wasted in unproductive ways. During the civil wars, for example, taxes on the commons wasted largely on war increased to intolerable levels. Especially heavy was the level of taxation under Henri III. In addition, the townsmen were hardpressed to maintain the defence of their cities. They had to look constantly to the strengthening of walls and fortifications. Citizens had to spend much of their energy on *corvées* or in the militia. Manufacture and trade decayed and were replaced by unproductive usury and real-estate speculation. In order to sustain themselves, the towns requisitioned grain from the countryside or forced the peasants to perform labour services. The towns as a matter of fact competed with local landlords in exploiting the peasantry.[90]

An illuminating example of the rivalry between nobility and town in this respect took place in Poitou in 1586. The city council of Poitiers refused to collect fifteen thousand *écus* from the townspeople for the maintenance of royal troops in Guyenne. Furthermore, they did not allow the money to be collected from the peasants in the surrounding countryside. The baron de Biron reported that the aldermen claimed that the king had exempted them. Indeed, the aldermen asserted that all the inhabitants of the town were noble and therefore exempt. Moreover, they would not allow the villages and bourgs of the region to be imposed upon. Biron notes that he responded by asserting that the taxes were for a public purpose, namely, the military. In a time of war no one could claim exemption; indeed, all the other towns and provinces had paid in obedience to the command of the king. Biron's position thus was much as one would expect up to this point. It is his subsequent remarks that are particularily noteworthy.

I saw in all this a cabal between the *officiers*, treasurers, mayor, aldermen, and principal inhabitants of the town to ensure that they are exempt while they will also be able to hold onto what is levied in the countryside. They stressed the misery of the people and I answered that there are two kinds of people, "le peuple maigre" that is, those of the countryside, and "le peuple gras," that is, those of the towns, who extract the substance of the poor people as well as that of the Church and the nobility.[91]

The notables of Poitiers had put themselves forward as the champions of the commons. Biron's response was to accuse them of hypocrisy. They wished to forestall the collection of tax on the commons in order to better exploit them themselves. The notables decried the suffering of the people, but in Biron's view, in doing so, the notables were hiding behind the term "the people." Certainly the poor people of the countryside were being exploited – milked dry by the well-to-do of the towns, the "fat cats," "les gens gras," who were battening on the Church and the nobility as well.

In arguing in this way, Biron was trying to sweep the responsibility of the crown and the nobility for the poverty and suffering of the peasants out of sight. However, his attack on the notables of the towns was justified. They, along with the nobles, made the commons and especially the peasants pay the price of the wars.

At the time of the uprising of the *Tard-Avisés* in the 1590s, the nobles were the main object of the wrath of the insurgent peasants. But the rural population complained also of the exploitation of the towns.

The towns, instead of seeing that justice is maintained, are indifferent to the ruin of the poor people because our ruin is their enrichment. They keep their goods and merchandise in their fortresses not subject to the brigands who infest the countryside. They sell these wares to us at whatever price they like, constitute *metairies* at a good price and then force us to pay double the ordinary rent. Perigeux has been taken by force, twice pillaged and sacked, Sarlat likewise. Bergerac has been reduced to the status of a village. Belvès, Montignac and other towns have also been captured and pillaged. Nonetheless today these fine ruins are richer than ever but all at our expense.[92]

The reference to *metayage* in this manifesto is especially noteworthy. Many peasants found themselves overwhelmed by debts as a result of the devastation of war and heavy taxation. In the south-west, share cropping on newly established *metairies* was often the only way peasants could continue to farm. Many more in Poitou, as well as Languedoc, Provence, Dauphiné, and Ile-de-France, were forced to sell off their land altogether.[93] The buyers were the most prosperous peasants, the bourgeoisie, or nobility.[94] The civil wars thus primarily benefited the nobles, but the bourgeoisie were able to console themselves by likewise turning on the peasantry. The civil wars thus had a paradoxical quality. They were a feudal reaction master-minded by the nobility, but at the same time they had the character of a kind of primitive accumulation in the capitalist sense of the term, involving the dispossession of a significant percentage of the rural petty producers by the bourgeoisie.

CHAPTER THREE

The Huguenot Republic

The nobility dominated both the Huguenot and Catholic parties throughout the civil wars. However, within the Huguenot party there was a constant tension between the aristocracy and the middle class. At first this conflict expressed itself in the realm of ecclesiastical differences. Following the massacre of St Bartholomew's Day, 24 August 1572, the bourgeois element in the Huguenot camp became more assertive. The leaders of the Huguenot towns elaborated plans for the defence of the largely Calvinist Midi more or less independently of the nobility. The Huguenot bourgeoisie defended the autonomy of their towns not only from the Catholic nobles but also from the ambitions of the Huguenot nobles. Indeed, the nobility suspected the towns of being secretly republican in sympathy. Although these conflicts tended to abate in the later stages of the civil wars, they never were fully extinguished.

It is commonly asserted that in the first decade of the civil wars, the clerical leaders and the aristocratic chieftains of the Protestant movement carefully eschewed political radicalism and that when demands for political change were made, they were couched in limited form. It was the massacre of St Bartholomew's Day, it is generally argued, that precipitated the appearance of more extreme theories of political resistance, which were embodied in the works of Hotman, Beza, and Duplessis Mornay.[1] It must be pointed out, however, that the Calvinists at the estates-general of Pontoise (1561) had already given voice to quite far-reaching constitutional proposals.[2] To have demanded that no war be initiated or new taxes collected without the consent of the estates-general was to take giant steps toward a constitutional government. Those who advanced such ideas must have had in mind the idea of a limited monarchy.

Two years later, an anonymous tract entitled *The Civil and Military Defense of the Innocents and the Church of Christ*, published at Lyons, argued for the right of the people to revolt against government for reasons of faith.[3] This view represented, a throwback to a more extreme and popular theory of religious resistance propounded by English exiles in the 1540s.[4] Such a view represented a break with the notions of the French Calvinist establishment, which vested the right of resistance in lesser magistrates such as the princes of the blood, the estates-general or the magistrates of provinces or cities.

IF WE ARE LOOKING FOR the democratic tendencies in the Calvinist movement in the 1560s, they will not be found in the arena of national politics, which, throughout that decade, was largely controlled by the princely and noble Calvinist families. It is rather within the realm of ecclesiastical disputes that democratic currents made themselves felt.

The Genevan Church, where Calvinism originated, was controlled by a consistory of elders and deacons who were self-selecting. This oligarchical body was reinforced by the Company of Pastors. In the French Church, likewise, the consistory of elders and ministers became the ruling entity of each established Calvinist church. The consistory was tied to the body of the Church in France through a system of local colloquies and provincial and national synods. Robert Kingdon has made known to us the existence of a democratic and congregationalist opposition to this structure during the 1560s, which was led by Jean Morély, a native of Paris who converted to Protestantism in 1547. In the 1550s, Morély moved to Geneva where he lived in a wealthy quarter of the city and associated with the elite of the Protestant community, including Calvin himself. At the time of the outbreak of the religious wars, however, he fell out of favour with the Genevan authorities. On his return to France, he published a *Treatise on Christian Discipline* (Lyons, 1562), in which he sharply challenged the ecclesiastical discipline of Calvinism in favour of a more grass-roots and popular form of order in the church.

Morély attacked as "oligarchic" or aristocratic that system of discipline that vested the authority of the church in the hands of the clergy. He called for an authentically apostolic order rooted in popular church government. The whole of the local church led by the ministry should participate in the disciplining of sinners. As Morély put it, "this power to throw out of the Church, to bar from its communion, to cut off from this body of the Lord, or to receive into this Church and replace in this company and community, is a sovereign power which belongs to each Church, as to a mother of a family in her house."[5] For this reason, he urged that it cannot belong to the pastors of their right. Morély further argued for the elective principle throughout the higher administrative structure of the church.

Morély's ideas horrified the leaders of Calvinism. Théodore Beza, Calvin's successor, directed all the guns of the Genevan church against Morély. Morély and his ideas were eventually suppressed, partly by persecution and partly as a consequence of the massacre of St Bartholomew's Day. But it is important to note that the violence of the reaction of the Calvinist leadership against him was based on the fact that his ideas actually found some support in France, particularly in the churches of the Ile-de-France.[6] The Morély affair thus represents an early example of the conflict between presbyterian and congregational forms of ecclesiastical order. Indeed, as Robert Kingdon has made clear, this conflict involved a clash within the Calvinist camp between the oligarchical and democratic principle not simply in religion but in politics.[7]

Hidden below the surface of an ecclesiastical quarrel was a fundamental political antagonism among Calvinists. At the root of this argument lay the question of whether aristocratic or bourgeois elements would control not simply the Calvinist church but the Calvinist movement. Appearances, however, can sometimes be deceiving. Not that one can doubt that Morély meant what he said. He was a humanist scholar and theologian who adopted the notion of congregational order in the church as a matter of principle. As a man of ideas or an ideologue, Morély must be understood as someone intellectually and emotionally committed to the democratic ideal. Moreover, from what we know of the history of the Calvinist movement, it is clear that there was a democratic current in it from its inception. It was only with difficulty that the elitist Genevan model was imposed on it in the 1550s.[8] The Morély affair reflected the fact that this current was still found in the French church in the following decade.

However, it is remarkable that at the very moment that the Morély question was at the focal point of polemical debate in the French Church, the Genevan model came under fire from a completely opposed quarter. The attack stemmed from the pen of Charles Dumoulin, who, in the aftermath of his falling out with the theologians of Geneva, put himself forward as the champion of Gallicanism. He denounced the Calvinist clergy of France as instruments of a foreign power whose design was to overthrow not only the ecclesiastical but also the constitutional order of France. As he put it, the purpose of the Calvinist ministers was "to reduce all this kingdom to the subjection and popular estate of Geneva, to change and overthrow the police of the Kingdom of France, even at the expense of the people of France."[9]

It would be easy to dismiss Dumoulin's attack as simply a canard. But Dumoulin was not alone among contemporary polemicists in attacking the Calvinists as enemies of the aristocratic and monarchical order in France. The upheavals of the early 1560s, furthermore, are enough to prove that at its base the Calvinist movement contained authentically democratizing elements. We cannot therefore simply dismiss these accusations.

How then are we to understand the Calvinist ecclesiastical order, attacked on the one hand as being oligarchical and on the other as being a "popular" threat to the traditional order of the government and society of France? We can begin by taking another look at Morély, or rather at his supporters. It is true that he apparently had some grassroots support from the churches close to Paris. However, his most prominent champions were Cardinal Odet de

Châtillon and Jeanne d'Albret, Queen of Navarre. These were hardly committed democrats. Why then were they supporting Morély? We can catch a glimpse of the answer if we take note of the intervention of Peter Ramus into the Morély debate. This occurred at the provincial synod of Lumegny-en-Brie a few months before Ramus's death at the massacre of St Bartholomew's Day. At the synod, Ramus supported the idea of more lay control of decision making in the church. But, as against the democracy of Morély, Ramus supported the idea of government by those of greater weight. In other words, those who counted most in the social and political sphere should also count the most ecclesiastically.[10]

Ramus makes explicit what is implicit in the support of Odet de Coligny and Jeanne d'Albret for Morély. One cannot doubt the sincerity of Morély's congregational and democratic opinions. But given the aristocratically dominated social structure of France, the implementation of Morély's ideas would have led to less democracy in the church rather than more. In practice, the application of Morély's proposals would have put the reformed church at the mercy of its aristocratic protectors.

The events of the 1560s made it evident that there was a fundamental antagonism between a Protestant aristocracy and a ministerial order of middle-class origin, whose outlook reflected the interests of the merchants and craftsmen who made up the great majority of the Calvinist followers. Faced with the overwhelming power of the nobility, it was Calvin's ecclesiastical discipline and not Morély's congregationalism that best safe-guarded the interests of the commoners. This antagonism was reflected in the conflicting views of Beza and the Calvinist ministry on the one hand and Louis de Condé on the other. These disputes involved matters both of ethics and of politics.[11] In both instances, Condé's hot-headed and impulsive actions offended the largely middle-class leadership of the reformed church and revealed a fundamental conflict in values.

It is not saying too much to argue that it was the Calvinist discipline that made it possible for the reformed leadership to hold its own in the face of a nobility dominated by aristocratic values. It is true enough that the majority of ordinary laymen were excluded from participating in the government of the church by this discipline. The consistory and synods that were at the heart of this ecclesiastical order were controlled by notables, merchants, and ministers. But they were at least commoners and not nobles. Moreover, the vesting of authority in the provincial and national synods ensured that commoners in the church had an instrument that gave them at least co-equal power with the nobility at the national level. Morély's congregational order at best provided for a decentralized and democratic ecclesiastical organization at the local level. At worst it opened the way for aristocratic control at all levels of the Calvinist movement. In a world that was still feudal or aristocratic, the Calvinist ecclesiastical system provided the greatest possible influence for commoners. For this reason, Dumoulin, among others, saw it as a popular threat to the existing monarchical and aristocratic order. The matter of order in the reformed church was thus of great importance. It is not without reason that in this church alone did the question of order become a mark of faith.[12]

The Calvinist discipline was closely tied to the issue of the defence of the reformed movement. In the wake of St Bartholomew, an assembly was held at Nîmes to organize the resistance of the Protestants of Languedoc. According to the concluding document of this assembly, ecclesiastical discipline was to be considered as fundamental as the military regime and political ordinances in sustaining the reformed church.[13] The military commander of the Calvinist forces was instructed to maintain ecclesiastical discipline right through the ranks of his forces. Such a discipline, it was held, would ensure the security of the army of the reformed religion. Under the ecclesiastical discipline, the morale of the army would be bolstered so that five soldiers of the Calvinist army would equal one hundred of the enemy.[14]

Excommunication was a fundamental part of this discipline. According to the synod held at Nîmes the same year, the purpose of excommunication was not to destroy but to instruct and enlighten. Its objective was to ensure that the flock not be destroyed by recalcitrant sheep. The aim of excommunication was likewise to humiliate the excommunicant by shaming him so that he would in the end be reduced to obedience. The goal of this act was finally to make an example of the one who was purged so that others would be inspired to obedience by fear.[15] The reformed discipline was thus harsh and coercive. But it was a yoke that was necessary for the survival of the new faith in an alien and hostile world. Order, discipline, and obedience were the watchwords of this revolutionary movement of the sixteenth century, much as they are of similar movements in the contemporary world.

The massacre of St Bartholomew's Day led to the radicalization of Calvinist political thought as reflected in the works of François Hotman, Théodore Beza, and Duplessis-Mornay. Hotman's *Franco-Gallia* invoked the history of the French monarchy to argue for an elective and constitutional government. Basing himself on the historical approach to the study of French law that had become more and more popular, Hotman sought to demonstrate the limited nature of the authority of the monarchy ultimately responsible to the estates-general. Beza and Duplessis-Mornay, likewise reverting to scholastic political theory, argued for the principle of popular sovereignty. But by doing so, they by no means recognized any democratic right to revolt, let alone to govern. Rather, they maintained that this original right had been delegated to the inferior magistrates of the kingdom.[16]

Such was the position of the mainstream Hugenot leadership at the level of political theory. However, more radical voices were also heard. An excerpt of Etienne de la Boétie's *Discours sur la servitude volontaire* was published in a Latin text under the pseudonym Eusebius Philadelphus in 1574. The compilation was quickly translated into French as the *Réveille-matin*. The passage of La Boétie's *Discours* that was included in this work called for the revolt of the many against the tyranny of one-man rule.[17]

The publication of the full text of La Boétie's work by a Calvinist minister, Simon Goulart, in 1576 included a text that repudiated not only one-man rule but the structure of society that based itself on such rule. In this celebrated passage, La Boétie rejected the whole structure of subordination and hierarchy that stemmed from the ruler and that kept the majority of the society in thrall.[18] La Boétie's attack can be taken as an assault not only on the traditional feudal hierarchy but also on the bureaucracy and networks of clientage of the early modern French state itself. The repeated publication of the *Discours* at Geneva during the 1570s undoubtedly reflects a current of republican sentiment in the Protestant camp in the wake of the massacre of St Bartholomew.

In the aftermath of St Bartholomew, Huguenot political discourse became more intransigent. When the queen-mother arranged a meeting with Pierre de Malas, seigneur de Hiolet, a Huguenot *conseiller* of the parlement of Toulouse, she began the interview with the observation that the Huguenots had now lost many of their adherents. She claimed that there were few Huguenots left and that they were of low estate. Hiolet defiantly answered that it was true that the queen no longer had to deal with a prince, admiral, or other seigneur, but rather with the younger sons of noblemen or poor nobles. As well, he noted pointedly, she had to deal with shoemakers, tailors, masons, locksmiths and blacksmiths who, alongside the petty noblemen, took great pleasure in bearing arms and going to war.[19]

Also in the wake of St Bartholomew, Calvinist nobles and bourgeoisie constituted themselves into what Jean Dellumeau and Janine Garrison have called the United Provinces of the Midi. Like the Protestant federation of the Netherlands, this was a quasi-independent state governed through its own estates-provincial and estates-general. Garrison has masterfully reconstituted the workings of this state within the state;[20] however, some contradiction appears to exist in Garrison's analysis of the social composition of the leadership of this Huguenot federation. While her charts and graphs show a clear predominance of notables and ministers in the estates provincial and general, she insists on the predominance of the nobles, a predominance that was capped by the emergence of Henri IV of Navarre as Protestant protector.[21]

I have no quarrel with her account of the way in which Henri of Navarre gradually subordinated the Protestant estates-general to his control. However, she seems to have given short shrift to the "democratic moment" in French Protestantism following the massacre of St Bartholomew, although she does take notice in passing of certain "fleeting democratic sentiments" in 1572 and 1573.[22] According to Garrison, the assembly of Millau was dominated by the nobility; furthermore, she tends to minimize the degree of conflict between the nobles and commoners. But the *Journal d'un protestant de Millau*, a contemporary record of the events, remarks on the sense of division between the nobles and the ministers and notables at this meeting.[23] At the assembly of Montauban that followed, according to the historian La Popeliniere, the nobles of the region were well received but their sense of liberty was out of sympathy with the sense of equality that reigned among the third estate.[24]

Garrison does note the so-called *Reglement des religionaires ...*, first published as part of the *Reveille-Matin* and subsequently published by Léon Menard in his history of Nîmes.[25] Menard ascribed it to an assembly held at Nîmes in May 1572. Garrison more correctly attaches it to the months following St Bartholomew's Day. Although she makes little of it, she does at least recognize that this document was of exclusively bourgeois origin.[26]

The preamble of the *Reglement* calls for the election by voice vote in each town held by the Calvinists of a major who will be vested with the defence and the police of the population. This measure is announced as expedient, given that France at the moment is governed by a tyrant. It would not apply, notes the *Reglement*, if the government were restored to good order or if a foreign prince, endowed with the evident signs of a liberator, were to intervene and deliver the kingdom. Resistance to tyranny and appeal to a liberator were standard features of Calvinist resistance theory.

Likewise the call for popular election of *majors* seems to stem from the same source. The usual recourse of resistance thinkers was to invoke inferior magistrates against a tyrant. Calvin himself advocated this recourse. As Quentin Skinner has pointed out, the last paragraph of Calvin's *Institutes* provides for the election of magistrates to defend the populace against tyranny.[27] The *Reglement* develops Calvin's point into a full-fledged sketch of an alternative government founded on a league of cities. According to the *Reglement*, the major was to govern with a council of twenty-four from the town or surrounding area. Councillors could be either nobles or commoners. The major and council would then select seventy-five others who together would constitute a court of appeal in major criminal cases. The ordinary business of war and administration was to be handled by the major and the council. On the other hand, the latter had to call the assembly of one hundred together to decide on matters of peace and war, fresh taxation, and new laws. The major and council of twenty-four were to be elected annually.

The majors and councils of each town were to meet together to elect a general who was to be empowered, according to the document, with the authority of the Roman dictator. The nomination of the general was to occur in the assembly of the towns, which would meet twice a year to discuss matters of state. They would do so in the manner of the Amphictony of ancient Greece. Once the emergency was over, the general and all other military officers were to surrender their offices and retire to private life or lesser office.

Popular control over those who were socially or politically superior was to be insured by the provision that any citizen could bring an accusation before the major and council of twenty-four against any noblemen or member of the government thought to be conspiring against the reformed religion or the civil authority. If an accusation was made against a major or a member of the council, the matter was to be judged in the assembly of one hundred. The accused should not be offended by the accusation made against him but rejoice at the opportunity to demonstrate his innocence to his co-religionists.

The *Reglement* of 1572 did not profess to be an alternative constitution for France as a whole, but was designed rather to regulate the affairs of a defensive league based on the towns of the Midi. It did not exclude the participation of the nobility but brought them under control. Ultimate power was to be vested in the populace who were called upon to elect their governors in annual elections. The *Reglement* was, of course, never implemented. However, it reflected and articulated the popular current among Protestants in the Midi in the wake of the massacre of St Bartholomew's Day.

The influence of the towns in the Protestant camp was observable even before the massacre. In 1567, at the time of the second civil war, for instance, the consulate of Nîmes exercised a powerful influence in Protestant councils. The noblemen who commanded the Protestant forces in Languedoc felt themselves compelled to act with the advice of the consuls of Nîmes. Indeed, two consuls were dispatched to the camp of the Protestant army to act as advisers to the noble commanders. At the national level, the admiral Coligny and Louis de Condé ordinarily sought the approval of Nîmes prior to making important decisions.[28]

AT THE HEART OF PROTESTANT resistance was La Rochelle. It was here, especially during the siege of 1572–3 after St Bartholomew, that the bourgeois and democratic spirit of the Protestant movement found its ultimate expression. From the 1520s on, the government of the town had been in the hands of the royal governor. The failure of the revolt of the gabelle had only reinforced the power of the tough baron d'Estissac, who feuded with the municipal councillors and built a citadel in the heart of the town at the expense of the townspeople (1555–7). Although Estissac's successor, Gui Chabot de Jarnac, was more conciliatory, he did not hesitate to call in reinforcements when he felt his authority threatened by the Protestants. At the behest of Jarnac in 1562 and 1565, the Duke of Montpensier and, three years later, Charles IX intervened to ensure royal control of the city. The Protestant *coup de main* of 1568 put an end to Jarnac's government.[29] From that point until 1628, La Rochelle became a virtually independent city-state.

In the ten years following the *coup*, power in the town passed to the assembly general, where it seems that all the heads of families took part in the decisions. The most important matters, including those of peace, war, and alliance, were decided by this body. During the siege of 1572–3, failure to notify the general assembly of certain negotiations with the enemy gave rise to outraged protests.

The frequency with which the assembly met and the charged atmosphere that reigned during its sessions are largely explained by the state of siege and revolutionary passion that marked this period.

The massacre of St Bartholomew saw an influx of six thousand Calvinist refugees into the city. The Rochelais, who themselves numbered only twenty thousand, reorganized the civic militia, enrolling the refugees into cavalry and infantry units, saw to the provisioning of the city, and created a council of war. The siege of the city began in December 1572 and continued until June 1573. From February on, the duke of Anjou accompanied by Louis de Condé, Henri of Navarre, and most of the grand nobility of the kingdom took their place in the ranks of the besiegers.[30] An atmosphere of desperate courage and religious exaltation animated the mass of those defending the city. A profound current of hostility to the nobility ran through the ranks of those under siege.[31]

François de la Noue at first tried to intervene with the Rochelais on behalf of the king. He was rudely rebuffed by the defenders who feared a trap. De La Noue then agreed to command the besieged Protestant forces. But the distrust of the populace was so great that he and other nobles felt themselves called upon to leave the city at the beginning of March.[32] The next months saw an intensification of the siege, culminating in massive assaults on the town at the end of May and beginning of June. The most detailed account of the siege is to be found in Massiou's *Histoire de la Saintonge*.[33] Massiou's breathtaking narrative of the defence of the city justifies our calling it an epoch of bourgeois courage against an army led by the combined strength of the assembled high nobility of France. The last great assault occurred on 11 June and ended in complete failure.

The repercussions of these events were felt all through the Midi. In a letter written in the autumn of 1573, the baron de Forquevaux expressed his opposition to a peace with the Huguenots in the wake of the failure of the siege of La Rochelle. Such a peace, he believed, would only intensify disorder in the kingdom. The king ought to have pursued the war so as to annihilate the Huguenots. As a result of the failed military effort, the clergy, nobility, and people of Languedoc were, he asserted, virtually in despair. The third estate, according to the baron, was not without the fantasy of allying itself with the Huguenots because of the excesses of the Catholic soldiers and an infinitude of subsidies invented each day in order to draw money out of them.[34]

The diffidence of the Huguenot townsfolk toward the nobility continued through the 1570s, as evidenced in the April 1576 joint meeting of the estates of the Calvinist nobility and a provincial synod of the churches of Rouergue. The nobles argued that the meeting should urge that certain strongholds held by the Catholics around Millau be dismantled. In turn, the estates should agree that other strong points held by the Protestant side likewise be dismantled. Finally, Millau should be garrisoned by three hundred soldiers commanded by a governor chosen by the nobility. The outlying areas would pay the costs of this garrison force.

The spokemen for Millau vehemently opposed this proposition. They agreed that the strong points should be abandoned. On no account, however, would they allow a garrison to be established in Millau, claiming that the town could defend itself with its own forces. They would have no governors other than the consuls. According to the chronicler, "these good fellows [the nobles] had proposed that in order to injure the town. Their purpose was to install an armed force and governor into the town as they had long since designed to do. So much was this the case that this nobility thought it would die of spite when they were unable to arrive at their end and object."[35]

In 1577, it seemed that the alliance between Montmorency, governor of Languedoc, and the Huguenots was on the point of collapse. According to Montmorency, the reason for this was the ambition of those among the Huguenots who wished to govern and direct matters in such a way as to dishonour and subvert the lords and the nobility whose enemy they were.[36]

Montmorency urged Henri of Navarre and Condé and all others who had commands to beware of the situation, since they soon would be treated the same way if the ambition of those who wished to change governors and establish a popular order was not punished. The whole of the nobility ought to be concerned for this matter affects them all. We have heard, said Montmorency, that their plan is to attack one of the lords and in this way to shake the sense of obedience that reigns. They think it will be easy for the commoners and towns to lay down the law to the nobility and force it to live under their control. This matter thus touches everyone, and it is in everyone's interest not to allow it. They ought not to permit those who are not fit to be judges in a court to have authority over matters of war. For they are nothing in reality without the arm of the nobility, captains, and men-at-arms, who ought to demonstrate their disposition to act appropriately by not subjecting themselves to the command of those who cannot judge their valour and merit.[37]

At the political assembly of the Protestants held at Anduze in 1579, Montmorency again attacked the ambitions of the third estate – this time denouncing the reformed ministers. The ministers, said Montmorency, ought not to have the power to contravene the decisions of the assembly, to arm the people, or to control the government of the towns or strongpoints held by the Calvinists. It is rather the nobility who ought to have such authority. Otherwise the people, under the influence of the ministers, tend to favour a republic. As a result they are unwilling to recognize the authority of the nobility or of the magistracy. This is the reason for all the upheavals and illegalities.[38]

The state of relations between the Protestant nobility and the towns may be judged from the example of Millau. The citizens there were in a permanent state of conflict with the Huguenot captain Larcis. On 7 July 1578 Larcis and his company invaded the city and proceeded to beat up the inhabitants. Overcoming their first surprise, the inhabitants rallied in arms and gave chase to the invaders. Larcis and his band all escaped except for one cavalier who was imprisoned.[39]

The war kept Larcis from giving his full attention to his feud with the inhabitants of Millau. But by the fall, a peace between Catholics and Protestants was arranged, and Larcis determined to fall upon his enemies in earnest. He allied himself with the captain Talosaie, also said to be a Huguenot. Backed by a company of sixty or eighty, the two captains pillaged the peasants and robbed the merchants of the region of Millau. Despite the declared peace, they took likely victims prisoner and held them for ransom. Many in the region believed that some of the merchants of Millau received Larcis's booty and so were helping to maintain him.

Upset by the calumny, the citizens set a trap for the brigands on the road outside the city. On the night of 9 November, they surprised Larcis and his followers, who were making their way back from a raid on the peasantry of La Montaigne. The militia of Millau forced the brigands to take flight, leaving their prisoners and booty behind.

Outraged, Larcis determined on revenge. He made an agreement with the commendatory abbot of Nant Monsieur de Froissinet, whose land lay adjacent to Millau. Larcis agreed to install Froissinet as governor of Millau when he had conquered the city, in return for permission to cross the abbot's land.

On the 11 November, Larcis quietly placed an experienced company of two hundred in a house close to the old bridge leading into the city. Larcis and a noble companion dressed themselves like poor peasants while concealing pistols under their garments. They circled the walls to make it appear that they were approaching the city from the faubourg La Montaigne. On the bridge they were stopped by the guards who asked them from where they came. As they responded "From La Montaigne," each of them suddenly seized a guard. But when they tried to discharge their pistols, these misfired, and so they were overpowered. Larcis managed to escape, but his companion was made prisoner.

Five days later, Larcis returned with a group of his followers, and they succeeded in killing one of the guards near the gate of the city. The militia vainly gave chase. But such was the level of frustration in Millau that the plebians revolted against the consuls, attacking the chateau and killing the imprisoned young noble who had been caught on the bridge. Larcis, unable to attack Millau, did not cease his plundering. According to the chronicler, there was not a *metairie* of Millau that escaped assault, Larcis carrying away all the moveables and livestock.[40]

WHAT WAS THE NATURE of the regime installed in the towns governed by the Calvinists? We can form a pretty fair picture from the sketch provided by Janine Garrison in a recently published history of Montauban.[41] The year 1562 saw the Calvinists seize the city and expel the clergy and notables who supported the Catholic faith. The new rulers then found themselves forced to defend themselves against three successive sieges imposed by the Catholic enemy. Armament, provisions, and supplies had to be secured to support the siege. The walls and fortifications needed to be reinforced and raised. The fauborgs, which could not be defended and which could provide a cover for the besiegers, had to be burned down. Women and children were mobilized alongside men to defend the walls of the city. The ministers' sermons inflamed the population with civic and religious zeal. Montauban was transformed into a political-religious dictatorship.

At last, the third siege was lifted by the arrival of news of peace in April 1563. With the return of peace, the fortifications of the town were reduced and the Catholic faith and royal authority in part restored. But the consuls refused to surrender all the weapons in the town arsenal. Attempts to force the Calvinist church into the suburbs were rebuffed.

It was during the second and third religious wars (1567–70) that Montauban became a bastion of French Protestantism, turning into a stronghold of the reform situated in opposition to Toulouse, the Catholic citadel in Upper Languedoc. Montauban tied together the Calvinist churches of Gascony with those of lower Languedoc.

In 1567, the Catholics were once again expelled or forced to accept conversion. The surrounding villages were conquered, and the tithe was collected to ensure the defence of the city. The consuls and ministers restored the dictatorship of the first civil war. The leaders of the Calvinist community were recruited from among the notables, merchants, and notaries. The Calvinist ministers advised and assisted the civil leaders. The walls and fortifications were once again raised up, their maintenance becoming an obsession of the Montalbanais. The church of St Louis was turned into a weapons foundry. Munitions, weapons, soldiers, horses, forage, and supplies were manufactured or gathered for the Protestant army in the field. An immense financial sacrifice, which was not always willingly made, was imposed. Tensions developed continually between the Montalbanais and their noble Huguenot governors. Two of these governors, Montbartier and Rapin de Thoiras, were expelled from the city by the population. Their crime was ostensibly extortion, but more seriously they were felt to be threatening the new-found independence of the commune.

After St Bartholomew, Montauban became a virtually independent city-state, one of the capital cities of the United Provinces of the Midi. The political assemblies of the federation met in the city in 1574, 1577, 1579, 1580, 1581, and 1584. The Montalbanais showed themselves fanatically devoted to the Huguenot cause. By means of religion, they were able to live like the citizens of an independent republic.

Like an Italian city-state, Montauban reached out to control as much of the countryside as it could. In this way it provided itself with the economic and financial resources necessary to its defence. At the same time, the ministers of the reformed faith subjected the spiritual and religious life of the subordinated communities to the control of the town.

The ongoing wars of religion were centered on the struggle between the citizens and the bishop of Montauban, who had been expelled from his see. At stake was access to the tithes and taxes in the region. The noble captains and the companies they commanded were the instruments by means of which the struggle was carried on by both sides. Fear, insecurity, and suffering marked the climate in which the citizens of Montauban experienced the wars. The enemy within was feared as much as the enemy without. Suspicion and denunciations, arrests and expulsions were commonplace. The city was bled white by the fiscal demands placed upon it, as well as by the ongoing economic malaise. The rural population's suffering was worse still; they were exploited and pillaged at every turn.

Tensions continued between the city and the nobility. Duplessis-Mornay spent fifteen months at Montauban trying to be its governor in the mid 1580s. When he left in 1586, he called it the most disorderly city in the kingdom. Even his wife was humiliated by the consistory of elders and ministers, who refused to allow her to take the Eucharist because of her extravagant dress and hairstyle.

The population bridled under the yoke of consuls and ministers. The ruling oligarchy narrowed. In 1586, it was startled by the appearance of posters that went up throughout the city calling for a rising of the population against the regime. Six years later, in 1592, the plebians defied the magistrates, killing two nobles who were accused of treacherously surrendering a strong point to the enemy.

In his memoirs, Saulx-Tavannes claims that in 1587 the Huguenots offered to conclude an alliance with the Duke of Guise, the darling of the Catholic bourgeoisie, against Henri III. The object, according to Saulx-Tavannes, was to create a federation of cities based not on religion but on resistance to royal taxation. He argued that the leadership of the Huguenot party was in the hands of the bourgeoisie of the towns, and claimed that the Huguenots wanted to create a popular state. Saulx-Tavannes asserted that the offer was made by de la Noue and was refused by Guise.[42]

Saulx-Tavannes's report demonstrates the link contemporaries were able to make between the bourgeois roots of the Huguenot movement and the emergent Catholic League. His observations, however, were somewhat out of date by the 1580s. By then Henri of Navarre had assumed control of the Protestant federation. Increasingly, representation at the Protestant estates was based on provinces rather than on cities. Moreover, the members were more and more chosen from those who could be relied on to support the designs of Henri. The democratic or democratizing moment of French protestantism was a memory. Saulx-Tavannes's fears of a popular republic at this point were somewhat preposterous.

At Nîmes, the transition to a more oligarchical government was manifest within the consulate itself. There, the *avocats* were traditionally given first place. The gentlemen who sat on the council always protested this order of things. An opportunity to change the arrangement occurred when Montmorency became governor. On 13 November 1588, the nobles asked Montmorency to give them first rank among consuls, as well as other honours that would allow them to control public affairs. Montmorency, who tried as much as he could to favour the nobility, decided that first rank among consuls should alternate between nobles and *avocats* and *procureurs*. The *avocats* were so outraged by Montmorency's decision they walked out of the *hôtel de ville* altogether. In reaction, the nobles, assisted by the local garrison, blew up the house of the leader of the *avocats*.[43]

La Rochelle, on the other hand, appears to be the exception to the trend toward the reassertion of royal power over the towns. In 1592, Henri of Navarre appointed Artus de la Roque to be *sénéschal* and governor of La Rochelle with regard to matters of justice. But the *corps de ville* objected to the terms of appointment, which in their view threatened their privilege to be free from a governor or garrison. In spite of their refusal to consent to his appointment, de la Roque tried to enter the city with a small escort, making his appearance unobtrusively near the dinner hour and taking rooms at the Inn of the Three Merchants. But his arrival did not go unnoticed. The bell of the city hall sounded and the people armed and assembled themselves, amid a great deal of murmuring and commotion because the entry seemed one of intentional surprise. The mayor, accompanied by the throng, made his way to the Inn of the Three Merchants where he confronted de la Roque, remonstrating that de la Roque ought not to have entered the city in such a fashion and that he should make his exit at once. De la Roque, fearful that he would be attacked under cover of night while he was leaving, tried to reason with the mayor to allow him at least to pass the night in the town. But the mayor refused his request while the clamour of the crowd increased. De la Roque was escorted outside of the town, his way out lit by torches.[44]

The same year, the king attempted to impose a tax on La Rochelle by blocking the estuary with ships. He commissioned two captains to place five or six ships at Chef-de-Bois to collect the imposition. The Rochelais attacked this blockade both by sea and by bombardment from the landside, forcing the captains to lift the blockade.[45]

The next year, 1593, the nobility of Aunis demanded the formation of an extraordinary council for the government of La Rochelle in which they would be given a deliberative and decisive voice. Furthermore, they asked for one of their number to preside over the town council in the absence of the mayor. They justified this proposition by citing the Spanish threat, against which, they argued, all must unite. The consuls rejected this proposal out of hand, saying that the town council sufficed for matters both ordinary and extraordinary.[46]

As the century closed, La Rochelle still stood as a virtually independent city-state republic, open to the sea. Indeed, the last years of the century saw an intense agitation on the part of the merchants and artisans to participate in the *corps de ville* alongside the notables. This was the prelude to a second democratic revolution in 1612–4.[47]

The nobility, we can conclude, controlled the Protestant as well as the Catholic side in the civil wars. Nonetheless, it seems that in the United Provinces of the Midi, particularly in the years immediately following St Bartholomew, the towns experienced a period of republican and even democratic effervescence. Over time, this current tended to weaken in most of the cities under Protestant control. But at La Rochelle, nourished by its access to the sea, the sense of independence and republicanism lived on into the next century.

CHAPTER FOUR

The Commoners' Revolt

We are fed up!

The commons of Gascony

In 1576 the chronicler of the Huguenot town of Millau noted: "In these times in the Auvergne, despite the fact that the headquarters of the Protestant princes were located there, a grand assembly of nobles, all of whom were papists, took place. These nobles did great harm and committed all manner of extortions on all of the people, men as well as women, and likewise on the peasants. This was so much the case that the peasants, having lost control of their senses, assembled and attacked, killing forty or fifty of the nobles."[1] The nobles, we are told, rallied in turn, killing one hundred or more peasants. Is this account fact or hearsay? It is hard to know. It is matched by another report from St Maixent the same year: "In this time, it is said that the commons of Gascony, Agenais, Quercy, and Perigord have risen and taken up arms. They have adopted as their motto these words: 'We are fed up'."[2] No readily available evidence exists that would corroborate this rumour. Its source may, in fact, stem from the inhabitants of St Maixent, who were themselves on the edge of revolt.[3]

These accounts are not important in themselves, but in so far as they reflect a growing mood among the commoners of the kingdom, they are significant. For fifteen years they had suffered under the blows of a civil war that showed no signs of coming to an end. Noble violence, heavy taxes, and economic regression were common afflictions of this period throughout the Kingdom, but especially in the Midi. I have already noted the way the towns of the Protestant Midi had taken advantage of the massacre of St Bartholomew to secure a large degree of urban independence for themselves. This did not free them from the burden of war, but it did at least ensure that they would be fighting and paying mostly on their own terms rather than on those of the nobility. The late 1570s were to see something quite new. In these years there emerged for the first time among the populace movements that took up a position independent of the two sides of the religious conflict. Because both the Protestant and Catholic sides were dominated by the nobility, the popular upheavals of the late 1570s tended to ignore the religious question altogether. Rather they directed their anger against the nobility and the monarchy.

At Beauvais, it is true, the initial disorders took the form of a revolt against the merchant drapers, rather than against the nobility. In 1577, the workers in the cloth industry were victims of a grain shortage that made bread expensive and work difficult to obtain. In the month of December, an edict was published devaluing the currency and effectively reducing wages. As many as four thousand workers rebelled, seizing the market and the principal quarters of the city. They attacked and pillaged the houses of some of the drapers and forced the release of those among their leaders who had been put into prison.[4] While it was the merchant drapers who bore the brunt of popular wrath on this occasion three years later it was the monarchy. When a royal *commissaire des aides* arrived in the town to impose a new subsidy on the inhabitants, a riot broke out in which the *commissaire* was nearly killed.[5]

It was the soldiers passing through or garrisoning the towns who most immediately represented a monarchy that oppressed rather than protected the population. Thus, in 1575 the bourgeoisie of Limoges refused to allow the governor, the duke of Ventadour, to establish a royal garrison. His attempts to impose such a force were frustrated by the mobilization of the urban militia and the rest of the citizens in a stout defence.[6]

At Caen, the population did not cease to complain of the garrison quartered on them. In 1577, this animosity burst forth in a riot in which the ensign of the commander was killed. When the soldiers tried to pursue the assassin, a crowd placed itself between the fugitive and the soldiers so that he was able to make his escape.[7]

At Mondidier in 1578, when a regiment of troops passed through the suburbs on its way to the siege of La Fère, a peasant recognized among the crowd of soldiers a horse that had been stolen from him. When he tried to reclaim it from the soldier holding its bridle, the rest of the soldiers went to the aid of their comrade. Likewise, the bourgeoise who had come to watch the troops pass came to the assistance of the peasant. A general mêlée ensued, in which shots were exchanged and several soldiers and inhabitants were wounded. But it was the bourgeoisie who stood their ground. The soldiers fled the scene, abandoning their baggage to the townsmen.[8]

Châlons-sur-Marne was garrisoned in 1576 by a company of German *reiters* who disturbed the town and the countryside by their violence and pillaging. One day in summer, a peasant came to Châlons to demand justice for the murder of his father. The townsfolk assembled to hear his claim and accompanied him to see the commander of the *reiters*, Colonel Ambloff, the brother of Gaspard de Schomberg. Trying to calm the population, Ambloff observed "that in time of war one cannot ask for or have recourse to justice." On hearing this, the peasant at once drew his dagger and plunged it into Ambloff's chest crying, "Let it be war then, since justice has no place here!" The *reiters* took to arms, but the bourgeoisie defeated them, killing some thirty in the process. One of the favourites of the king, otherwise anonymous, attempted to intervene. Rising from a sickbed, he tried to bring the bourgeoisie to their senses. For his trouble, he was insulted, arrested, and held as a hostage in case of reprisal. The notables and bishop were able to restore order only with great difficulty.[9]

Despite their increasing alienation from Henri III, the Catholic bourgeoisie were no less suspicious of the nobility than were the Protestant townsmen. Thus, in 1576, at the time when the nobles and clergy attempted to constitute the first Catholic League, the reaction of the Catholic bourgeoisie was resolutely negative. At Châlons-sur-Saone, for instance, the town assembly declared itself openly hostile to such a league, denouncing it as a threat to the institution of monarchy. It solemnly protested against the ongoing violence countenanced by the nobility, and resolved to organize an energetic resistance against a league based on the nobles and clergy, the costs of which would have to be borne by the third estate.[10]

It is only in 1578 that the Catholic bourgeoisie of the north began systematically to distance themselves from the monarchy. The estates of Burgundy, followed by those of Normandy, Brittany, and Auvergne, energetically protested the ever-mounting tax burden. Meanwhile, in the Midi, the estates of Languedoc refused to pay the *crue*. In certain quarters, it was felt that a vast uprising was even then in the offing.[11]

The next year saw a rising of the peasantry near Caen. In January 1579, six hundred peasants invaded Caen and disdainfully returned the *mandements* for the taille to the *élus*.[12] The tax collector was attacked at Matragany when he tried to carry out his function, as were the military when they tried to restore order. Antoine Seguier, the royal commissioner sent to investigate the troubles, reported that poverty was at the root of the problem. The way in which the taille was apportioned was also in question. According to Seguier, "The injustices perpetrated in the apportionment of the taille stem from the *élus*, the assessors and sergeants of the tailles but especially, and this is the essential factor, from the excesses of the 'rich' at the expense of the poor."[13]

The year 1579 also saw popular mobilizations in Provence. At Solliès the inhabitants had long been at odds with Palamède de Forbin, the local seigneur. In reaction to having been forced to sell his mill and a great deal of land in order to pay his debts to the commune, de Forbin did everything he could to undermine the government of the town. He insisted on appointing the captain of the town militia and revoked the militia's privileges and rights to exercise justice. The inhabitants rebelled, forcing de Forbin to take flight, and pillaging and demolishing the chateau. Elsewhere in Provence, commoners burned the chateau of the Baudemont at Cuers, assassinated the seigneur de Calles as well as his sons, forced the seigneur de Mons to flee his estate, and burned chateaux at Sainte-Maxime and Bauduen to the ground.[14]

These attacks were an outgrowth of the wars that had swept Provence during the previous ten years. At the beginning of the 1570s the count de Carcès had been appointed lieutenant-governor of Provence. He and his followers, called Carcistes, terrorized Provence in the ensuing years. Those who suffered from the ravages of the Carcistes called themselves Razats, "those poor wretches who were despoiled of their goods as if a razor had passed over the top of their heads."[15]

The Carcistes were overwhelmingly an aristocratic party, although they were able to count on the support of the indigent proletarians in many towns. The heart of the Razat party, on the other hand, was the merchants, lawyers, and artisans, found especially at Brignoles, Draguignan, and in the towns along the coast from Hyères up to Grasse and Nice. They were able to enlist certain nobles on their side and, from 1574 on, allied themselves with the Protestants in the region. The social cleavage between the two sides was exemplified when both parties were called before Catherine de Médicis, each to tell its side of the story of the feud. The Carcistes were unable to find a lawyer from the middle class to make their case to the queen-mother. On the other hand, the count of Carces refused to debate with the Razats because they were, he claimed, "men of no account."[16]

The risings of 1579 were thus a popular reaction to the ravages of the Carcistes, with the climax occurring in April, when the inhabitants of the bailliage of Guillaumes and the *vigueries* of Grasse and St Paul de Vence took up arms and forced the Carcistes to take flight.[17] A remnant of the Carcistes numbering some seven or eight hundred men encamped at Cuers. The militia of La Vallete, Solliès, Toulon, and Ollioules elected captains and proceeded to attack this force. The Carcistes took to their heels, and the militias were able to seize strong points at Pierrefeu, Le Cannet, and several other places. The commoners then disbanded, promising to reassemble if need be. The Carciste leader de Vins attempted to revenge these defeats by besieging Hyères but without success. The commoners of Hyères then took to the field again, with the militias of Theonez, Grasse, Saint-Paul, and Vence, and routed the army of de Vins, killing more than one hundred of his men.[18]

The year 1579 also saw widespread popular ferment in the Vivarais. The unrest there appears to have been provoked by popular exasperation against the behaviour of soldiers and nobles, as well as against the staggering burden of royal taxation.[19] The first signs of peasant resistance had begun to appear four years earlier, in a year of terrible war and famine. The countryside was despoiled by the soldiers of both religions who cooperated with one another. In the summer of that year, 1575, the syndic of the Catholic estates noted the tax revolt growing among the Catholic peasants to the west of Largentière. The peasants refused royal demands for taxes, as well as all other impositions. Leaguing together they resisted the sergeants and commissioners sent by the estates to carry out fiscal collections. Two years later, in June 1577, six parishes in Sablières and Petit-Paris rose and massacred the local garrisons. The Catholic commander in the lower Vivarais noted, "I have received warning that the twenty-two parishes which have rebelled are on the point of joining the Huguenot party and have massed in force. If something is not done, there will be a rash of these evil beggars. I am sure that they could still be assembled for some purpose if properly handled on our part."[20]

By early 1579, the peasants had found a leader in Jean Rouvière who came from a small town to the west of Aubenas and may have been a notary or lesser merchant. From this time onward, the revolt seems to have been based on an alliance of the peasantry with the petty bourgeoisie of the small towns who were not represented in the provincial estates.

Rouvière styled himself "procurator of the petitioners of the third estate." In February 1579, he drew up a petition to the king on behalf of the people of the countryside of the Vivarais. It opened with an enumeration of the atrocities committed on the commons by captains, soldiers and nobles. Men had been buried alive in manure, thrown down wells, garrotted, and burned alive, while women had been raped, their children kidnapped and held to ransom. In all manner of ways, the property and belongings of the commons had been destroyed or pillaged. The Protestant and Catholic garrisons had imposed more taxes on the commons in one year than the amount of the royal taille in thirty years.

The petition demanded the establishment of a special court to deal with the crimes of the military. Additional officers of the *prévôté des marechaux* ought to be appointed to police the countryside, with their salaries assured so as to guarantee that they would act against the soldiers. The document called for the election by the communes of a syndic of the *plat pays*, since the syndic of the estates could not be relied upon to protect the interests of the peasantry. The new syndic should have the right to sit in all the public assemblies of the province. This demand parallels those made earlier in the Auvergne and the Velay. Indeed, it is noteworthy that the *plat pays* had finally gained entry into the adjoining estates of Velay three years earlier.

The text protested against the nobility's support of the soldiers of both the Protestant and Catholic camp. The nobles, according to the complainant, were helping to support and maintain those who were disrupting law and order. The king should prohibit the nobles from giving the soldiers of both sides shelter in their manors or any other support. Moreover, the king should insist that the nobles exercise justice in their lands and seigneuries, employing proper judges and officials in order to do so. If the nobles refused to give up their support for the warbands, the governors and lieutenants of the *prévôt des maréchaux* should attack their strongholds and seize the wrongdoers. If these officers needed assistance, they should assemble the communes by the sound of the trumpet.

The document further complained about new and illegal taxes and exactions. It asked for the remission of the taille for a ten-year period. It charged the fiscal officers of the estates with fraud. A new and honest controller should be named and the tax imposed should be collected by a *procureur*, notary, and ten elected representatives. Finally, the petition took up the problem of debt. Parishes had been forced to borrow money in order to pay ransoms or arrears on loans. Usurers were charging exorbitant interest on these debts. According to the petition, the peace of 1577 required that debts arising from the war were to be paid by the side that had incurred them rather than being passed on to the community as a whole. During the past civil war, both sides had used the same agents to raise money. Now the parties had united to shift the burden onto those who had no part in the conflicts and who had never been consulted about the raising of taxes.

While in no sense a revolutionary document, the petition does embody an articulate and intelligent representation of the point of view of the rural commons, as opposed to that of the nobility and its allies. Particularly impressive is the way it proposes specific institutional remedies to deal with the complaints of the commons: a syndic to sit in the estates, a special court to address the violence of the military, the election at the local level of tax assessors. Evidently, the petition was composed by Rouvière and other representatives of the small-town bourgeoisie.

In response, the king promised to put a stop to violence and corruption, but refused to concede any of the principal demands advanced in the petition. The royal reply apparently did not satisfy the peasants. Indeed, by the fall of 1579 the revolt seems to have become general in the Vivarais, with Protestant and Catholic parishes actively collaborating with each other. In return, the monarchy made preparations to use force against the rebellion. Guillaume de Joyeuse, the lieutenant general of Languedoc, whose Vivarais estates at Saint-Sauvur had been attacked by Protestant rebels, arrived at Pont-Saint-Esprit. At the end of November, he wrote to Catherine de Médicis.

I am going to Vivarais, where I am told that most of the people have refused to pay the *taille* to the King this year, and want none to be imposed. They speak of nothing but killing the *receveurs* and their agents when asked to pay the King's *deniers*. Those of the one religion are as much involved as those of the other, and those who have not suffered depredations from either party are the ones most to blame. There is need to act at once, Madame, so that this fire will not spread from neighbourhood to neighbourhood. I understand, Madame, that there are some petty ruffians who call themselves syndics or deputies of the *pays*, and who pester Your Majesties with remonstrances full of frivolous requests. While awaiting a reply, they persuade the people to pay nothing and promise them to obtain exemption. They seem to be able to hold the people firm in the view that they should pay nothing.[21]

Joyeuse's hand, however, was stayed. Instead, Rouvière was able to arrange for the meeting of local assemblies of nobles, clergy, and representatives of the towns. In return for guarantees of peace, Rouvière and other delegates who represented the peasantry swore to pay the taille, tithe, and seigneurial dues once again. At a meeting at Largentière on 9 February 1580, it was agreed to establish a special militia under the command of a local seigneur in order to enforce law and order. This decision appears to have met the demands in the petition drawn up the year before.

Shortly thereafter, François Barjac, the Protestant seigneur of Pierregourde, led the Catholic and Huguenot forces of the *plat pays* along with his own followers against the great fortress of Crussol overlooking the Rhône, clearing out its band of marauders. Even then the rebellion in the lower Vivarais appears to have been dissipating. By late spring of 1580, all trace of it was lost.

The forces of order having dealt with the rebels in lower Vivarais now turned their attention to the Huguenots in upper Vivarais. This austere and mountainous region was a bastion of Calvinism much like the Cevennes further to the south. Unlike the Cevennes, most of the population made its increasingly precarious living by subsistence farming.[22] Like their neighbours of the eastern Velay, their relationship to the nobility and bourgeoisie of Le Puy and the valley of the Loire was marked by continual tension. Largely excluded from the benefits of the commerce between Le Puy and the Rhône valley, the peasants and artisans of the small bourgs of upper Vivarais chaffed under the attempts of the elites of the Velay to control them. The ecclesiastical interference of the bishop of Le Puy, the seigneurial control of the Vicomtes of Polignac, and the judicial power of the *sénéchaussée* of Le Puy were equally unwelcome. The inhabitants of this region joined the attack on Le Puy in 1562 alongside the population of the bourgs and villages of the east of the Velay.

At the focal point of the Huguenot resistance in the Vivarais was the town of St.-Agrève. This bourg of three thousand inhabitants way up in the high country of the Vivarais was the epitome of a great agricultural entrepôt of the mountains. Located at the mid-point between the wheat country to the west in the Velay and the wine region of the Rhône, it was the most important way station for the muleteers who ensured the trade between the two areas.[23] The notaries and great merchants who dominated the town jealously guarded its independence. Recurrent attempts on the part of Le Puy to force St.-Agrève to pay taxes to the estates of Velay were rebuffed in the decades prior to the religious wars.[24] Political autonomy soon came to be confused with religious dissidence. The last will and testament of the judge of St.-Agrève, Jehan de Reboulet, dating from the 1550s, calls for the reading of the psalms in his house on the day of his death.[25]

St.-Agrève became a stronghold of the Huguenot party with the outbreak of the Wars of Religion. So important was the town to Le Puy that it was garrisoned by troops from the estates of Velay.[26] It was repeatedly taken by the Huguenots, who were deeply entrenched in the surrounding bourgs and countryside. In January 1579, the town once again came into Protestant hands as a place of surety.[27]

Following the pacification of lower Vivarais, the leaders of the Catholic party in Vivarais and Velay determined on the reduction of St.-Agrève. The reasoning behind this decision emerges clearly in the account of the siege by the secretary of the king, Charles de Figon, entitled *Le vraye discours du siège, prinse et totale ruyne de la ville de Sainct Agrève*.[28] According to Figon, the Calvinists, who, he notes, were very numerous in this border region between Velay and Vivarais, could not have chosen a better site to fortify than St.-Agrève, as it dominated all the other sites in the region around it. Based on their control of St.-Agrève and the forts and bourgs in the neighbourhood, the Calvinists were bent on subjugating the whole region between the Loire and the Rhône. According to Figon, the Huguenots insisted on collecting taxes and tithes throughout the area, "which they were imposing according to their pleasure and will like kings and sovereign princes ... even though the one or the other of the said two regions are not without governors, great lords, gentlemen, prelates and other good and notable personages ... to oppose the above said."[29]

The Huguenots of the Vivarais, like the Catholics, were led by noblemen. The four-hundred-man garrison of St.-Agrève, for example, was under the command of Jean de Chambaud from an impoverished if ancient noble house. Moreover, we note as well in the Protestant camp such relatively insignificant seigneurs as François de Barjac, Seigneur de Pierregourde, Noël Albert, sieur de Saint-Albin, and Jacques de Saint-Priest, sieur de Saint Romain. The principal seigneurs of the Vivarais seem all to have been Catholic.[30] The distinguished historian of the estates of Vivarais, Auguste Le Sourd, notes furthermore that in the Huguenot estates there were no barons at all, and indeed, few figures of significance, either in title or wealth.[31] The expedition against St.-Agrève was based on the assemblage of the combined resources of almost the entire high nobility of Vivarais and Velay against the Huguenot upstarts.[32] Moreover, just before the siege of the town, Chambaud, the noble commander, abandoned the garrison in a vain effort to seek help elsewhere. The overwhelmingly aristocratic force of the Catholic party overran the garrison within a matter of days, delivering the inhabitants of the town to their fate.

The upheavals in the Vivarais were closely watched from across the Rhône by the *juge mage* of Romans – Antoine Guérin[33] – since a parallel rebellion in the Dauphiné, of which Romans was at the heart, was likewise reaching its climax. The Dauphiné revolt has attracted the attention of a number of historians including Le Roy Ladurie,[34] who can be consulted for a detailed narration of its course. Rather than dwelling on the events at Romans, it would be more helpful to provide a clearer picture of events that took place elsewhere in the province. In Le Roy Ladurie's account the focus is so much on Romans that the fact that the revolt embraced the whole of Dauphiné has been slighted. Above all it would be useful to offer a more precise sense of the chronology of the struggle in the Dauphiné as a whole.

The causes of popular protest were similar in both Vivarais and Dauphiné. The violence of cavaliers captained by Protestant or Catholic officers, heavy taxes, both official and unofficial, noble oppression, and a sense of political and social exclusion led small producers in both provinces to take up arms. Le Roy Ladurie tends to minimize the influence of heavy taxation, claiming that if inflation is taken into account it was no heavier in the 1570s than in the 1540s. But Daniel Hickey has shown that Le Roy Ladurie's observation is true only if official taxes are taken into account. If the subsidies demanded by Protestant and Catholic warlords are included, the level of taxation is found to be much higher.[35]

In contrast to the Vivarais, the weight of seigneurial dues appears to have been an important issue among the peasants of the Dauphiné. It was in the regions where these dues were heaviest that the highest level of rural unrest was recorded. But it was the dispute over the taille that especially distinguishes the upheaval in Dauphiné from that in the Vivarais. In most of the Dauphiné, the *taille personelle* was the rule, meaning that taxes were assessed on the basis of the social station of the individual. Thus, the lands of nobles and ecclesiastics were exempt from the taille while lands belonging to commoners were not. While this in itself was unfair, what enraged the commons even more was the growing number of wealthy commoners who were able to gain exemption because of ennoblement or because of their status as professors or judges. Even more galling was the increasing acquisition of commoner land by the privileged. Not only were the peasants deprived of their property, but the land subsequently became exempt from the taille. The burden of taxation was thus shifted upon those commoners who continued to own property.

Until 1548, the urban bourgeoisie was able to avoid paying the taille on its holdings in the countryside. The peasants were thus embittered against the bourgeoisie, as well as against the first and second estate. However, an edict of that year imposed the taille on urban property owners, which resulted in a gradual rapprochement between the peasantry and the bourgeoisie. By the 1570s the two groups were actively cooperating with each other in their common quarrel with the privileged over the question of taxation. Assemblies of villagers, as well as of townsmen, were held with growing frequency to draw up *cahiers* related to the taille.[36] By 1574, there were demands not only for redress on the matter of the taille but also for the right of the third estate to meet separately from the privileged orders. Two years later, the third estate demanded the right to assess and collect the taxes imposed upon it. By 1578 a close collaboration had emerged between bourgeois and peasant assemblies. This was an important development, since the leagues that began to emerge in 1578, calling for armed resistance to military and aristocratic violence, arose out of the experience of these assemblies of the preceding decade. Resistance to taxation spilled over into resistance to the military, to the king, and to the nobility.

The first signs of armed resistance appeared as early as April 1578. The inhabitants of the bourgade of Pont-en-Roians, both Protestant and Catholic, acted in concert to expel the Protestant captain Bouvier, who refused to abide by the terms of the peace of Bergerac that had brought the sixth religious war to an end. Following his expulsion from the town, Bouvier attempted to install himself in the chateau du Pont. But the peasants of the region forced him to abandon this stronghold as well.[37]

In the summer of 1578 an anti-fiscal movement led by Jean Faure (Barletier) began to surface among the plebians at Montélimar to the south. The townspeople there formed a league that refused to pay the taxes imposed by the estates of Dauphiné. Moreover, they demanded that the Parlement of Grenoble order a review of the accounts of the town. In this way, the plebians threw down the gauntlet in front of the oligarchy.[38]

By October, leagues of peasants had become active in the countryside around Montélimar. On 1 November, a crucial meeting of the general assembly of Montélimar took place, attended by some eighty members of Faure's (Barletier's) urban league. Also in attendance was Coste, the spokesman for the peasant union that had formed in the region. His wrath was directed onto the heads of the soldiers of both the Protestants and Catholics, but particularly the Protestants, who were preying upon the commons in the region. In order to demonstrate the moderation of the peasants, Coste declared his willingness to submit the peasant league to the direction of the Parlement of Grenoble and the lieutenant-governor Maugiron.[39] The plebians of Montélimar themselves rallied to the support of Coste. So too did the *vice-sénéchal* of Montélimar, Jacques Colas.

Colas was the son of an *avocat* of Montélimar. Around 1572 he had attended the University of Valence. De Thou, who was there about the same time, describes him as "an impassioned orator, bold and presumptuous, who seemed prepared to risk everything in order to elevate himself."[40] By supporting the moderate program of Coste, Colas was able to direct the popular movement in the region of Montélimar away from any radical challenge to the established order.

The notary of St Antoine, the chronicler Eustache Piémond, dates the appearance of a league at Valence as early as October 1578,[41] but it is only in the new year that it began to make itself felt. At that time the peasantry to the north of Romans took the initiative. Marsas was a village that had suffered much persecution as a result of its attachment to the Protestant cause. By January 1579, its inhabitants had formed a league with the nearby village of Chantemerle, as well as with other nearby communities. The peasant league, numbering in the thousands, acquired weapons from a hardware merchant in Romans. Indeed, growing ties with the lesser merchants and craftsmen of Romans helped to bind the villages together. The rank-and-file of the league rallied to the peal of church bells or to the call of trumpets of wood fashioned in the Swiss manner. Their first attack was against a company of light horse commanded by Jean de Bourelon, seigneur de Mures and governor of Embrun. This company was attempting to make its way through Marsas on the way to Flanders. After losing some men and horses to the villagers the company was forced to take refuge in the chateau of Jarcieu. The peasants then attacked the company of Henri d'Angoulême, Grand Prior of France. Harassed by the rustics, this company of nobles was forced to detour away from the site of the insurgency.

It was in this context that, the next month, February 1579, the plebians under Jean Serve Paumier rebelled against the oligarchy of Romans. Paumier almost immediately assumed leadership of the peasant leagues to the north of the city. According to the account of Antoine Guérin, some fourteen thousand peasants followed Paumier from the villages around Romans and to the north in the Valloire.[42] According to the same account, Paumier instigated the revolt of Valence of 15 February that followed the upheaval of Romans within five days.

It is quite likely that the rebels of Valence were inspired by the events at Romans, but the outcome at Valence was quite different. Already in January the inhabitants had refused to do guard duty, pointing to the edict of peace that was supposed to be in force and to the large garrison in the town that was so expensively maintained. On 10 January, Maugiron demanded two hundred pioneers, provisions, boats, and gun powder for the siege of Soyons. This provoked murmuring and unrest in the population. On 4 February, the consuls asked Maugiron to evacuate his troops from the city so they could be replaced by the urban militia. Maugiron refused until a miller, Chevalier (alias Boniol), aroused the population against the garrison. Maugiron's cavalry, as well as two companies of infantry, were expelled.[43]

According to Piémond, the revolt at Valence differed from that of Romans in that at Valence, despite ongoing tensions between radicals and moderates, the government of the city remained in the hands of those who were "most honourable."[44] In other words, the expulsion of these royal forces was not accompanied by the overthrow of the oligarchy.

The same month, Colas led twelve hundred men of the popular league of Montélimar in an attack against the Protestant noble brigand Laroche, who held the chateau of Roussas. Although Laroche was able to obtain the assistance of about thirty nobles, after four days he was forced to take flight.[45]

At the beginning of March, Paumier commanded a force of four thousand peasants against another noble brigand, Laprade, who was holed up at Chateaudouble east of Valence. Maugiron, the lieutenant-governor, decided to march to the aid of the peasants in an attempt to keep control of the movement. After several weeks, especially in the face of Maugiron's cannon, Laprade was forced to capitulate. Dismissing the captains who had led the peasants, Maugiron adjured them to abandon any further enterprise against the king's will. They answered that on the contrary they had acted to enforce the king's edicts against Laprade and the other garrisons in the country. Moreover, they asked Maugiron to help them to pursue their *démarche* with respect to the reform of the taille.[46]

While Maugiron and his forces were occupied by the siege at Chateaudouble, the bourgeoisie of Grenoble acted to secure their city against his return. On 15 March, the consuls ordered the inhabitants to arm themselves. Four days later, they established a special citizen militia of three hundred men to protect the city. On 27 March, Maugiron returned from Chateaudouble to find the walls of the town heavily defended by the citizens who refused to readmit his troops. Infuriated, Maugiron insisted on a meeting with the consuls in front of the *Palais de Justice* the next day. At that meeting, he warned the consuls of what could happen to those who took arms against the king, especially to the inhabitants of a town such as Grenoble, which was the seat of a parlement (which was considered a royal council). The consuls responded that Grenoble was part of a union of towns that included Vienne, Valence, Romans, and others whose purpose was to liberate themselves from the garrisons that occupied them and to live at peace according to the will and edict of the king. Their intent was to free themselves from the intolerable cost of maintaining these garrisons and to undertake to defend the towns themselves while maintaining their obedience to the king. Good patriots that they were, they were obedient both to the king and to Maugiron as governor of the city. Finally, they noted that, like the rest of the union, they intended to pursue the just remonstrances contained in the *cahiers* of the people. In light of this response, Maugiron tried to put the best face on the new situation. He offered to assist the townsfolk in advancing their remonstrances, adjured the consuls to be modest, and expressed the hope that there would be a reconciliation of the nobles, clergy and commons at the upcoming estates.[47]

Vienne it may be noted had not yet joined the general movement; however, at the end of April 1579 the inhabitants there forced the departure of their military governor thereby joining the revolt of the town.[48] It is important to take note of the province-wide dimensions of this movement of expulsion of royal garrisons and officials. The complement to the peasant attack on soldiers was the movement in the towns of Vienne, Valence, and Grenoble against royal representatives and military forces quartered on the inhabitants. If anything, the expulsion of the garrisons from the town was a more serious act of disobedience to the king than the attacks against passing bands of soldiers or on the chateaux of Chateaudouble or Roussas. In any event, the queen-mother saw the two as closely linked. Writing to the king, she reported not only that the peasants had made attacks but that "very upsetting movements have begun to take place in Dauphiné; according to what I have been told, all the towns have banded together; all the soldiers, your own as well as those of the Huguenots, have been chased out of their garrisons ..." [49] Thus, in the eyes of those in authority, the consuls of Valence or Grenoble were as culpable as the artisans of Romans or the rustics of Marsas. In their representations to the queen-mother, the town notables sought to distinguish their behaviour from that of the craftsmen and peasants, especially in so far as the latter's actions threatened their power or reputation. Yet in terms of the law they were on equally shaky ground, considered in a state of rebellion by the nobles and the queen-mother – all the more so as Paumier, as the representative of the plebians of Romans and of the peasants of the environs, and the consuls of Grenoble pressed the same grievances with respect to the taille.

The estates of Dauphiné, opened its meeting on 19 April 1579, in the wake of the popular upheavals of February and March. The highlight of the meeting was the speech of Jean du Bourg, the spokesman of the third estate who presented the commoners' *cahier* of grievances. Composed of forty-four remonstrances, this document was based on an earlier *cahier* drawn up for presentation to the estates-general of Blois in 1576. Like the earlier text, this one reflected the extensive consultations with the villagers in the Dauphiné that had gone on between October 1578 and the beginning of April 1579. However, this document marks the first inclusion of specific peasant demands: the demolition of useless chateaux, prohibition of the hunt in the fields and vineyards of the peasantry, and the return of common woodlands, marsh, and pasture usurped by the nobles. At the heart of the document was the demand that the taille be imposed on those of the privileged who held commoners' land. Du Bourg also insisted that the third estate be allowed to elect its own *procureur*, which would endow it with a separate identity in the estates, where it was outnumbered by noblemen and clerics. Likewise, he insisted that the number of fiscal agents or *commis* chosen by the third estate be doubled to increase the influence of the commons in the assessment of taxes.

The popular upsurge in Dauphiné was reflected in the confident and assertive tone adopted by du Bourg's *cahier*. As Le Roy Ladurie points out, in this remonstrance the timeless values of justice and equality were placed ahead of custom or tradition. But du Bourg goes further, to assert that "the situation at present is greatly changed and unlike that of the past. When necessity requires it, as in the present, there is not a law, statute, custom or privilege which ought not to be superceded ..."[50] In the tradition-bound sixteenth century, such an assertion of the need of change could only be the product of a powerful social movement.

If we compare du Bourg's *cahier* with the protest drawn up by Rouvière in Vivarais, it becomes evident that the former achieves a much broader articulation of the demands of the commons. Undoubtedly this is a reflection of the greater strength, depth, and unity of the popular movement in Dauphiné as compared to that in the Vivarais. Rouvière spoke only for the bourgs and villages that were excluded from the estates of Vivarais, while du Bourg put forward the demands of the whole commons, including the governing elites of the principal towns of the Dauphiné. On the other hand, the commons of the Dauphiné were fighting for what the Vivarais already had, namely, the *taille réelle*.

The clergy at the meeting of the estates showed itself willing to pay taxes on the commoners' land that it would acquire in the future. The nobility, however, adamantly refused any concession on the matter of taxes. On the other hand, both the privileged orders were prepared to concede the right of the commons to elect delegates to advise the lieutenant-general alongside the nobility and clergy. The third estate was not so easily placated. Speaking for the commoners, du Bourg called for a strike by the third estate against the payment of taxes and the arrears on the debts incurred by the province. The refusal of taxes, coupled with the expulsion of garrisons, quite clearly established a common front of the third estate, rich and poor, urban and rural, against the privileged, as well as against the monarchy.

It was in this super-heated atmosphere that the peasants in the Valloire north of Romans attacked three nobles who had provoked them, killing one and burning two of their manors to the ground. At the same time, the judge, chatelain, and clerk of the barony of Clérieu were murdered. The urban bourgeoisie did all it could to disown these acts; however, in the eyes of the increasingly frightened nobility, the bourgeoisie was entirely compromised.

Lesdiguières, the chief of the Huguenots, used the excuse of the rising of the peasants to raise several new bodies of cavalry. The Catholic side tried to do likewise. Meanwhile, Jacques Colas did what he could in an effort to restore the unity of the third estate under the leadership of the bourgeoisie. While the nobility – Protestant and Catholic – girded for war, Colas issued a manifesto in May calling for unity among the third estate. In his appeal, Colas recalled that it was the commons that bore the brunt of taxation, whether imposed by the king or by the Catholic or Protestant parties. The third estate was being bled infinitely more than was the nobility and, therefore, had the right to take up arms to see that the royal peace was maintained. It was true, according to Colas, that as a result of the peasant rising in the Valloire, the nobility distrusted the third estate, but that should not cause the latter to lose heart. Rather, the third estate, the consuls of all the towns and rural communities, should be convoked to an assembly organized by the cities of Valence, Romans, Crest, and Montélimar. Colas thus called for a meeting in which the urban elite in conjunction with the rural notables would recover control over the popular movement. This assembly would then invite certain nobles and clergy to join them in settling the affairs of the province.[51]

In mid-July, Catherine de Médicis arrived in Dauphiné to try to restore order. But since she entirely sided with the nobility, she was unable to accomplish a great deal. She called Colas "presumptuous and foolish" and qualified du Bourg as a "fomentor of faction." Her attempts to enforce an agreement at the provincial estates that met in August ended in failure. Notable are the arrests at that time of a surgeon named Bastien and an *avocat*, Pellegrin Gamot, on her orders. Bastien was accused of threatening the nobles with the fate of the nobility at the hands of the Swiss. Gamot was denounced as being a Swiss agent actively promoting the notion of revolt in the towns and countryside. It is noteworthy that rather than disowning Gamot, the consuls of the principal towns intervened in his behalf. At about the same time, Innocent Gentillet, who was the principal religious adviser to Lesdiguières, was likewise intriguing among the peasants of Valloire. In the preface of his translation of Josias Simmler's work on the Swiss republics, which appeared in 1579, he responded to the charge that the establishment of a republic always led to anarchy.[52] "One might conclude the opposite," said Gentillet, "seeing the confusions into which monarchies so often fall. That is why a well-administered monarchy should be praised, provided that republics well governed by laws are likewise not condemned. For if monarchy degenerates into tyranny, however much one makes excuses for it, or hopes for its success and conservation according to the lights of God and men, on the contrary, one must expect a more horrible scandal in it than in aristocracies or democracies which are experiencing tumults."[53]

The queen-mother left Dauphiné in September. Far from pacifying the province, her departure left Dauphiné in as great a state of ferment as ever. The peasants spoke of refusing the tithe and seigneurial dues as well as taxes. Romans was in a state of perpetual tumult. In the market, peasants and artisans elected captains from their ranks as popular leaders. The insurgents spoke of a march on the provincial capital Grenoble.[54]

In November, the estates tried to impose the taille once again. The representatives of the third estate complained of the bad harvest and refused to pay. Each would pay what he owed, they announced, when the king satisfied the demands they had made in the *cahiers* they had presented to the estates. The king, they concluded, did not intend that any levy be imposed on the people.

Following this refusal, the parlement ordered the arrest of the representatives of the rural communities. But so great was the popular reaction, which went to the point of open calls for revolt, that the court was forced to release them.[55] While these events were taking place, reports began to circulate that the seigneur de Tournon was massing troops to crush the rebellion.[56] Two months later, in January 1580, rumours surfaced that the nobility of the province was secretly raising companies to put down the commoners.[57] In February, finally, came the *coup de main* of Antoine Guérin at Romans.

The massacre at Romans seems to have taken the heart out of the rebellion. For several months afterward, the peasantry, in alliance with the Huguenots, resisted the nobility and the crown.[58] Many were killed at the siege of Moirans at the end of March 1580. The following September, the last stronghold of the peasant league, the fort of Bouvoin, capitulated to the army of the duke of Mayenne. The revolt of the Dauphiné was over.

The stated aims of the revolt had been limited. No one had advanced the idea that the clergy or nobility pay taxes the way everybody else did. It was only asked that they pay taxes on the commoners' land that they had acquired. Moreover, proposals for a reform of the estates went only so far as a demand to allow the third estate to deliberate separately from the first and second estates. Likewise, there was no call for the third estate to assess taxes on itself but only to have a greater voice in the process. Du Bourg, the ideologue of the movement, went only to the point of claiming a functional equality between the third estate and the privileged orders. On the other hand, there is no denying the democratic influence of Swiss republican ideas among the plebians and the rural population. According to Le Roy Ladurie, the leader of the plebians of Grenoble was Gamot, who deliberately sported all the paraphernalia of popular and democratic revolt – the green branch, the rake, and the Swiss trumpet. He had dozens of these instruments manufactured and distributed to the rural folk.[59] The surgeon Bastien spoke for more than himself when he threatened the nobility with a massacre after the Swiss manner. The threat of turning Dauphiné into a Switzerland, idle though it may have been, was commonly held. It demonstrates that among the commons the idea existed of a society of equals or of one in which there would no longer be a system of orders.

The suppression of the revolts of 1579 did nothing to erase the causes of popular discontent. Consequently, it is not surprising that agitation continued elsewhere through the next decade. In 1582 peasants in the Comminges rose up against heavy taxation and the oppression of the military. Some of the villages threatened to turn Protestant if that would free them from the heavy weight of taxation.[60] The same year, many peasants in the area of Abbeville were arrested for refusing to pay the gabelle. Reporting to the town council, the mayor noted that many townsmen as well as peasant women had raised protests with him. He continued: "Remonstrances over these matters have taken place even in the public market by large numbers of women from the villages armed with scythes who had been impelled to march to the city following their husbands who had been taken here as prisoners, some having been killed, others wounded."[61]

In 1587, five years later, we hear of armed bands of peasants in the Forez who forced the retreat of Protestant gendarmerie trying to penetrate into the region.[62] Already the year before, a league of bourgs and villagers had organized itself in the region of Toulouse. On 28 May, the capitouls of Toulouse received word from the bourgs of Chateaudorry, Gunette, Gonelles, and other places of the formation of defensive leagues. The spokesmen for these associations explained that they had to defend themselves because their governors were absent and that nothing could be expected from them in any case.

A league was organized for the diocese of Toulouse itself. Each community was required to raise a body of horse and infantry to come to the assistance of whoever was attacked. The tocsin was to be sounded continually from bourg to bourg in order to effect a general mobilization. Those who failed to respond would be denounced to the lieutenant-general, the *sénéschal* of Toulouse, or to the parlement. At the sound of the tocsin, the consuls would repair to the countryside to mobilize or to give assistance to the rural population. Nobles were also obliged to respond to the tocsin, and if they refused, were likewise to be brought before the authorities.

The reference to governors who are absent or useless makes clear that the formation of this league undoubtedly began as a popular initiative. But as it became increasingly organized, the league lost its initial popular impulse. By 1587, it had come under the control of the duke of Joyeuse and the local military and political authorities.[63]

A fiscal strike by the inhabitants of the Uzège took place between 1582 and 1592. The population beat to death the archers sent to collect taxes. In the Aigoul and Epernou in 1587, insurgents hidden in the bocage threatened to crop the ears of the *sergent des tailles*.[64]

In 1588, the year of the revolt of the Catholic League, Caen witnessed a popular riot over an increase in the gabelle. Inhabitants of the town were joined by crowds of peasants, who flocked into the city from the surrounding countryside. As a result, the rate of the gabelle was reduced. Significantly, Caen was one of only two towns in Normandy that refused to join the League.[65]

By the 1580s, the continuation of the wars began seriously to undermine the economic condition of the urban as well as the rural population.[66] The quartering of troops on the urban population led to a growing estrangement between commoners and military, in which religion was beside the point. In 1585, Agen rebelled against the attempt of Marguerite of Navarre to make the town a citadel of resistance against her husband Henri.[67] The same year, Issoire revolted against the sieur de Randon, who was the governor and a League sympathizer. Having been called to the side of the duke of Guise, he left the garrison in the hands of the sire de Charnay and the sieur Chaterelle. In mid-June, three hundred townsmen took up arms, forced the first consul to lead them, and expelled the hundred-man garrison. In the next few years the politics of Issoire revolved around the question of the readmission of a governor. The popular party, led by a disgruntled family of notables, the Aulteroche, accused the patricians of selling the city out to the Sire de Randon in order to massacre the plebian men and to force their wives and daughters to marry soldiers. The Aulteroche urged the populace to accept the local seigneur d'Alègre as governor. The patricians countered by championing the ideal of municipal independence, compelling the people to swear not to accept a nobleman as governor.[68]

At Béziers in 1584, the town rebelled over the policy of quartering troops on the population. Several of the soldiers of the garrison were wounded and one was killed. In reaction, Montmorency ordered the gates closed until three o'clock the following day. He commanded the hanging of the ring leader and lodged a whole company of soldiers at the ring leader's house, effectively demolishing the place. He ordered that a tax be collected on the population and that those who refused be forced to billet troops.[69]

Perhaps the most striking of these conflicts between the urban population and the military occurred at Millau in 1586. Relations between Châtillon, the governor of Rouergue for Henri of Navarre, and the citizens of Millau had become more and more bitter. The inhabitants wanted to guard the walls of the town themselves. Instead they were forced to surrender their weapons to Châtillon's troops and to quarter this force in their houses. They complained that "disarmed and denuded of the principal means of defence they appear to be in a servile rather than in a free condition ..."[70]

Châtillon himself arrived in the city in July. For the next six months, the inhabitants were forced to maintain three thousand infantry and cavalry, who quartered themselves at the expense of the inhabitants while pillaging the countryside as well. Some of the inhabitants left the city in exasperation. When this was brought to Châtillon's attention, he responded: "It is all one and the same thing! He who does not want to stay, let him leave. I am resolved that if only twelve remain they will carry the whole charge. If these twelve are reduced to six and the six to three or even down to one it will be necessary for them to decide to maintain us. And when nothing is left then we will move." When Châtillon's lieutenant, the seigneur de Saint-Auban, tried to remonstrate with him, Châtillon answered: "Oh well, they haven't begun to eat one another yet!"[71]

The inhabitants were threatened, beaten, pillaged, forced to pay ransom, terrorized, and bled dry by the soldiers quartered and billeted on them. The garrison openly said that the town had become the property of Châtillon because the kingdom was in the process of being divided up.[72] Popular anger finally boiled into an uprising – an open confrontation between the populace and the garrison in January 1587.[73]

In the Narbonnaise, it is clear that the inhabitants of the bourgades were driven by the instinct for survival rather than by religious fervour. Puisserguier expelled its garrison in September 1586 because of its oppressiveness. Cabestaing went over to the Protestant side in January 1587 for the same reason. Likewise, Perinhan revolted against its garrison for the same cause at the beginning of April 1589.[74] Seizure of grain could lead the peasants to revolt against their

Catholic masters and to submit themselves to those of the opposite camp. Thus, in the summer of 1589, the principal bourgades of the Narbonnaise deserted Joyeuse and went over to Montgomery because the latter had seized their grain.[75]

In many quarters, the revolt of the League appears to have had little effect on this popular agitation. Around Carcassonne in the fall of 1589, the peasants became increasingly agitated by the pillaging of the garrison of the town. They invaded the town in large numbers, demanding redress. Only an attack by the garrison was able to subdue and disarm them.[76] At Saint-Estienne the same year, the populace expelled its League garrison. Their revolt was not out of any sympathy for the Protestant or Politique faction, but simply a way to get rid of the garrison quartered upon them.[77]

In Provence, the seigneur du Muy Jean de Rascas was assassinated by his subjects in 1588, after they had begged him to no avail to send away a company of Gascons whom he employed as a garrison.[78] At Barmes the next year, peasants massacred the seigneur and his family and destroyed the chateau. At Mane, peasants claiming to be on the side of the League destroyed the chateau. The villages in the region of Grimaud meanwhile revolted against the seigneur of St Tropez.[79]

Popular agitation in the late 1570s and the 1580s manifested itself in many places in opposition to the dominant elites. The leadership of the clergy – Catholic and Protestant – as well as that of the aristocracy was increasingly questioned. Political demands were voiced independently of the ruling ideologies. Admittedly, the popular unrest of these years was localized, diffuse, and inconclusive; moreover, it was to be eclipsed by the upsurge of a new coalition based on a resurgent Catholicism. Nonetheless, the popular agitation of these decades was to become a prelude to the much more widespread upheavals of the 1590s.

CHAPTER FIVE

The Democratic League

... a popular government and a republic
... in my very beard

the duke of Mercoeur
Journal of François Grignart

Was the League a popular movement? Of course. The Day of the Barricades, May 12 1588, witnessed the mobilization of tens of thousands of ordinary Parisians against the king. Many modern historians, however, have preferred to look not at the rank-and-file but at the leadership of the League, asking, "Was the leadership of the League drawn from or close to the common people?" Certainly contemporaries especially the supporters of Henri of Navarre, thought so. The *Manifeste de la France aux Parisians et à tous le peuple françois* exclaimed:

Consider, I beg you, the state of your city today which only lately was the most celebrated and opulent of Europe. Into what hands has it fallen? And under what governors? ... If you seek out the hounds of this hunt you will find that they are only those who move from door to door to add their piss to the sewers, beasts of the butcher and carnage, the filth and most vile excrement of your city. Some of this kind have seized control of one fortress, others have gotten control of another, in order to acquire a guarantee against the magistrate and to rob everyone with all the more impunity.[1]

In more recent times, Henri Drouot pictured the leadership of the urban League as a secondary elite of merchants, *avocats*, and *procureurs*, who formed into a bloc resting on the masses against an upper crust of urban notables and office holders.[2]

A reaction against even this view has developed in the last few years. Thus, we have Robert Harding insisting on the clerical nature of the league,[3] Phillip Benedict underlining the predominance of members of the urban elite in the League of Rouen,[4] and Robert Descimon refusing to believe in the implacable hostility of the leaders of the Paris League toward the nobility.[5]

Descimon argues that the League sought not only to recover the independence of the towns but also to restore the balance between officers and notables. The growth of the state, according to Descimon, had broken the harmonious alliance between these groups by multiplying the number of officers fortifying the *noblesse de la ville*.[6] By looking at the League in this way, Descimon has helped us to understand the congruence between the religious and the political objectives of the leadership of the League. Defence of Catholic piety went hand-in-hand with a struggle to re-establish the autonomy and social equilibrium of the town. But granting the significance of Descimon's insight, has he not simply turned Drouot's thesis upside down? The latter argued that the leaders of the League were merchants and holders of lesser offices who were resentful of their exclusion from the ranks of the notables. Descimon agrees with Drouot on the social origins of the leadership of the League. He merely argues that their objective was not to raise themselves up to the level of the notables but to pull the latter down.

As for Phillip Benedict, he has reminded us that the League ought not to be reduced to its radical wing. In certain places or at certain moments the League was the creature of urban notables. Harding's view, that the League was a religious rather than a social movement, is harder to swallow. Must we choose the one or the other? In trying to sustain this line of argument, Harding notes rather feebly that the Leaguers of St Malo were republicans of a sort rather than democrats.[7] As if that were not radical enough in sixteenth-century France!

Descimon and Eli Barnavi have captured the mercurial nature of the League in their recent study of the assassination of Barnabé Brisson, the president of the Parlement of Paris.

What was the League ...? A movement of religious opposition first of all, the offensive arm of the French Counter-Reformation. A purely political opposition also, and in this respect a reaction of the body social against absolutizing centralism: for the nobles an attempt at "feudal" division; for the towns a manifest desire to consolidate their threatened traditional autonomy; for the provinces, the dream of lost liberties, of fiscal privileges, judicial rights, of political autonomy likewise. A movement of social opposition finally where orders and classes grapple with one another in a confused mêlée, nobles against the crown, lesser office holders against grand robins; those without office, commoners, against the nobility, everyone against the kind of life led by the court, against waste, corruption, taxes ... The League, it is all these things simultaneously, at the same time and in different degrees, according to the people involved, the social stratum, the moment, the political context, local and international.[8]

The League, then, was a complex affair. There can be no doubt of the religious impulse that lay behind it, impelled it, and helped to bind its elements together. Militant counter-reformation Catholicism inspired its preachers and apologists and helped to mobilize its tens of thousands of adherents. It was as much a religiously based movement as was Calvinism in its heyday almost thirty years earlier. But whereas the one was directed against the Church, the other was aimed at the state.

The League was in part a conspiracy of nobles – those of Guise, Mayenne, Joyeuse, Aumale, Villars, Chevreuse, De Vins – to carve up the kingdom into so many quasi-independent fiefdoms. The nobility – Catholic and Protestant – had been in a state of anarchy for almost a generation. The League provided the opportunity to turn that anarchy into a political system. But it likewise provided occasion for parlements to defy the monarchy, for towns to reclaim their eroded liberties, for provinces to try to establish regional govern-ments. The League represented a massive revolt against the outrageous tax burden imposed by Henri III and the dissolute and corrupt government of this same king.

In its social aspect, it embodied feudal reaction, a revolt against the urban notables by petty officials, merchants, and craftsmen, and an explosion of popular hostility against privilege and the privileged, including the nobility. As to the leadership of the League in Paris, no one has more carefully studied it than Eli Barnavi. Through his analysis, one is able to follow step by step, the evolution of the movement from one that enjoyed the collaboration of the nobility and magistracy to a regime of radical upstarts. Barnavi holds, as does J.H. Salmon before him, that the core of its leadership was composed of Drouot's lesser officers and merchants.[9]

Recent historiography, as I have noted, focuses on the leadership of the League. It has virtually ignored the base of the movement. But there is no doubt that the leaders of the League based themselves on the mass of merchants and artisans in Paris and in other towns. The Day of the Barricades was not simply a Spanish intrigue or a conspiracy of a small group of Catholic zealots. The entry of the Swiss into the city led to a rising en masse of the inhabitants. In part, this upheaval was a religious revolt. But it must also be seen as part of the broader pattern of popular rebellion against military occupation and oppressive fiscalism, which is a common thread in the history of sixteenth-century urban France.

IT IS THE POPULAR and democratizing League that is of interest to this study. This is the league of the lesser bourgeoisie, which based itself on the people – above all, on the urban plebians. Indeed, the strength of the popular element of the League needs to be reiterated. The very weakness of the institutional Catholic Church, whose resources had been sapped by Calvinist attacks, tithe revolts and the alienation of ecclesiastical property, made a popularly based Catholic movement more feasible. It is this league of the unprivileged that was to be always an uneasy participant in the league of nobles, clergy, and magistrates.

The popular basis of the urban League can be seen at Angers, where the League took power without major difficulty in 1589. But its takeover was facilitated by the collapse of the ruling caste of municipal officers and the institution of a more representative regime five years earlier.[10] Beauvais, which had been a staunchly Catholic town through the religious wars, quickly became a League town. Its Catholicism was dictated by the Calvinism of the nobility in the surrounding countryside.[11] At Limoges, the League failed to capture the government, but the revolt it orchestrated in 1589 is a striking example of an uprising against a ruling oligarchy by a coalition of lesser bourgeoisie and plebians.[12]

At Troyes, the seizure of power by the League represented no more than a transfer of the government into the hands of one group of notables as against another. However, the period of the League witnessed acute tension between this new oligarchy and the plebians. The opposition took the form of a conflict over the threat that the politiques and Protestants living in the towns represented. In 1590, the politiques unsuccessfully attempted a rising. In the aftermath of this failed *coup*, some of those involved were put in prison while others, those among the most distinguished, were placed under house arrest. The populace attacked the prison and massacred thirty-seven of those held there. It then assaulted the dignitaries being held under house arrest.[13]

At Toulouse, March and April 1589 saw an uprising of a secondary elite of lesser officials and merchants based on the populace, which sought to overthrow the authority of the capitouls, parlementaires and the rest of the notables.[14] Having failed on this occasion, fresh attempts to seize the government of the town were made in September[15] and October.[16]

In contrast, at Laon a new government was installed that had a definite popular cast. Thus, already in September 1588 we find the cathedral canons of Laon endeavouring to forestall the installation of a commune.[17] Self-government had been suppressed by the monarchy at the beginning of the fourteenth century. The League provided the occasion for its revival.[18] In this revived commune, the mayor and council who were installed had to govern with a popular assembly general.[19]

Le Puy in the Velay was vehemently a League town, its inhabitants bitterly opposed to its politique bishop. But they likewise maintained their distance from the noble-dominated estates of the Velay, which also supported the League. Indeed, anti-noble feeling mounted from 1591 onward.[20] At Auxerre, meanwhile, the royalist bishop barely escaped with his life at the hands of a populace inflamed by the sermons of the lower clergy of the city.[21]

Rodez was also a bastion of the League, with its bishop, François de Corneillan, seigneur of Rodez, a champion of Catholic extremism. But the triumph of the League soon turned into a bitter struggle between the bishop and the inhabitants over municipal rights. The bishop plotted to reduce the traditional autonomy of the bourg. His brother, Jean de Corneillan, who was governor of the town, endeavoured unsuccessfully to take the town from the inhabitants by force. The bishop was made a prisoner by the urban League. The episcopal palace, which made it difficult to defend the walls of the town, was demolished. Meanwhile the League nobility ravaged the *metairies* of the bourgeoisie in the countryside.[22]

The council of the League in Paris proved too pro-Spanish and too republican for the tastes of the Duke of Mayenne and was therefore replaced in 1589 by a council of state more amenable to the will of the Duke.[23] At Lyons, however, the provincial council of the League remained a creature of the government of the city. Only in 1593 did the duke of Nemours succeed in subordinating it to his authority.[24]

In the meantime, the conflict between Mayenne and the *Seize* of Paris had shifted from the realm of national to municipal politics. In August 1591, elections under the control of Mayenne resulted in the nomination of a conservative city council. Two days later, the radicals prevailed, and a new roll of electors chose aldermen more acceptable to the *Seize*.[25]

As early as 1590, the League in the Agenais split over control of the finances of the movement. The conflict took the form of a struggle between the council of Agen and Charles de Montluc. The lieutenant general of Guyenne wrote to the king that Montluc had lost his grip on the town. The people had dismantled the forts Montluc had built in the city, claiming such defences were contrary to their privileges. Montluc no longer dared enter the town because doing so would put him at risk of falling into the hands of "that people who at all times, as your majesty knows, are ready to undertake something."[26]

By the next year the municipal elite that controlled the League in Agen had become fearful of the populace. In October 1592, an ultra-League faction that showed dangerous democratic tendencies came into the open. Calling itself the "red crusade," it opposed the power of the consuls and protested the weight of taxation.[27]

Provence seems to have been particularly agitated. Under the banner of the League, a popular revolt occurred at Arles that forced many nobles and bourgeoisie into leaving the city.[28] Similar events took place at Aix.

The relationship between the League and populist politics is nowhere better illustrated than in Salon. The leader of the ultra-Catholic and democratic party at the time was the Cordes family. The Cordes were brought close to the League as a result of the intrigues of the Baron de Vins, who, along with the countess de Sault and the count de Carces, was the chief of the aristocratic League in Provence.

The appearance of the League provided the occasion for mobilizing the democratic party in Salon. The democratic struggle against the oligarchy had been going on throughout the sixteenth century. In 1581, the ruling elite had been able to get an *arrêt* from the Parlement of Aix abolishing universal suffrage. Not only were the plebians thereby excluded from the vote but the political power of the Cordes family was likewise curtailed.

The outbreak of popular revolt at Aix became the signal for the popular rising at Salon. Jean de Cordes and a former rival, Jean-Antoine de Brunet, assumed leadership. These two had the support of the mass of the population and the Carcistes among the nobles and bourgeois of Salon, in addition to the peasants of nearby village communities.

On the other side, the politique first consul, Eyguesier de Confoix, proved to be a resourceful and determined opponent. Realizing that Sunday, 28 August, was the likely day of the popular revolt, he called the town council together the day before to warn the consuls of a probable rising and to ask for twelve arquebusiers to stand ready with the consuls around the clock.

The sedition broke out the next evening at six o'clock following Vespers, when all the Leaguers assembled on the Place des Ormes. De Confoix and his men tried to confine the insurgents to the public square. Indeed, de Confoix boldly led the arquebusiers into the square to try to disperse the mutineers. But the riflemen panicked, forcing de Confoix to take to his heels and to enclose himself in the chateau. From there, he organized a stout defence with the help of the politique bourgeoisie and nobles. The whole town was in a state of siege. As night fell, the gates were opened and the villagers from the surrounding countryside poured into Salon, equipped with clubs, pitchforks, and scythes. The besieged were filled with a sense of despair, but de Confoix was able to convince them to hold out. They were rewarded by the arrival of troops loyal to the king who forced the Leaguers to abandon the siege. Many of the Leaguers were compelled to take flight.[29]

The democratic revolt at Marseilles likewise began under aristocratic auspices. Its leader, Charles Casaulx, acted under the protection of the redoutable Christine d'Auguère, countess de Sault. But once Casaulx had entrenched his government, he made Marseilles into a virtually independent republic. During the five years of his government, most of the bourgeoisie and merchants became his bitter opponents. He imprisoned many of them, seized their property, or forced them to leave the city. Only a small handful of the bourgeoisie and merchants were prepared to give him their support. The real foundation of his power was his popularity with the mass of the population.

Despite the hostility of most of the wealthy, Casaulx's government was intelligent and beneficent. Casaulx dealt with the subsistence crisis that afflicted the inhabitants of Marseilles by buying grain and ensuring the public distribution of it. He resorted to forced loans and arbitrary taxes deemed necessary to feed and defend the population. As far as he was able, he undertook public works, particularly to improve the town's system of sanitation. He completely reorganized the system of poor relief, while going as far as to create a *Hôtel des monnaies* and a *cour de justice souveraine*.[30]

Meanwhile, far to the north, the citizens of St Malo had revolted against their seigneur. In 1589 the inhabitants assaulted the chateau of the town and killed its governor. Using their adherence to the League as justification, the

St Malouins made the town into a virtually independent republic.[31] The townsfolk not only undertook to defend their city but engaged a troop of horse to police the countryside. When the new bishop, Bourgneuf de Cucé, arrived in the city he was imprisoned under suspicion of being a politique. But the truth was that the St Malouins, having rid themselves of their governor, were not prepared to accept anyone else in authority over them. All attempts by the leader of the League in Brittany, the duke of Mercoeur, to assert his authority were rebuffed, with successive delegations from the town sent to try to forestall him from entering the town. In a climactic interview, Mercoeur categorically rejected the St Malouins' demands for self-government. "I cannot nor ought I to authorize it," said Mercoeur. "You yourselves would not want to counsel me to do something so prejudicial not only to my authority as governor but to the very dignity of kings. And I fear if they one day left their graves that they would reprimand me for having allowed a popular government and a republic to form itself as it were in my very beard."[32]

The 1590s thus saw the existence of more-or-less independent urban republics at Marseilles and St Malo under the banner of Catholicism and similarly independent cities like La Rochelle and Montauban under the banner of Calvinism. More generally, the opening years of this decade saw France divided not simply between rival groups of nobles but between two urban leagues or federations – the one Protestant and the other Catholic.

The Protestant towns were not able to organize themselves as a body apart from the Huguenot nobles, who tended to dominate the Calvinist political assemblies. Only the religious synods dominated by the Calvinist ministry were largely free from noble control. As for the urban League, its capacity for self-organization was inherently limited by the fact that it was by definition anti-centralist in character. Given this nature, the inability of the League towns to organize concerted action followed of itself.

The popular League was not limited to the towns. In Normandy and in Perche, Maine and Brittany, the peasantry was also swept into the movement. Angered by the fiscal demands of the king and the excesses of the military, peasant assemblies and militias began to appear in 1586 throughout Normandy, notably, in the pays de Caux and in the Lieuvin near Evreux, Conches, and Bernay. The bourgs and villages not only armed themselves but defied the king and the Parlement of Rouen by refusing to pay taxes. The ultra-Catholic nobles of these regions sided with the peasants and undertook to lead them. Nobles or servants of the king who defied them were liable to attack. Perhaps as many as sixteen or eighteen thousand peasants enrolled in these village militias. Dying down temporarily in the course of 1587, this movement reappeared, stronger than ever, in 1588 and 1589.[33] Nor was this insurgency confined to the countryside. In July 1589, these *Gautiers*, as they were called, attacked the chateau de la Tour about a league west of Falaise. The bourgeoisie of Falaise gave their full support to this assault and subsequently had to pay an indemnity to the seigneur of the place.[34] Likewise the citizens of Bernay leagued themselves with the *Gautiers*, giving them refuge at the moment of their defeat. As a result the town was besieged and taken by assault.[35]

The *Gautiers* got their name from the village of La Chapelle-Gautier, whose peasants took the lead in resistance to the military and the fisc. The leaders of the movement were some of the wealthier peasants, curés of the villages, and veterans of the wars. It was the local Catholic nobles who enrolled the *Gautiers* under the banner of the League. The climactic conflict took place at the siege of Falaise, where the royal army under Montpensier encountered a force of some five or six thousand rebels, among whom were perhaps two to three hundred nobles under Brissac. Many of the peasants – perhaps three thousand – were slaughtered; the rest surrendered or took flight. Notably at the critical moment of the struggle, the peasants were abandoned by Brissac's nobility.[36]

In the Perche, events unfolded in much the same fashion. In 1590 supporters of Henri of Navarre occupied the town of Mortagne. At once the peasants of Bazaches, Saint-Hilaire, and Saint-Céronne mobilized to oppose them. Under the command of Chenet-Hayot, an inhabitant of Bazaches, the peasant militia assembled at the hamlet of Ronnel, which they transformed into a fortified camp. At this news, some fifteen hundred royalist troops immediately marched on Ronnel, storming the barricades of the defenders, setting fire to the village, and forcing those peasants who could to run for their lives.[37]

In Brittany, the peasants, crushed by unending war, likewise threw their support to the League. Miserable, devout, and Breton-speaking, they detested equally the Protestant or royalist towns and the nobility. Ordinarily, peasants in sixteenth-century France had a low sense of class consciousness, but the situation in Britanny in the 1590s was far from ordinary. Decades of war in which the peasants had been victimized by nobles, and a sense of common misery, common faith, and common culture, helped to produce a shared sense of grievance against the nobility and the rich townsfolk. An unusually high sense of class awareness was the result.

The peasants followed the army of the League like a hungry wolf. Thus, in 1589, Mercoeur surprised the count of Soissons at Chateau-Giron. The peasantry, some two thousand in number, arrived too late to participate in the battle. Noting their discontent, Mercoeur urged them to join in the siege of a nearby chateau where some of the enemy were holding out. Having no provisions, the besieged soon agreed to surrender. But the peasants refused to honour the terms of the surrender, attacking and killing the prisoners.[38]

The same year, Mercoeur undertook the siege of Vitré, a Calvinist stronghold. Under the leadership of their captains, some twenty thousand peasants mobilized in the hope of doing battle with the Huguenots and of sacking the town. Lavardin, one of the leaders of those besieged in Vitré, tried to flee to Rennes, but he and his troop were ambushed by the peasantry along the way, and much of the troop was destroyed. Only Lavardin and a handful of other survivors made their way to safety.[39]

When Mercoeur gave up the siege of Vitré, the peasants refused to obey him. They continued the investment of the city, and that failing, barricaded themselves in their villages. The prince of Dombes, supported by cavalry and cannon, was dispatched in order to suppress them. He had to reduce them parish by parish, using both fire and sword.[40]

It was in lower Brittany that the mobilization of the peasantry was widest and deepest. As many as twenty thousand joined the rural militias of the League, laying siege to the royalist stronghold of Brest. In order to combat these militias, many of the nobility of the region united near Lannion under the orders of the sieur de Kergommard. In several engagements, they were able to rout some three or four thousand insurgents. As a lesson to the others, the sieur de Kergommard ordered some of the captured peasants to be strung up and left hanging from trees. If we are to believe the account of a contemporary, this was enough to cower the peasants in this region.[41] The island of Bréhat, likewise defended by its peasantry, fell to the nobility under Kergommard.

But these actions dealt only with the rebels on the north coast of Brittany. According to a contemporary, almost the whole of lower Brittany was in revolt. "The peasant communes being armed have colonels and popular tribunes who lay down the law to the nobles who live in the area."[42]

The seizure of the chateau of Kerovzère is a good example of the ferocity of the peasant insurgency in this region. This chateau, owned by Pierre de Boiséon de Coethizon, was the stronghold of the royalists in the region around Saint-Pol-de-Léon. From it, Coethizon and his band of forty nobles and soldiers raided the neighbourhood. They kidnapped people in the area and were mortally hated by the peasantry. Led by several gentlemen in November 1590, the peasants mobilized and invested the chateau. Cannon having breached the walls, Coethizon began to treat with the nobles on the other side for terms. But the peasantry became incensed at the idea of a generous accord between those in the chateau and the nobility who had conducted the siege. According to a contemporary account, "they threatened to kill everyone, even the nobility of their side, if the latter accorded liberal terms to the besieged. They wanted the lot of them exterminated."[43]

Two of the besieged noblemen, Goesband and Kerandon, left the protection of the chateau to negotiate at another fortress about half a mile away. Hearing of this, the peasantry attacked the fortress. Kerandon tried unsuccessfully to escape on horseback but, was beaten and literally torn to pieces by the peasantry, who took away parts of his body to display like trophies. Goesband, protected by the nobles, was able to save his skin.

After several days, the chateau surrendered; nevertheless when the besieged left the chateau, the besieging nobles had all they could do to save themselves from the wrath of the peasantry. One of these nobles was wounded by a pitchfork thrust into his neck, while another received an axe blow that nearly split his skull.[44]

Meanwhile, in September, two months earlier, the peasantry had scored a bloody victory against the nobility at the Chateau of Roscanou near Quimper. Robert du Châtel de Kerlech, "one of the brave gallants of Brittany," had married his cousin Claude du Châtel. Wishing to bring his bride back to lower Brittany but aware of the peasant insurgency, he travelled with an escort of eighty other noble friends and relatives. On the way they stopped at the chateau of Roscanou, the lady of which was despised by the local peasantry and suspected of being a royalist. As soon as du Châtel's party dismounted, word spread through the surrounding country that royalist cavaliers had arrived at Roscanou. The tocsin began to ring in all the parishes for miles around. By evening, thousands of peasants had surrounded the chateau. The wedding party nonetheless made merry, laughing at the rustics. The latter blocked all the roads from the chateau, making it impossible for the noblemen to leave. They then set fire to the building, forcing the nobles one by one to leave the shelter of the chateau to face the pitchforks and halberds of the peasants. In total, sixty nobles met their deaths in the fire and massacre. The bride herself had her neck pierced by a pitchfork.[45]

The Waterloo of the Breton peasantry came at Carhaix. Weakly defended, it was overrun and pillaged by royalist troops in September and raided once again in November. News of this second attack led to the mobilization of thousands of peasants to the sound of the tocsin. They marched toward Carhaix without order or discipline, the advanced elements forcing Lanridon, an old noble soldier, to lead them into battle. The royalist forces sought to lure the peasants into a trap by appearing to retreat. Understanding the ruse, Lanridon tried to hold the peasants back, but they accused him of cowardice, threatened to kill him, and forced him into battle. Wave after wave of peasant infantry was slaughtered by the royalists. When fresh peasant levies arrived from outlying parishes the next day, they were taken by surprise and massacred in turn.[46] This setback temporarily turned the tide against the peasants. A contemporary reflecting on this rout noted:

This defeat of the peasants of Carhaix ... reduced their arrogance and pride, for they were all disposed to a revolt against the nobility and the towns, not willing to be subject to anyone, of which they openly boasted. It is certain that if they had returned victorious from Carhaix as they had promised, they would have thrown themselves on the residences of the nobles without pardoning anyone who might have been of a condition higher than themselves. In doing so, they said that they would make everyone equal, without one having power or jurisdiction over another.[47]

The defeat at Carhaix did not put an end to peasant mobilization in Brittany. Two years later, we find five or six thousand taking part in the siege of Brest.

As before, their anger against the Protestants and royalists was transformed into fury against their own noble commanders.[48] Indeed, they were quite capable of attacking the forces of the League itself. Thus, when Saint-Laurent, governor of Dinan, was defeated by the royalists, his soldiers fled in disorder. The peasantry attacked the retreating troops, killing several hundred.[49] A League force under D'Aradan travelling from Guémené to Hennebont was set upon and attacked by two thousand peasants.[50] Peasant insurgency continued in Brittany until the end of the civil wars, merging itself with the popular insurgency that arose throughout France in the mid 1590s.

IN SO FAR AS THE TOWNS of the League were prepared to accept leadership, it was to Paris that they looked. Barnavi has unearthed and published a proposal, which he dates between 1585 and 1588, to organize a federation of urban adherents of the League.[51] The proposal begins by noting that Paris as the capital city has living in it merchants from all the towns of the kingdom. These merchants are generally used by the provincial towns as intermediaries, whether on matters relating to commerce, justice, or the court. The document proposes that these merchants be used as emissaries, between the provincial towns and the council of the League of Paris. At first they could serve as simple intermediaries but with time and experience they could be given powers to deliberate and to resolve matters affecting the whole "Union." The deputies would be resident in Paris but without additional expense. The result could be the creation of a kind of estates of these towns. The estates would be in continual session without being apparent to the public eye.

The League was built on a fragile alliance of the urban population and peasants with the ultra-Catholic nobility. We have noted the tension that tended to undermine this alliance. One of the most direct reflections of this underlying friction is the pamphlet literature of the League, its most notable feature its hostility toward Protestantism and the centralized monarchy. Many of the pamphlets recall the writings of the Huguenot theorists, who called for limiting the powers of the monarchy and enlarging the powers of the estates-general. But throughout much of this literature, an unmistakable undertone of hostility to the nobility is apparent.

In his *De la vertu de noblesse* (1585) Jean de Caumont tries to redefine the nature of nobility. That which is noble, he states, is not different in kind or nature from that which is not noble. It is simply an excellence of quality or an outstanding faculty. Nobility flows from rightful actions or good works, which reduce themselves to the honouring of God. Thus, it is those who honour God who ought to be considered noble or gentlemen. It is only such who deserve the title of nobility.[52]

Echoing Caumont is Mathieu de Launoy in his *Remonstrance ... à la noblesse de France* (1589). According to Launoy, humankind as a whole has been drawn and extracted from the same mass. Rejecting any notion of nobility based on blood, race, or lineage, Launoy argues that nobility is a personal quality rooted in the intensity of one's faith. Thus, the degree of one's nobility is based on the measure of one's spiritual zeal. Only Catholics can pretend to the title of nobility.[53]

The estates-general of 1588 provided the occasion for the publication of a number of pamphlets that called for the reform of finance, justice, and religion. One of these is the *Bon advis et nécessaires remonstrances pour le soulagement des pauvres du tiers Estat*, which urges the estates to relieve the burden of taxation on the commoners. The work is marked by a profound hostility toward the nobility. The nobility are described as the men of war, on behalf of whom the taxes are raised on the backs of the third estate. Since the beginning of the reign of Henri III, taxes have never been higher, while the existence of the kingdom has been put into question by civil war and foreign invasions. The nobility have not acted to deal with these disorders but in fact some of them have joined the factions that are fomenting disorder. Meanwhile, the poor have to pay. Finally, the author of the tract noted that while the League serves true religion, the Protestants and politiques cause the troubles.[54]

Another remonstrance that reflects the point of view of the radical League is the *Articles pour proposer aux Estatz et faire passer un loy fondamentale du royaume* (1590). The treatise, apparently written at the instance of the *Seize*, was sent to all the cities that were part of the League. The author calls for the promulgation of the decrees of the Council of Trent, insists that only a Catholic can be considered a legitimate king of France, and calls for the estates-general to limit the power of the monarchy. The provinces will be governed by lieutenant-generals elected by local estates according to forms determined by the estates-general. The local estate will also have the responsibility to see that the provinces are governed according to the ordinances issued by the estates-general.

From our perspective, what is most interesting is the attitude of the author of this treatise toward the nobility. The proliferation of the nobility, the author argues, has been one of the principle reasons for the increased burden on the people. Accordingly the dukes, counts, and marquises, whose titles were created at a time not specified, are to be suppressed by the estates-general, the number of nobles is to be reduced to that of the ancient Kingdom of the Franks, and the estates-general is to have the right to decide whether or not to legitimate all royal grants of land, money, or privileges.[55]

Oudart Rainsart's *La representation de la noblesse hérétique sur le Théâtre de France* (1590) was written to convince politique noblemen supporting Henri of Navarre to join the League. Nonetheless, this work, too, is filled with hostility toward the nobility, stating that the ancestors of the nobility of the present acquired their titles by acts of brutality and robbery. According to Rainsart, it is monstrous that the nobles who are supposed to defend the Church and the liberties of the people are largely in the party of atheism. The wars have killed so many virtuous nobles that it is easy for the Valois to enslave the people and for the evil nobles to increase their power and wealth. The title of noble, like that of king, is given by the people, and thus the nobles, like the king, can be deposed by the people.[56]

The radicalism of certain elements of the League is apparent in these pamphlets. Contemporaries were well aware of this current of subversion. Arnaud D'Ossat, a diplomat, noted in his *Discours sur les effets de la Ligue en France* (n.d.) that "the people wish neither a sovereign nor a nobility and recognize neither a prince nor a gentlemen. Even the most insignificant inhabitants of the countryside wish to remove themselves from their obedience."[57] Another work, the *Quatre excellent discours sur l'état present de France* (1593), remarked that "the whole people of the Kingdom and especially those of the cities who received from the monarchy only the right to pay taxes and serve it have only the idea of liberty in their head ..."[58] The clergy sustained the revolt, but the nobility did not, understanding that if there was no longer a king each village would get rid of its gentleman.[59]

Although this clearly was an exaggerated view, an element of truth lies behind it. The nobility were frightened by the extremists in the League. The duke of Montpensier noted that "the designs of the Leaguers tended only to reduce France to a popular confusion and to wipe out the prerogatives and dignities of all the nobles of the Kingdom."[60] According to Mayenne in 1590, the violent and injudicious domination of the bourgeoisie was becoming uncontrollable. The nobility was becoming estranged from the League, "for there is no jealousy which touches to the quick the heart of a Frenchman than the apprehension of a popular and tumultuous state and the establishment of a republic in which there is no longer a distinction of ranks and qualities."[61]

Earlier, the duke of Nevers took note of the republican spirit he detected among the towns of the urban League. According to Nevers, such republicanism was inherently self-destructive. Nevers believed that those towns that tried to establish themselves as republics would not be able to sustain themselves. If they tried to unite in a union for their protection, each would refuse to submit to the decisions of all the rest. Having rejected the yoke of royalty, he argued, would they find it acceptable to submit to an urban authority of lesser dignity? The little republics of Italy in the end had fallen under the domination of princes. Virtually the same thing had happened to the free cities of Germany, for most of them had had their territories annexed by their neighbours the great princes. The same thing, he argued, would happen to those in this kingdom who desired to establish republics. They would find that they could not have access to the countryside, carry on trade, or practise law. Divisions would appear among the citizens, because those who had something to lose would become angry when they saw themselves at the point of ruin. Such discontent would create disunity and cause the loss of the government of the city. Threats and secret intrigues, he concluded, would lead to surprise attack on the cities, to their sack and ruin.[62] Nevers here appeared to have been whistling in the dark. But in their very elaboration, his predictions reflected his anxiety over the unruliness of the towns. There is no question that their turbulence and independence tended to alienate elements of the nobility from the League.[63]

The alienation of the nobility by the radicals alarmed some of the more conservative leaders of the League. Louis d'Orleans's *Second advertissement des Catholiques anglois* was designed to mollify them. D'Orleans noted that one of the major difficulties of the League was that it had frightened the Catholic nobility by its apparent desire to create a popular government. He repeatedly denied that this was the objective of the League. On the contrary, the League sought to preserve the monarchy and nobility. D'Orleans noted that some of the activities of the *Seize* were a threat to the League. Some were thieves, some overly ambitious, while others wrote seditious books. By their actions, many of the *Seize* were creating the impression that the League wished to create a democracy.[64]

Henri of Navarre in particular played upon the elite's fears of the apparent radicalism of the League. He made especially good use of the pen of Duplessis-Mornay to stir the disquiet of those with wealth or privilege. In December 1588, he addressed the delegates to the estates-general in a letter composed by Duplessis-Mornay.

What will the appearance of the Kingdom be if this evil continues? What will happen to the nobility if our government changes, as it indubitably will? One sees it even now: the cities out of fear of partisans will reinforce their defences, no longer permit anyone to command them, form themselves into cantons in the Swiss manner. No one wishes this I am sure, but the war will force this result in the long run. I already see the beginnings of it, to my great sorrow ...[65]

He wonders about the fate of the cities once they have overthrown the old order in the name of liberty. He asserts that they will have the whole of the nobility against them if they do so. The peasants, he argues, will only await for an opportunity to sack the towns. He warns the *officiers* that the offices of the state that they now control as personal property will be lost if the monarchy falls. Without the monarchy, he cautions, the bourgeois will be unable to carry on trade, guarantee their property, implement judicial decisions, or defend their towns. As a result of the split between nobles and towns, the people will not be able to find repose. It is the people, according to Duplessis-Mornay's letter, who are the foundation of the state. But without the monarchy the people cannot protect themselves against the oppression of the nobility and the taxes imposed on them by the towns. In short, Duplessis-Mornay argues that the monarchy is indispensable to the peasantry and bourgeoisie.[66]

Elsewhere, addressing himself to the bourgeoisie, Duplessis-Mornay notes: "Today it has become a heresy to be politic; thus, order, which has enabled the towns to flourish, is held in contempt. Tomorrow it will be an unpardonable crime to be rich."[67]

It was the contradictions that Duplessis-Mornay pointed to that were to ensure the defeat of the League. Despite the half-hearted attempts to create a federation, to bolster the estates-general, and even to envision a republic in place of the monarchy, no alternative government emerged from the revolt of the League. Indeed, the League was based on the desire for autonomy of the towns and the aristocracy. United only by a common animosity to the Protestants and the state, they could not and would not find an alternative to the monarchical order.

On the other hand, if we consider the League from the perspective of the popular movements of the sixteenth century, it is evident that it was the largest insurgency yet seen of the commons. Revolts occurred in both town and country. In some towns radicals tried and sometimes succeeded in displacing the more moderate leaders of the Catholic faction. The more radical faction was able to produce a number of treatises that gave vent to the popular hatred of the nobility. Finally, at least some leaders of the urban League thought about the possibility of a federation of the towns or dreamed of a republic. They could envision a new scheme of things based on a limited monarchy or no monarchy at all. They could visualize a new state of things in which the power of the nobility would be reduced if not eliminated. But they lacked the wherewithal to implement their fantasies.

CHAPTER SIX

The Croquants' Revolt

Liberty! Liberty!
Long Live the Third Estate!

Jean Tarde's *Chronique*

Revolt by the commons wore several disguises in the course of the religious wars. At the beginning, it adopted the guise of militant Calvinism. In the period of the League, it took on the appearance of Counter-Reformation. In the critical years 1579–80 in the Vivarais and Dauphiné, it unveiled itself for the first time as a revolt independent of both the Protestant and Catholic religions and of the elites that championed them. It was in this latter form that it was to manifest itself once more in the 1590s. On this last occasion it was to reveal itself as a nation-wide movement against the continuation of the civil wars. As such, it represented a repudiation of the nobility as well as of the clergy. In most places, it marched under the banner of royalism, but in some towns and provinces it displayed itself as a democratic wave against all authority.

THE POPULAR MOVEMENT of the concluding phase of the civil war occupied especially the years 1594–5, but there were premonitions even at the height of the League. For example, Provins in Champagne was a town supposedly firmly in the camp of the League. But when grain merchants attempted to buy up the grain in the market to supply the army of the League in 1589, a popular sedition broke out.[1] In the town of Reims, as early as 1590, relations between the League garrison and the townsfolk were extremely tense. Soldiers fired on a group of masons, who counter-attacked using their tools as weapons. In the faubourg, Cères Herbin Callemont was heard to cry, "We ought to kill the captains who are allowing these disorders."[2]

Châlons-sur-Marne and Sainte-Menehould, likewise League strongholds in Champagne, revolted against the League nobility soon after the assassination of the duke of Guise. Châlons expelled the seigneur de Rosne and his troop on 31 December 1588. A few days later, the inhabitants of Sainte-Menehould surprised the garrison of the seigneur de Mondreville. Both towns declared for Henri of Navarre as a way of justifying the recovery of their municipal independence.[3]

That the restoration of municipal autonomy lay behind these urban risings is confirmed by the cases of Langres and Meaux. In Langres, the royalist bishop had arranged for the submission of the town to Henri of Navarre, but when the latter tried to introduce a company of two hundred and fifty as a new garrison, the townspeople rebelled once again.[4] In Meaux, the garrison that controlled the town wreaked destruction on the neighbouring villages. In 1590, these villages, such as Nanteuil-lès-Meaux, Quincy, Mareuil, and Monthyon, began to fortify themselves in order to defend themselves against the pillaging of the soldiers.[5] One morning, three of these troops were discovered hanging from a tree less than a league from Meaux. On one was pinned the couplet: "For having been taken at Monthyon / You will have a rope under your chin"[6] Having barricaded themselves behind their fortifications, the villagers refused to pay the taille and other exactions demanded by the chiefs of the League. In mid-June, St Pol, the governor of the Brie for the League, attacked Quincy with two thousand men and two cannons. The village was overrun and pillaged but only after bitter resistance that caused the deaths of fifty of the besiegers.[7] In 1591, when the inhabitants of Jouarre declined to pay the taxes demanded by the League, the town was attacked and pillaged by the garrison of Meaux.[8] A year later, it was the townsfolk of Meaux who revolted. Arming themselves, they attacked the garrison and forced the soldiers to abandon the city.[9]

Around Senlis in 1591, a group of peasants calling themselves "les francs museaux" refused to recognize the authority of either the League or the royalists. In the course of that year, as well as the next, several of them were captured and hung at Senlis.[10] Likewise, we hear of "francs-museaux," as well as "châteaux-verts" and "lipans," in Normandy.[11]

In 1592, Rouen came under siege by a royalist army. Shortage of bread led to popular riot and pillaging in April. The imposition of new taxation soon afterwards provoked new disorders. Insurgents claiming the support of four thousand inhabitants besieged the *palais de justice* and the *hôtel de ville*. They were dispersed by men-at-arms.[12] A full-scale sedition broke out at Caen in March 1593 against the *Cour de aides* of the League which refused to recognize exemptions from the taille on land that the townsfolk exploited for themselves.[13]

At Limoges, a town held by the League, a popular riot took place at the time of the municipal elections. A crowd assembled before the *hôtel de ville* demanding that neither Huguenots nor Leaguers be named as magistrates. A pitched battle with the authorities ensued in which the latter were able to regain the upper hand.[14]

Far to the south, the Labourd was in a ferment. The inhabitants of Espelette rose en masse in 1591 against their seigneur, besieging him in his chateau. The

League nobility of the region intervened to save him. At the same time, the commoners in the neighbourhood supported the insurgents of Espelette. The magistrates and governor of Bayonne hastened to interfere demanding the punishment of Leaguers and calling for a truce.[15]

Hostility against the nobility was not confined to towns occupied by the League. Castres, a Huguenot stronghold, was the site of a popular upheaval incited by the cruelty of the count Montgomery. On the evening of the 31 May 1591, Montgomery was standing near his residence in the company of the seigneur de Pujol and the seigneur de Monteson. He was approached by Pierre Dupuy, a royal notary and syndic. Dupuy spoke some words to Montgomery, who responded by beating Dupuy over the head with his baton. Dupuy made his way home with his head covered in blood. Word of what had occurred soon spread through the city and led to an immediate mobilization of the townsmen. Montgomery's residence was attacked and invaded and Montgomery forced to flee across the neighbouring roofs and gardens. A house-to-house search for the fugitive was made, which led to the vandalizing of several shops when the shopkeepers showed reluctance to open their premises to the vigilantes. The people stood at arms through the night. The consuls and notables were gradually able to calm the population. Toward three o'clock in the morning, it was arranged that Montgomery would leave the city in the company of two other noblemen.[16] The anger of the population of Castres did not explode out of nothing. There had been numerous acts of violence against townsfolk prior to Montgomery's assault on Dupuy, including one against the widow of a bourgeois of the city.

In Champagne in 1593, the villagers at Villemorien revolted against the pillaging and extortion of the League garrison at Bar-sur-Seine to the north.[17] Speaking of the violence and brigandage of the League a local chronicler remarked, "it makes one believe that if our princes of the League, do not soon vouchsafe to grant peace everyone will take up arms."[18] Indeed, the same source noted that a certain Dandenot had taken and occupied the priory of Viviers and was collecting the fruits of it like a seigneur. Poor shoemakers, vinedressers, and metal workers were occupying the residences of nobles whom they had forced to flee.[19]

An insurrectionary wave against the League developed in Champagne the following year, 1594. The townsmen of Reims had become increasingly disenchanted with the League. After the abjuration of Henri of Navarre, the civic militia refused to serve the League any longer. In early February 1594, open fighting broke out between the citizens and the League garrison in which several were killed or wounded.[20] At Tonnerre, the inhabitants smashed the garrisons of Chablis, Vezelay, and Saint Florentin, which had been sent against them.[21] At Bar-sur-Seine, the citizens rioted against their garrison.[22]

The chronicler of these events in Champagne kept himself abreast of parallel developments elsewhere. With evident satisfaction, he noted the coincident rising of the *Bonnets-Rouges* in Burgundy, the *Croquants* in Gascony, and the

Tard-Avisés in Auvergne.[23] Immediately following, he reported how the soldiers of the chateau of Chamay had killed more than thirty villagers of Cléry and La Vacherie because they, too, were at the point of taking up arms in revolt.[24] At the village of Arrelles, thirteen League soldiers tried to arrest some of the villagers. When one fired his arquebus and hit one of the children of the village in the eye, the villagers tore the soldiers to pieces.[25] The monsieur de Gramont, governor of Bar-sur-Seine, accompanied by a strong escort, attempted to enter the village of Vauldes. Twenty arquebusers from Ricey bolstered the resistance of the inhabitants to this intrusion, one of these marksmen shooting Gramont in the head and causing the invaders to take flight.[26]

At Easter the townspeople of Noyers revolted against the League and were able to beat off an attempt by the League army to retake the town.[27]

In the region of Montsangeon, the whole countryside was in arms. Saulx-Tavannes invaded the region, his troops burning and pillaging the villages and raping the women. Treostondam carried on what Saulx-Tavannes had begun. When villagers in many places barricaded their communities, they were accused of wanting to exterminate the nobility. A bourgeois witness, however, claimed they were only trying to defend themselves. In October, the League chieftain, the duke of Nevers, reported that the peasants of Châlonnais were barricading their villagers even against those who desired to protect them.[28]

Further north, Beauvais was increasingly restless under the League. This discontent was especially directed against the Spanish garrison. In February 1594, the populace rioted against their presence.[29] By the summer, virtually the whole population yearned for a capitulation to Henri of Navarre. On 14 August, this found expression in yet another riot against the garrison.[30] That very month, the townsfolk of Laon expelled their League garrison. According to Mayenne, "they even rushed to do violence to their men-at-arms in order to advance the capitulation ..."[31]

The conversion of Henri of Navarre was the turning point at Amiens. As one bourgeois noted: "Shortly thereafter, the people, seeing that the princes did nothing to ease the burdens of the afflicted people, and seeing that in the end the princes had conducted their business at their expense, abandoned them to their confusions and resolved to recognize and render obedience to the King."[32] A revolt initiated by the wool combers and brushers led to the liberation of the city.[33] The minutes of the town council note that, the king having become Catholic, "the reason for carrying on the war ceased to exist. That is why the people today revolted and took up arms – in order to recognize the king."[34]

By 1594, ACCORDING to Drouot, Burgundy lay exhausted by the civil wars.[35] The peasantry were unmercifully pillaged and oppressed, while the towns were bled white by renewed fiscal pressure from above and the outcries of the poor from below. The popular movement that took shape in Burgundy, like that in Champagne, assumed the character of local attacks and uprisings. The steady pressure the commoners of Burgundy exerted was perhaps as effective as or even more effective than the large and diffuse uprisings of the Midi in bringing peace.

Drouot admits that the abjuration of Henri of Navarre played an important role, as did the intrigues of his supporters. But Drouot underlines the decisive part of the popular revolt in the overthrow of League power in Burgundy. He points out that without this force, the conspiracy of the *politiques* would have been to no avail.[36]

In March 1594, the first signs appeared of the collapse of the authority of the League oligarchies in the towns of Burgundy. The vinedressers, long the allies of the Catholic magistrates, began to reject their tutelage. Forbidden to leave Dijon for fear, it was said, of the royalists, the vinedressers assembled in protest. Men, women, and children numbering three hundred rallied and attacked the watch at the porte d'Ouche. Artisans at Dijon and Châlons threatened the magistrates with death. The clergy, especially the Jesuits, became objects of popular execration. At Beaune two hundred Beaunois wearing white scarfs attempted a *coup de main*. In April and June, an uprising was planned for Autun. By summer, Mâcon, Auxerre, and Avallon had opened their gates to the king.

The revolt at Beaune is exemplary. Hostility to the League had been in evidence since March 1594, but it was not until February of the following year that the townsfolk were able to concert a popular rebellion. The city was held for Mayenne by a strong garrison under the seigneur de Montmoyen Edmond Regnier. The approach of the royal army led by the mareschal de Biron provided the occasion for the uprising. It was precipitated by Regnier's attempt to imprison the leaders of the plot and to disarm the population.

The bell of the town clock gave the signal, and the mayor appeared in the street wearing a white scarf and crying "vive le roy!" Women and children poured from their houses, likewise crying "vive le roy!" and using whatever they had in hand as weapons. After a pitched battle, the townsfolk were able to clear the soldiers from most of the city. The entry of Biron facilitated the capitulation of the chateau. Notably, those of the garrison who fled into the countryside were killed by peasants who came running toward the city in arms at word of the insurgency.[37]

The revolts at Beaune and Dijon in mid May 1595 took place in the name of the king, but this was because appeal to the king justified revolt against the oppression of the League and its soldiers. A useful counter-example is the town of Villefranche, at one time a staunch Leaguer city. Having capitulated, the townspeople were dismayed to learn that the king intended to introduce his own garrison into the city. Villefranche once again immediately exploded into a popular rebellion.[38] Although it failed, this rebellion does demonstrate the independence of the political aspirations of the urban population from the rule of the king as well as of the League.

Signs of peasant unrest appeared as early as 1592 in Burgundy. The next year, the peasants of Pommard, Volnay, Meursault, Auxey, Santenay, Saint Aulbin, Gamay, and other communities mobilized to the sound of the tocsin on sight of a man-of-arms. Thirty of the men-of-arms of Mayenne were slain by the peasantry of these communes when they tried to collect taxes. In February and March 1594, the rural mobilization of peasants spread to the Beaunois and Châlonnais, where the vinedressers dug fortifications and equipped themselves with cuirasses. Auxey turned its church into a fortress. The valley of the Saône likewise witnessed popular upheaval. The communities of the Mâconnais mobilized themselves. To block the route of Mayenne near Tournus, Ornano reinforced his troops with some twelve or fifteen hundred villagers, who called themselves the "Bonnets-Rouges." In May an uprising occurred at Bar, which involved the surrounding peasantry.

These uprisings were localized and spontaneous movements of villages grouping themselves into associations of mutual aid. Here and there, a noble may have undertaken to lead these rustic companies, but for the most part their leaders were chosen from the ranks of the peasants themselves. The leaders came from the category of rich peasants, which in some measure guaranteed that the aims of such groups remained limited and moderate.

There were, to be sure, challenges to the rights of property. In June 1594, peasants were accused of grazing their cattle on the seigneurie of Saint-Clément. Attempts to expel them were met with violence. The owners of the seigneurie, the canons of St Vincent, were forced to hire soldiers to drive the peasants off.[39] Events such as these, however, were the exception. The object of the peasants was to put an end to the looting and violence of the military, that is, to attack those who opposed peace. More often than not this led to support for the forces of Henri of Navarre, who was the beneficiary of the universal desire for peace among the rural and urban population.

But popular support for the king was limited and contingent. A year after the capitulation of Dijon to Henri, for instance, the oppressiveness of the royal garrison made it as unpopular as the soldiers of the League had been.[40] In July 1596, the populace was so fired up against the garrison that the latter was forced to seek refuge in the chateau.[41]

TO THE SOUTH, LYONS suffered under the governorship of the duke of Nemours. The city was in the grip of economic crisis: taxes that were higher than those under Henri III, a scarcity of provisions, and a corresponding inflation of prices. Nemours was determined to maintain himself at whatever cost. Accordingly, on 19 September 1593, the city rebelled and Nemours was made a prisoner.[42] But the overthrow of Nemours did not by itself bring the city to the side of Henri of Navarre. In February 1594, a group of politique notables staged a *coup de main* that found popular support and brought the city over to the side of Henri IV.[43]

On the occasion of Lyon's capitulation, Antoine Du Verdier explained disaffection from the League as a result of the people "having been ever since dominated and oppressed more and more by thirty little princes who were as many tyrants in as many provinces or towns: indeed there was not a hamlet which under their authority did not have yet other petty tyrants, and the people were sore oppressed by exactions and insupportable taxes."[44]

In Dauphiné, the middle years of the 1590s were to see a recrudescence of the hostility of the nobility and the third estate over the taille. Indeed, the language used on both sides of the argument was more bitter and sharp than it had been in the 1570s. Dauphiné remained quiet for the most part, but here and there were signs of popular rancour.[45] This debate, which is important in itself, has to be seen in the context of the popular unrest that was sweeping over large parts of France at the time.

At Digne in Provence, the whole town revolted against the League governor after he made fresh demands for taxes.[46] At Sellon the next year, a popular uprising forced the evacuation of the forces of the count de Carces, ensuring the return of the police of the town to the consuls.[47] At Aigues-Mortes, when the governor Bertichières refused obedience to Henri IV, the latter had no other choice but to prompt the consuls into organizing a popular uprising against Bertichières. But having done so, the consuls then demanded the restoration of municipal liberties, including the abolition of the office of governor itself.[48] The year 1595 also saw in Provence the pillaging of the chateau of Tourrette by the inhabitants of Fayenne. Likewise, the chateau of Saint-Martin-de-Castillon was demolished in January 1596 in the course of a popular uprising.[49]

In Languedoc, popular reaction to the aristocratic League's control of municipal life is likewise evident. When Henri de Joyeuse, count of Bouchage, tried to garrison Avignonet in the Lauraguais, the consuls refused to admit his men-in-arms, "seeing that this is a preliminary to wishing to capture and to tender the inhabitants subject and slave."[50]

In tandem with this movement in the towns, the 1590s witnessed an increasingly organized resistance from the bourgs and villages in the Languedoc. In the Haut-Biterrois, a league of twenty-four bourgs and villages made up of both Catholics and Protestants took form. It protested against taxes while establishing a system of self-defence centred on Caux, providing itself with the necessary finances by a process of self-taxation. The twenty or more villagers or bourgades who united themselves in this fashion refused to pay the taille. The consuls – unlettered peasants such as Joseph Mas of Faugières, or Serguières and Cassan, syndics of Roujan – were at the heart of the resistance. Tirelessly they levied the dues necessary to the league, travelled to the general assembly, and pleaded their case before the magistrates of the region. Unlike the leagues that emerged elsewhere, it appears that no rural bourgeois or notable undertook or was allowed to lead them. Nonetheless the peasants were able to draw up a charter of liberties, which they presented to the gentlemen of the region.[51]

In the meantime, the rural leagues of Comminges became active once again. The roots of these associations may be traced back to mid-century. Their formation at that time was in reaction to the increasing burden of taxation. The peasantry was particularly agitated by the unequal character of these taxes, which were imposed by the bourgeoisie and nobles in the estates of Comminges. In an effort to placate the rural population in 1560, the grievances of the third estate of Comminges gave voice to the complaints of the peasantry over taxes but also against the oppression they suffered at the hands of the nobility.

In 1568, official status was conferred on the syndic of the villages of Comminges. The *sénéchal* of Toulouse called upon him to convoke representatives from the villages to discuss a call-up of men to fight the religious war in Languedoc.[52] In 1582, the estates of Comminges reported armed risings of the villages against tax gatherers and clashes between the peasantry and the soldiery.[53] Some villages, it was said, were ready to become Protestant if doing so would free them from taxes.[54] In 1586, indeed, some of these villages collaborated with the Protestants in an attack on Saint Bertrand de Comminges.[55]

At the beginning of the 1590s, the organization of the peasant leagues of Comminges for purposes of defence increased. The leaders of the peasants made every effort to represent the leagues as associations of self-defence. In appealing in 1591 for recognition to the parlement and to Villars, the king's lieutenant in Guyenne, they reiterated the orthodoxy and obedience of those who adhered to their league.[56] They sought to restore the existing order, which was being threatened by those who, under the guise of war, were killing, raping, pillaging, and committing sacrileges at the expense of the people.

The articles of the syndicate of the villages of Frontignes, Sauveterre, and Pointis help us to understand the organization and objectives of the leagues more clearly. In the first place, these articles specified that an inventory be drawn up of the soldiers and weapons in each village. The village consuls were to establish a magazine of powder and lead based on the number of soldiers and arquebuses. These were to be distributed to the soldiers when they were called out. In addition, each arquebusier was to equip himself with a store of cord, bullets, and powder, according to his means. The soldiers of each village were to be led by a military chief, who was to command them when they were called to assist a neighbouring community. The expenses of each troop were to be met by the village from which they came. Each community was to appoint a bursar to keep account of these expenditures.

The militia of the associated villages were to take no property, not even provisions, against the will of any of the inhabitants of these communities. Those accused of doing so were to be arrested by the local consuls and handed over to justice for punishment. The expenses of trial were to be paid by the communities involved.

Catholic soldiers passing through the region were to be provided with food and lodging, but if they began to pillage and rampage the village, militias were to be marshalled against them and they were to be handed over to justice. All other soldiers and marauders were to be dealt with summarily.[57]

The articles of this syndicate reflect quite a sophisticated level of organization among the peasants of Comminges. Indeed, it would seem that decades of war carried on by the nobility had led to the gradual militarization of the society as a whole, including the peasants themselves. It is evident that large numbers of peasants had possession of firearms and knew how to use them. Furthermore, it is plain that the leaders of this rural population had some sense of military organization. This should come as no surprise since, if modern history has taught us anything, it is that peasants can be effectively organized and that the chief means of doing so is precisely protracted war.

The leaders of the peasantry of Comminges had made it a point to represent the purposes of their association as conservative. But that is not how they were seen by the nobility and third estate of Comminges. In the middle of January 1592, the estates of Comminges hastily assembled to deliberate on the articles of the peasants. Notice had to be taken "as a result of certain leagues and articles newly drawn up by certain unavowed individuals in large numbers who are demanding nothing but the ruin of the country and the overthrow of the state of the Church, nobility and third-estate."[58]

Having heard the peasant articles, the third estate of the towns withdrew and after long deliberation decided to denounce the rebellious peasants. Some of the nobles called for immediate and harsh repression "of articles and associations without leaders to the prejudice of the public." Others, more moderate, sought first for conciliation and, that failing, for coercion. It was finally decided that a noble and bourgeois from each of the regions affected would jointly confer with the leaders of the leagues and order them to desist and disband.[59]

No sooner were these resolutions taken than a delegation of eight popular representatives came before the assembled estates. Two of these, Vidal Cestec and Bertrand Seintgès, were described as general syndics of the confederation of the countryside. They declared their aim to be to put an end to the ravages from which they suffered, stating that they had been authorized to do so by the parlement and the lieutenant-general of Guyenne. They affected not to know the identity of the author of the articles that had so disturbed the members of the estates. Spokesmen of the estates urged them to disband their association, seeing that they would be assisted "in all things." In turn, the representatives of the peasants declared themselves ready to leave their league in order not to cut themselves off from the "body" of Comminges. They promised to determine who was prepared to leave the league and who was not. Finally, they agreed to submit their *cahier des doléances* to the next meeting of the estates in order that their complaints be set right.[60]

What were the contents of the articles that so alarmed the estates? We know what they were from the fact that they were subsequently condemned by the Parlement of Toulouse "as tending to license the people to every disorder and to subtract it completely from obedience to the magistrates and superiors ..."[61] According to the parlement, certain disorders had led the population to league themselves together, to assemble in arms under elected syndics, to oppose the passage of men-in-arms, to refuse the orders of the lieutenant-general, to organize an administration of the countryside, to oppose those who did not obey it, to control all coming and going through their districts, and to attack all those not authorized to do so.[62] Although tendentious, this list of articles represents a fair summary of the military articles for Frontignes, Sauveterre, and Pointis.

What was alarming about these ordonnances was not that they directly offended or menaced the nobility and the towns, but rather that, put into effect, they would give the peasantry a degree of organization that would be much more threatening than occasional verbal or even physical attacks on the nobility or the bourgeoisie.

One fraction of the peasants of Comminges was again prepared to make common cause with the Huguenots. This fraction continued to refuse to pay the taille. In November 1593, three or four hundred, calling themselves *Croquants et de la Conférence* (*campanère*), took part in the pillaging of churches and the seizure of ecclesiastical property.

Another current under Jean Désirat, a rural merchant, appears temporarily to have adopted a more conciliatory approach, cooperating with the estates and the League. Désirat urged those peasants who looked to him for leadership to respect the Church and the seigneurs and to pay their taxes. He even undertook to send troops of infantry to the aid of the marquis of Villars, the head of the forces of the League in Bigorre.

In the event, a still unified rural league of Comminges was in existence in 1594. In March, Désirat demanded the lowering of the taille, the conclusion of a truce with the Huguenots, and, in default of that, the confiscation of the property of the Church in order to pay the troops. At that moment, Désirat appeared before the estates of Comminges under a safe conduct. From the account of his appearance, it is evident that the villages of the region were still in arms. Once more, their insurgency was based on resistance to the pillaging and violence visited upon them. But added to this was a fiscal grievance against the towns. The countryside, according to Désirat, was forced to pay for the garrisons maintained in the towns. Désirat complained that the taxes for their maintenance ought to be paid for by the towns as well as by the countryside. Désirat also implied that the garrisons bore part of the responsibility for the destruction visited on the countryfolk. Indeed, it emerges that some of the armed peasantry had even undertaken to attack the towns.[63] Once again we see confirmed that in the sixteenth century the commons and especially the peasants and rural bourgeois saw their enemy to be the urban oligarchies, as well as the nobility.

To the east and north of Comminges at the other extremity of Languedoc, popular unrest mounted in the Velay in 1594. The people of Le Puy were increasingly restive under the domination of the League oligarchy. On 15 June, one hundred and fifty women took the *juge mage* of Le Puy hostage in his own court. They refused to pay the taxes they had been assessed, claiming that they did not have the means to pay them if they were also to feed their children.[64] The same day a riot of the "menu populaire" broke out against the stocking-makers. The latter had obtained a decree prohibiting the populace from making gloves and stockings. Hundreds of such items were confiscated. Burel, the chronicler of Le Puy, commented that "there was much tears and lamentation among these poor people!"[65]

The end of October saw yet another popular tumult. On the twenty-seventh, Jean Mauzac, servant of the merchant Louis Mialhet, was to be hanged. At the foot of the scaffold, he lamented that it was his master who had set him to stealing. "They are sparing my master and mistakenly putting me to death." The populace attacked the provost at the place of execution and forced him to take to his heels. They then assembled at the residence of the governor and at the common court of Le Puy, where they threatened, "If you think you can trick us by executing the small time thieves while sparing the big timers, we will cut the throats of all those who tolerate them!"[66] The chronicler of Le Puy sided totally with the commoners.

God has illumined for us the treason that many of the rich have committed while always protecting themselves against poor people, saying in their manner of speaking: "these commons will betray us and only seek an opportunity to pillage." What a smoke screen these rich use in protecting themselves against the poor inhabitants! But they needed the poor when the city required defending and without them would have been lost. As you see in this instance with respect to the big time thieves and the rich they have always sought to destroy the enemy within in order to pillage and sack us and cut our throats and the throats of our children. And still they do not want to see justice done! But God will punish them.[67]

The radicalism of Burel was that of the popular League. The League held aloof from the peasant insurgents who appeared in the Velay in 1595. Burel calls them "Croquants" or "Tard-Avisés" after the peasants who had risen in Guyenne. Although it is likely that they also saw themselves in this light, there do not appear to have been actual links between the movement in

Guyenne and that in the Velay. It would seem then that the movement in the Velay had its own momentum. Like the peasants in Guyenne, the Croquants of Velay kept their distance from both the Protestant and the Catholic camps. Indeed, it is noteworthy that Burel speaks of their movement as literally "another religion,"[68] implying that they consciously held themselves apart from the established churches.

The "Croquants" of Velay were at first encouraged by the governor M. de Chevrières and the royalist nobility. The Croquants sought to rally the countryside by attempting to supress the payment of the taille to the League. In May, twelve hundred peasants from the east of the Velay – the classic region of revolt – were mobilized under the command of Hector de Fay, seigneur de Verchières, and Jean de Chaste, seigneur de Saint-Just. While they attacked the chateaux and towns held by the League, they could not be prevented from also pillaging the chateaux of royalists. By the autumn of 1595, the governor M. de Chevrières had turned his own forces against them.[69] Le Roy Ladurie notes, in fact, that insurrectionary movements were general along the southern tier of the Massif Central at this point. In the Vivarais, Haute-Uzège and Gévaudan, the peasantry refused to pay the taille in 1593–5. The receivers sent cavalry against the delinquents, attempting to constrain them by laying waste to their property, quartering troops upon them, and seizing their cattle as movable goods.[70]

In the Vivarais, an anti-fiscal current made itself evident as early as 1592. Once again dissidence was focused on the small town. An assembly held at St Michel de Chabrillanoux in the summer of that year determined to oppose the levy of taxes by force of arms. In April 1594, a popular league reportedly occupied St Alban. Fay and Chaneac emerged as focal points of popular unrest. By the next year, the Boutières as a whole was greatly agitated. Tax officers were expelled from St Fortunat. At Montagne the receivers of the taille were murdered. The bailli of La Voulte declared that the consuls of Privas "have been cracked [*croquants*] and they are still cracked." The inhabitants of St Fortunat and Petit-Paris continued their refusal of the taille as late as 1596. In 1599, Arsac, Prat, and Chanteldouble were still on strike against the taille. The inhabitants of two villages close to Pradelles asserted that they would rather abandon their homes than pay.[71]

THE LAST AND GREATEST of the peasant upheavals of the 1590s, indeed, of the sixteenth century, was that of the *Tard-Avisés*, as they called themselves, or the Croquants as they were called by their enemies. The revolt engulfed Limousin, Périgord, Poitou, Saintonge, Angoumois, Marche, Agenais, and Quercy. In short, the whole of Guyenne rose as in the revolt of 1548 forty years earlier. Was the second revolt then largely an anti-fiscal rebellion as was the first? There can be no question that the rebellion involved a significant element of tax revolt. The insurgents denounced the officers of the king for imposing excessive tailles and subsidies to the ruin of poor labourers. But to conclude that this upheaval was essentially an anti-fiscal movement, as it was in 1548, is a great error. As we have seen, the revolt of 1548 itself had at least an undertone of anti-noble hostility. By the time the Croquants revolted in 1594–5 peasant hostility toward the nobility had become the dominant note.

The notion of this rebellion as on anti-fiscal rising has been imposed on the events of this upheaval by Y.M. Bercé, a student of Roland Mousnier. Bercé's view has been at least partially accepted by Le Roy Ladurie, who speaks of Bercé's "belles recherches."[72] The latter's treatment of the Croquants is to be found in his monumental study of the revolts of the seventeenth century in the southwest of France.[73] Bercé's view of the revolt of the Croquants is extended to all of the popular revolts of the last decade of the sixteenth century. In a style that could only meet with the approval of his mentor Roland Mousnier Bercé concludes that the peasants "did not put into question the vertical solidarity of society, fidelity to the local seigneur who one often sees take command of his tenants in order to give chase to enemy cattle thieves. The different sides knew how to utilise the peasant assemblies and to make them march according to local conditions, here for the League and there for the King of Navarre."[74] Bercé is certainly right that both sides sought to make use of the peasantry. But can we really agree after our own investigations that the peasantry of Brittany, Velay, and Comminges remained under the control of their seigneurs?

Bercé's need to downplay the anti-noble character of the revolt of the Croquants requires him to do extraordinary violence to the sources. Thus, he says that "the anti-noble theme and the myths of subversion are scarcely present in Palma Cayet, the best informed chronicler."[75] One may well ask what Palma Cayet actually says in his authoritative account of the uprising. He does note that the pretext of the revolt was the weight of heavy taxation, but he adds that it was likewise due to the pillaging of the nobles, especially those of the League.[76] Palma Cayet records that the people called the nobles "Croquans," saying that they sought only to "croquer" the people. The nobility turned this sobriquet around, labelling the rebels "Croquants."[77]

Palma Cayet observes that the representatives of the "Croquants" who presented the grievances of the insurgents before Henri of Navarre stressed popular discontent with the nobles, especially those of the League. They claimed that because their revenues were unequal to their expenditure, the nobles committed all sorts of crimes, imprisoning and torturing prisoners in their chateaux in order to extort the maximum in ransoms.[78]

While negotiations with the monarchy were underway, Palma Cayet reports that, "as a result of the injuries received the one by the other, the people and the nobility not being able to remain at peace, the people assembled once again ..."[79] In the light of Palma Cayet's account, one can only rub one's eyes in disbelief at Bercé's assertion that the anti-noble theme is scarcely present in this chronicle. In fact, in Palma Cayet's narrative, the leitmotiv is not merely anti-noble feeling but class hatred between noble and non-noble.

Bercé's obsession with the integrity of the vertical structure of French society leads him to a gross distortion of the evidence. He asserts that "the Croquants themselves believed that the seigneurs had the power to make their tenants adhere to the [peasant] assemblies."[80] As proof, Bercé notes that at the assembly of Abzac, Porquery received the mission "to go to the sieur de St Alvère to tell him on the part of the company that he ought to enjoin his subjects to join their assembly."[81] Bercé makes it appear that the peasants were making a polite request of a seigneur who was in control of his tenants. This interpretation is dubious at best. What were the true circumstances of Porquery's commission? St Alvère, along with eight other nobles, had attempted to spy on this assembly of seven or eight thousand insurgents. When they were discovered, the peasants attacked them to the cry: "Let's have at the crackers!" Using their arquebuses, the peasants opened up a massive fusillade against the fleeing nobles. Porquery was sent to St Alvère not to request that his peasants join the popular assembly but to announce that such would be the case. When St Alvère answered that he would forbid his tenants to join the assembly, Porquery warned him that the insurgent peasants would attack *en masse*.[82] The circumstances then of this request were that of an ultimatum in the midst of a spreading insurrection. To use these circumstances as the basis of the claim that the peasant assemblies had to ask the permission of the seigneurs to allow their tenants to join the assemblies is to twist the facts beyond recognizable form.

Bercé's perverse reading of the sources extends to the chronicle of the canon of Sarlat Jean Tarde. According to Tarde, cited by Bercé, "the army of the Croquants was not entirely made up of peasants and artisans. For a third were children of good houses or old soldiers who had carried arms during the previous wars. This consideration made the nobility advance, keeping the bridle of their horses in their hands."[83] Bercé's next sentence – "that in effect there were gentlemen who associated themselves to the assemblies" – might lead one to believe that the children of good homes and old soldiers were noblemen. In fact, Tarde's reference is an extremely important confirmation that the revolt of the Croquants involved not only peasants and artisans but also members of the small-town bourgeoisie, as well as rural notables.

Tarde, in fact, begins his account of the revolt by stating flatly, "This year the peasants of Perigord revolted against the nobility."[84] He reports an assembly of twenty thousand men on the plain of La Boule on the last day of May 1594, in which the crowd raised their hats at the end of their weapons to the cry of "Liberty! Liberty! Long Live the Third Estate!"[85] The Croquants of Guyenne no doubt had fiscal grievances, but to limit the reasons for the revolt to these represents a gross twisting of the evidence.

Loutchitzky long ago reprinted the conclusions drawn up in 1594 by the Parlement of Toulouse of the reasons for the uprising.[86] Heavy taxation certainly played a part, and pillaging, ransoms, and the quartering of soldiers by the military are also noted. But it is above all the oppression of the nobles in the form of unlawful demands for the payments of higher rents and seigneurial dues and the arbitrary imposition of new charges that is stressed. Refusal of payment, according to the parlement, had led the seigneurs to invite men-of-war onto the lands of tenants and illegally to seize their lands or persons. Finally, the nobles had refused to pay the taille and other taxes due on commoner lands that they had acquired.

It therefore seems evident that whatever other elements were involved, the "Croquant" upheaval was at bottom a challenge to the nobility on the part of the peasantry and the small-town bourgeoisie. On no account can it be assimilated to Mousnier's model of an anti-fiscal revolt that did not rupture the vertical order of French society. Indeed, the anti-noble tone of these revolts as compared with that of the gabelle revolt is an important measure of the degree to which vertical ties between lord and peasant had weakened over half a century.

It is perhaps not a surprise that the most judicious accounts of this upheaval come from the pens of Anglo-American historians rather than from those of the French. It is in J.H. Salmon's *Society in Crisis: France in the Sixteenth Century* that the best summary account of the Croquant Revolt may be found.[87] The seventh chapter of Richart Tait's Oxford doctoral dissertation on Matignon, the king's lieutenant in Guyenne, is an important supplement to the analysis of Salmon.[88] Both historians understand that the movement was based on class hostility rooted in the behaviour of the nobility during thirty years and more of civil war. Tait also underlines the hostility between the *plat pays* and the larger towns. The Croquants asked for the help of Agen and Périgueux, particularly demanding cannon to attack the chateaux and forts of the nobles. These demands were refused. Indeed, as early as April 1594, the rebels of the *plat pays* denounced the exploitation of the country-side by the larger towns of Guyenne.[89]

The hostility between *plat pays* and the big towns underlay the demand of the peasants of Périgord for a syndic of the *plat pays*. Such a demand, which was refused by the king, struck directly at the privileges of the leading towns – Périgueux, Sarlat, Bergerac. It echoes the conflicts that had taken place in the Agenais, Velay, and lower Auvergne prior to the civil wars. Such a demand was presented to the estates of Périgord by such smaller towns as Domme, Belves, Beaumont, and Issigeac as early as 1583. It was from the lower and less successful end of the lawyer, professional, and officer stratum, especially from the small towns, that the leadership of the Croquants was drawn.[90]

As to organization, Salmon quotes Tarde, who provides the best account of how the rebels marshalled their forces.

In their first assemblies they swore loyalty to each other and arranged to have the greatest number of parishes join them. To do this they wrote letters setting forth their grievances and sent them from village to village and from town to town. After declaring itself, each parish made up a company, elected its captain, lieutenant, and other officers, and provided itself with a flag and a drum. They marched to their assemblies in battle order, with drum beating and flag unfurled.[91]

Salmon remarks on their impressive equipment. Many armed themselves with pikes and arquebuses. At their height, the number of insurgents was estimated by the *sénéchal* of Périgord at one hundred thousand men.[92] There seems little doubt that, as the *sénéchal* put it, "part of [this force] speaks openly of ruining and exterminating the nobility."[93] Not only did they talk of attacking the nobles, they actually attacked their persons and chateaux.

Salmon, however, points out that the demands of the Croquants as formulated in February 1595 reflected a limited if nevertheless sophisticated program. The Croquants of Périgord asked for:

1 the proper administration of their benefices by the clergy;
2 an end to unjust oppression by the nobility;
3 the appointment of a syndic to preserve peasant rights and liberties;
4 the return of the level of the taille to its status before the wars;
5 a requirement that the nobility who had bought *roturier* land should pay taxes associated with it;
6 the substitution of the local *juge-mage* for the *élu* as a tax assessor;
7 a ban on the holding of noble titles by those who were not of the ancient *noblesse de race*;
8 judicial reform to prevent the nobility from using illegal influence upon higher tribunals;
9 the abolition of all new taxes.

The rebels, of course, acknowledged the authority of the monarchy and laid aside religious differences in the interests of class solidarity. According to Salmon, "the demands are in no sense those of a social revolutionary, but they indicate clearly enough that the peasantry were engaged in a conscious struggle with the *noblesse*, and that, while they did not intend to recast the structure of society, they wanted to modify its balance."[94] Salmon's remarks could apply to the struggles of the commons everywhere else in the kingdom. Here and there were individuals or groups who in their desperation dreamed of a revolutionary transformation of the social order. But the aim of most of the insurgents in the north as well as in the Midi were more limited and in proportion to their capabilities. Above all, they sought an end to the war, which they saw as benefiting the nobility and the privileged at the expense of the commons.

Despite the moderation of the demands voiced by the Croquants, the sense of peril felt by the social establishment was all too real. The very ubiquity and depth of rebellion by the mid 1590s could only alarm those who took a broad view of the affairs of France. The relief felt by these elites at the suppression of these tumults is manifest in the words of congratulation of September 1595 addressed to Henri IV by Jean Nicolay, the first president of the *Chambre des Comptes*. "Sire, it is no trifle for a great prince such as you to have in the face of the revolt of an infinite number of cities and the virtually universal uprising of your subjects to have in so short a space of time ... regained the heart of so many people ..."[95]

Looking back on the history of the religious wars, we can conclude that from start to finish the wars represented a kind of class war from above. On the other hand, the wars were marked by three great popular upsurges – the Calvinist revolts of the 1560s, the League rebellion, and the popular movements of the 1590s. Each of the movements in turn galvanized a greater proportion of the population. Moreover, each in turn appears to have put into question an essential element of the established order. The Calvinist Revolt attacked the Church, the League attacked the state, and the movement of the 1590s attacked the nobility itself. At the end of this process, the dominating institutions of French society were badly shaken. It would take all the skill of Henri of Navarre to restore the myth of monarchy. It would also take not only the adherence of the elites but also the acquiescence of the commons.

CHAPTER SEVEN

A Society of Orders in Crisis

Such was the impact of popular rebellion in the 1590s that for the first time it became a significant theme in print. It is taken up for example in Pierre Constant's *La cause des guerres civiles en France*.[1] Constant chastized all the estates for midsdeeds that had contributed to the war. Having reproached the clergy, nobles, and merchants, he turned his fire on the artisans and "mechanics." According to Constant, their pride, gluttony, drunkenness, defiance of the sumptuary laws, impatience in adversity, and felony against the king had helped to unleash the tempest of the wars. The felony of the plebians against the monarchy, according to Constant, lay in the fact that, under the pretext of religion, the majority of craftsmen had improperly and thoughtlessly sought to reduce the monarchy to a popular state.[2] If we are to believe Constant, the object of the popular stratum on both the Protestant and Catholic sides was to overthrow the monarchy in favour of a popular government, using religion as a pretext.

François l'Alouëte's *Des affaires d'estat, des finances, du prince et de sa noblesse*, published at Metz two years later, reflected a still deeper level of anxiety. Harking back to an old refrain, L'Alouëte complained that places of honour in the state and in the court had been usurped by avaricious peasants and commoners. The old families had no place, no longer enjoying the honour of paying court to the king.[3] Such a lament, it appears, returns us to the grievances of the nobility at the beginning of the civil wars.

The old nobility, L'Alouëte continued, no longer had the favour or authority over the people that they once had. This devaluation of influence had occurred because "every little mechanic" was passing himself off as a noble. Everyone carried the titles and arms of nobility, or rather all the glory and dignity of the nobility was being annihilated.[4] L'Alouëte's complaint, to be sure, was a commonplace, but one that arose from the reality of the power of the bourgeoisie, which continued to grow unabated during the civil wars. At the highest levels, this reflected itself in the entry of bourgeois notables into the ranks of the nobility. The arrival of these parvenus stimulated the celebrated debate over nobility of race as against nobility of virtue, which marked the civil-war period and its aftermath. Arlette Joanna lists some seventy-seven authors who dealt with the question between 1550 and 1615.[5] Much resented by the old noble families, the entry of the upper stratum of the bourgeoisie into the nobility may have been an essential safety valve, which made it possible to keep class conflict from turning into revolution.

The discomfiture of the nobles was not due simply to the entry of parvenus into their ranks. The nobles had been instrumental in initiating and continuing the civil wars. These wars were a form of class war through which the nobility was able to maintain its political and social ascendancy. But its ultimate position eroded still further as a result of the wars. True, the nobility was able to bolster itself by military commands, pillaging, and kidnapping for ransom. It was also able to recover certain seigneurial rights and to gain control of a certain amount of the land of the Church, as well as that of the impoverished peasantry. But it was the middle class – ranging from officers to merchants, well-to-do artisans, and rich peasants – that was the principal beneficiary of the civil wars.

It is undeniable that the wars seriously damaged commerce, industry, and agriculture and that the possibility of making profits from productive investment tended to diminish – even the appreciation of rent tended to stagnate. However, despite such adverse conditions, enterprising members of the middle class made money by speculating in commodities and by lending money to impecunious peasants and debt-ridden governments. It was the middle class that seized the lion's share of land taken from the Church or from the impoverished peasants. Indeed, the war accelerated the displacement of many of the rural small producers to the benefit of the middle class. Paradoxically, the wars were at one and the same time a seigneurial reaction and an important phase of bourgeois "primitive accumulation."

The walled towns, with their civic militias, hired mercenaries, and garrisons, were less directly affected by the destruction of war than was the rural population. Indeed, a large if undetermined fraction of the urban population rode or marched in the armies of the Huguenot or Catholic party. Others took part in the defence of their towns and cities in one capacity or another. The bourgeoisie became militarized in the course of the civil wars in the way that their forefathers had been during the Hundred Years War. Bourgeois cavalry companies led by middle-class captains even came to compete with the mounted troops of the nobility.

It is no wonder that L'Alouëte bemoaned the disdain with which the nobility was increasingly regarded. L'Alouëte took note of the increasing hostility of the peasants toward their masters. Tenants, he noted, were directly challenging seigneurial rights and jurisdiction. Indeed, according to L'Alouëte, everyone was ready to arm themselves in order to attack the nobility. L'Alouëte recalled that the peasants had almost succeeded in their attack on the nobility during the Jacquerie in France, during the Peasants Revolt in England and during the Hungarian Revolt of 1514, as well as on other occasions. "And does not one see," he concluded, "that they are seeking extermination [of the nobles] everyday by means of pillages, cruelties, tyrannical acts and murder ...?"[6]

Sensitivity to current events is also evident in Regnault d'Orleans' *Les Observations de diverses choses remarqués sur l'éstat, couronne et peuple de France*, published the same year.[7] D'Orleans opened his work by recalling a passage from Jean Bouchet's *Les Triomphes*.

Democracy is government by the whole people,
And these two things are, to be sure,
Subject to the great danger of rash alliance.
For in its weal the populace is inconstant.
Suddenly it attacks a seigneurie
And is obstinate in mutiny
And is desirious of foolish change,
Despising the great and their principalities.[8]

Popular sedition d'Orleans took to be a great evil, attempting to demonstrate the truth of this by recounting the history of popular revolts in France from the age of Charles VI to the time of the League. As a *conseiller* in the *siège présidial* of Vannes, d'Orleans must have been especially sensitive to the popular and republican seditions that had manifested themselves in the League in Brittany.

A sense of unease is apparent also in the treatise of David de Flurance Rivault on the estates of the kingdom, which appeared in 1596.[9] Writing from the perspective of a *bourgeois gentilshomme*, Flurance allowed that the nobility was superior to the third estate in both its lineage and its virtue. On the other hand, he asserted that members of the judiciary, as well as merchants who fought in the wars, could look forward to ennoblement.[10] In order to renew itself, the nobility must recruit its new members from the third estate. According to Flurance, "in the process of renewal the third estate is like a seedbed of wild plants by means of which the field of nobility is repopulated and in which they are in time domesticated, bearing fruits which gradually lose their commoner-like bitterness."[11]

Flurance thus placed himself squarely among those who championed the movement of the successful bourgeoisie into the nobility. But the converse to this position was his belief in the strict regulation of the third estate itself. The duty of the third estate, affirmed Flurance, is that of obedience toward those above them.[12] Disobedience of tenants toward their seigneur, he anounced, rendered their property forfeit, as well as making them subject to even more severe punishment. Such disobedience, he declared, injured not only a particular lord but all seigneurs who as a consequence might be affected. The whole nobility, therefore, continued Flurance, should ensure that such misdeeds are punished. According to Flurance, "God himself works through such punishment."[13] The root of such disobedience, he avowed, ultimately lay in a lack of faith, which itself prepared the way for atheism.[14] The source of this lack of faith was rooted in the fact that not only were the people not well disposed toward the nobility, but that they opposed it at every turn and often rebelled in arms against it. As proof, Flurance reviewed the history of popular rebellion, starting with the Jews, Greeks, and Romans. He noted that France had greatly suffered from this "plague," citing the Jacquerie, the revolt of the *Maillotins*, and the *chapperons blancs* of Ghent. For good measure, he took into account the English Peasants' Revolt, the Zwinglians in Germany, the Hungarian Peasants, as well as the German Peasants War in neighbouring or nearby states.[15]

In the last two hundred years, he concluded, France in particular had had much experience of this disease. He was prepared to concede that popular rebellion did not precipitate the civil wars. On the other hand, popular enmity toward the nobility during the troubles had been stronger than had feelings of religious partisanship. Indeed, the people would not have become so commonly and openly disobedient if not for such feelings of animosity. The wars had exacerbated these sentiments. This fact ought to move the seigneurs, Flurance continued, to be on their guard with respect to the behaviour of their subjects, not only for their own good but for that of the state itself. They ought, Flurance cautioned, to keep an eye on the power and arms that the people have at their disposal for fear that the people will misuse them. As a result some terrible calamity might well occur, the smoke of which is evident already in several provinces of the kingdom. Concluded Flurance: "For there is no Moor so cruel, no Arab so inhumane, no Turk so innimical, no lost soul so desperate as this kind of fury which tyranizes, ransoms and overwhelms those who by fortune fall into its power. In these last years, those who have fallen into the hands of the Croquants, Tard-Avisés, and others who have abused the license to bear arms have had experience of it."[16]

The impact of the uprisings of the 1590s is apparent also in Pierre Charron's *De la Sagesse*, which was composed in the immediate aftermath of the Civil Wars.[17] Charron devoted one chapter to the "people" or the "vulgar" and another to sedition.[18] His treatment of the commoners amounted to a stream of learned invective against their rebelliousness. The people are the vulgar, the crowd, the popular lee, or those of low, servile, and mechanical condition. They are defined by their inconstancy, variability, irrationality, extremism, love of novelty, gullibility, and disloyalty. Furthermore, they are injudicious, envious, and malicious.[19] The people are the enemy of men of substance, contemptuous of virtue, and begrudge the happiness of others. They favour the weak and malevolent, wish ill to men of honour without knowing why, save only that they are men of honour.[20]

If we are to believe Mousnier, those who governed or were privileged during the Ancien Regime did so with the consent of the governed. This hardly agrees with Charron's view of the attitude of the people. They are mutinous at the first pretext toward their betters and prone to sedition, especially when they find a leader. They swell up, rise up, and are not to be tamed. Deprived of their leaders, on the other hand, they are immediately beaten, cowed, and frightened.[21]

If Charron is correct, the people were incapable of giving their political assent to those who governed. According to Charron, they have no regard for the public good or honesty. They are concerned only with their private interest, which they sordidly pursue.[22] They mutter and grumble ceaselessly against the state, being full of slander and insolent opinion against those who govern and command. The humble and poor have no other pleasure than to slander the great and rich, not by virtue of reason but on account of envy. They are never content with their rulers and the existing state.[23]

Charron's extensive treatment of sedition, which he defines as "a violent movement of the multitude against the prince or magistrate," reflects a similar sense of anxiety. He acknowledges that sedition might arise from oppression, but chooses, instead to harp on those who were its leaders out of less worthy motives. Those who have committed great crimes and who fear punishment and others who fear they might be attacked, unite together in order to ward off the expected aggression. Seditions, he admits, were created by necessity and famine. But he dwells upon the likelihood of a conspiracy of evildoers, who attracted a following under the pretext of liberty and the common good.[24]

More interesting is the practical advice Charron proffered to those faced with sedition. First of all, those who have revolted ought to be remonstrated with by appropriate spokesmen. If that does not work, Charron advises, arms and fortifications are to be resorted to, but in such a way as to allow the rebels time to come to their senses. According to Charron, the resolve of the rebels should be shaken by arousing both fear and hope. Try to divide the insurgents and to recruit spies amongst them, he suggests. Win over others, he urges, by granting some of their demands and by making beautiful-sounding promises in ambiguous terms. Punish the ring leaders, he concludes, but be clement with the mass of rebels who surrender.[25] One cannot help concluding that Charron's advice was the fruit of first-hand experience.

Charron's obvious hostility to the multitude sprang no doubt from his own bitter experience with the radicals of the League, but likewise from the popular upheavals of the closing years of the century. But hostile to the people though he is, Charron is almost as implacable to the traditional nobility. He distinguishes between a nobility based on birth and one acquired through virtue. Of the two kinds of nobility, he prefers the second to the first. Nobility by birth Charron considers a kind of empty vainglory. Personal nobility really belongs to the person who has acquired it through virtue and who is actually useful to others.[26]

However much he appears to have questioned the notion of nobility based on birth, Charron's definition of nobility in one way seems conventional. Brushing aside those who would see it as a virtue appertaining to the realm of politics, administration, literature, or learning, Charron seemingly holds to the traditional view that nobility is a kind of military virtue.[27] Likewise, he takes the same line at the beginning of the chapter he devotes to the military profession: "the military occupation and profession is noble in its cause for there is not more just or universal service than the safeguarding of the repose and greatness of one's country."[28]

However, in the very next paragraph he launches a stinging attack on the martial arts – the essential activity of the noble order.

But on the contrary one could say that the art and practice of mutually doing one another in, killing one another, the ruin and loss of one's own species seems contrary to nature and the result of the loss of one's senses ... What folly, what madness it is to cause agitations, create hardship for so many people, run so many risks by sea and by land for something so doubtful as the outcome of war; to hasten so avidly with such asperity toward death which is everywhere to be found, and, without hope of burial, to proceed to kill those whom one does not hate and whom one has never seen. But from whence comes this great madness and passion against those who have not committed any offense against you? What frenzy and mania it is to put one's body, time, repose life and liberty at the disposition of someone else ... And this for a cause which one does not know to be just and ordinarily is unjust. For wars are usually unjust ...[29]

By attacking the notion that military action is a virtue, Charron is putting into question the *raison d'être* of the nobility as an armed caste. At the same time, as we have seen, he casts doubt on the hereditary nature of nobility.

Charron's attack ought to be seen as part of a more general ideological assault on the nobility, which has been brought to light by Ellery Schalk.[30] Schalk explains that the medieval view of nobility as a kind of virtue based on the profession of arms continued to be current in France until the outbreak of the religious wars. During the early phases of the war, the relationship between virtue and nobility became the subject of increasing debate. However, it was only in the 1590s that virtue began to be counterposed as an alternative to birth as the basis of nobility. Bourgeois critics such as Charron were prepared to admit that even the virtuous progeny of a butcher or vinedresser could become noble. In reaction, according to Schalk, defenders of the traditional nobility began to stress pedigree in a self-conscious way as the basis of nobility. Schalk, it should be noted, regards this ideological mutation to be the result of the widespread popular challenge to the nobility as a class that took place in the 1590s.[31]

In Dauphiné, as we have seen, the mid 1590s witnessed only minor disturbances. Nonetheless, the political and social atmosphere was by no means peaceful. The *procès des tailles*, which had played such a critical role in precipitating the revolt of 1579–80, came to the fore once more. The estates again were the arena of violent argument between the representatives of the third estate and the nobility. Indeed, the prolongation of the fiscal dispute over half a century of civil strife led to an extraordinary degree of ideological polarization between the second and third estates.

Whereas in other parts of France the confrontation between nobles and commoners took the form of the clash of arms, in Dauphiné class war remained at the level of a conflict of ideas carried on by means of speeches, pamphlets, and judicial proceedings. But it took place with the memory of the revolt of 1579–80 very much on everyone's mind – all the more so as it unfolded at a time when commoners and nobles were at one another's throats elsewhere in France. The conflict of ideas in Dauphiné at the time was all the more sharp for that reason.

A typical expression of the point of view of the nobility may be found in *Les escritures et defenses des gents de la noblesse de Dauphiné*.[32] From the start, this work played on the memory of the events of 1579–80. It underlines the confirmation of the privileges of the nobility by Catherine de Médicis at the time of her visit in 1579. In reaction, the author of the treatise argues, the third estate incited the people to revolt.[33] The author accuses the third estate of long harbouring a deep-seated hatred of the nobility, attacking it as being the real oppressor of the people by means of financial and commercial fraud and the practice of usury.[34] As to the effect of the wars on the commoners, he denies that the nobility as a whole has ravaged the people. Only some of the nobility ought to be considered responsible; other noblemen have in fact helped the commoners. Noting the many commoners who have served as captains, the author points to the violence that they had perpetrated on the people. He concludes by reiterating that it is not the order of the nobility that is the cause of the evil but rather the war and the disorders themselves.[35]

The case of the bourgeoisie is nowhere expressed more eloquently than in the work of Claude Delagrange, *liéutenant particulier* of the *bailliage* of Saint-Marcellin.[36] Delagrange begins by noting that the nobility attributes the miserable condition of the third estate to the infelicity of the times, to popular errors, or to the very nature of civil wars. The nobility, Delagrange observes, deny that the misery of the third estate ought to be attributed to themselves. The nobles, he notes, claim that they are poorer than ever save only about thirty of them who profited by the wars while they were carrying out their duty. On the other hand, Delagrange continues, the nobles point to a thousand commoners who held commands and against whom they make no complaint – to which Delagrange responds: "They do not say who has incited the wars, who has kept them going, who has prevailed by them, nor the means by which they found themselves invested with and have taken possession of our goods."[37] Here we have repeated the perennial accusation of the bourgeoisie that the civil wars were a conspiracy of the nobility against the commons. But Delagrange invests this accusation with a sweep and eloquence that is unprecedented. "We will speak here [only] of a certain number" of nobles, adding caustically, "We will omit the most civilized." "How many are there who, to have the substance of their neighbour, have beaten him, had him consumed by passing companies of troops, arranged the confiscation of his livestock so as to pay the whole of the taxes assessed on his village."[38] Those who have enriched themselves in this way, Delagrange avows, keep their deeds to themselves. They claim nevertheless that only thirty of the nobility took advantage of circumstances in order to enrich themselves and that these were only doing their duty. Delagrange sarcastically notes that if this is true then there were not more than thirty who performed the heroic exploits that the nobles were claiming for themselves.[39] According to Delagrange, the majority of noblemen were involved in acts of pillage. The evidence, he maintains would demonstrate that there has never before been such a ravaging of the property of the third estate as in these wars. Delagrange concludes by asking rhetorically, "Who [among the nobles] would oppose such a war which has so put them at their ease? Why would they not rather seek to prolong it in hopes of similar transactions at the expense of their neighbours?"[40] As Le Roy Ladurie has noted, in comparing the *cahier* of the third estate in 1576 with the speeches of the representatives of the third estate at the end of the century: "At a quarter of a century's distance anti-noble bitterness became clearer, more concrete, and detailed. Under Henri IV, the pride of the third, aware of its martial vocation, is more evident, the polarization between the two groups, nobility and commoner more acute."[41]

The martial pride of the third estate manifested itself when Delagrange took note of the thousand bourgeois who the nobles alleged to have held command in the wars. "Let them answer," says Delagrange cuttingly, "if these thousand of our estate have not accomplished exploits as soldiers in proportion to thirty nobles? Those of our order who fought not only on foot but also on horseback, were their hands immobile?"[42] Delagrange, we may note, denies that bourgeois soldiers enriched themselves. Those that had, he drily observes, at any rate pay their taxes.

Delagrange insists on the equality of the third estate with the nobility. The difference between nobles and other men, according to him, is not natural or substantial, because by nature, all men are alike. A beggar is as much a man as is a noble. All men are descended from a common father. Nobility is something that has happened to certain men accidently and has had a definite beginning.[43] When the nobility address us as if we were their subjects, notes Delagrange, we refuse to recognize it. We are not of this number nor are we their serfs or freedmen. We were born free, he asserts, and are subject only to the king. We do not spurn nor despise the noble, deferring to him in what by right he ought to be deferred to in. It is they who spurn us, Delegrange complains, considering us as serfs and unworthy, not qualified to complain or to make claims.[44]

The nobles, according to Delagrange, say that those who are noble retain their original innate nature according to which they are forever free and can never be reduced to a servile condition. Also mechanical work is prohibited to the noble. On the other hand, the plebian is a subject and enserfed man. Their propositions, asserts Delagrange, are not true. Those of the third estate, like the other estates of Dauphiné, are born free and retain their original innate and natural freedom, remaining such except if they are enserfed and subject by force or by special obligation. If the noble has always been free, so too is the commoner of Dauphiné. This is undeniable by virtue of the customary law whereby all inhabitants of the province are equally free from taxation. Those that have since been ennobled have a quality that is only a second degree of honour among the king's subjects, of which the ecclesiastics have the first and the rest of the people the third. However, neither the ecclesiastic nor the noble have lordship over those of the third estate as a result of this quality. Those of the third estate remain in their original freedom just as those of the other estates do.[45]

Delagrange retains the idea of a society of orders distinguished according to function. He also evidently believes that nobles and clergy deserve respect according to their function. He rejects, however, the conception of the innate superiority and lordship of the clergy and nobles over the third estate. Like the noble and the ecclesiastic, the commoner retains his innate liberty. In this respect, he is the equal to those of the first and second estate.

Unable to think beyond the society of orders, Delagrange invokes the concept of equality to turn the society of orders into a functional relationship between the three estates. In no sense can the first two orders claim an innate superiority over the commons of Dauphiné. Indeed, Delagrange asserts that it is precisely when the nobles do injury to the people that the society of orders breaks down. From such injury, he claims, in a somewhat contradictory fashion, arise the seditions that render the people equal to the nobles.[46] It is almost as if this primal sense of equality lies dormant within the society of orders until activated by the injuries done to the people by the nobility. The nobles bring sedition onto themselves, causing the dissolution of the society of orders and a reassertion of primal equality.

Delagrange's sense of equality is thus mainly latent and defensive. As such it is primitive compared to the conception of the third estate of 1789. Nonethe-

less, the vehemence and indignation with which he repeatedly sets it forth
is unprecedented for the sixteenth century. "There is nothing more crude
and arrogant," Delagrange notes,

than when they say that the noble retains his original and innate nature and the plebian
likewise remains in his first state. We would like them to tell us if the matter of which
a man is composed is other than his flesh, bones, blood and other parts of which
his body is composed and if the body of the noble is composed of some other matter
than the body of he who is of the third estate? We would like them to tell us if
the nobles when ennobled change their bodies and the original matter of which it
is composed? No one can believe that such a change takes place. They assert that
we remain in our first state in order to render us more vile notwithstanding that they
remain in the same state as us.[47]

No doubt Delagrange's declaration of equality here is rhetorical. But rhetoric
expresses a certain emotive reality that lies behind it. While he rejects the
notion of rebellion the force of his words however suggests a questioning
of the prevailing ideological order.

   If Delagrange's treatise strains the limits of the idea of a society of orders,
the work of Louis Turquet de Mayerne clearly exceeds them. Published in
1611, his *La Monarchie aristodémocratique* advocates a constitutional monarchy
dominated by the bourgeoisie.[48] This folio of over five hundred pages, most
of which dates from 1591, has been analyzed in an article by Mousnier entitled,
significantly, "L'opposition politique bourgeoisie à la fin du XVIᵉ siècle et
au début du XVIIᵉ siècle."[49]

   Louis's father Etienne Turquet was an Italian from Piedmont who between
1536–40 monopolized the silk market in Lyons. Louis converted to Protestantism and was obliged to take refuge in Geneva following the Massacre
of St Bartholomew. Later, likely when Henri IV became king, he returned
to Lyons. Apparently, he visited Paris regularly, where his son Théodore
practised medicine. In 1611, the latter became personal physician to James I.
Louis and Théodore had a family connection to the baron de Langerac, the
Dutch ambassador to France. Although it is not clear what his profession
was, Louis Turquet de Mayerne was probably a merchant like his father.

   According to Mayerne, the universe is bound by natural laws imposed by
God. Human society, which is part of this universe, is likewise governed by
law. Based on observation, Mayerne claims to know what kind of society
most conformed to the laws of nature. First of all, he attacks the idea of an
ordering of society by birth or race. In its place, he asserts the idea of equality,
which entails that the nobility should not be given precedence by virtue of
their birth. Rather the order of society ought to be based on talent and function.

   A nobility based on race declines or dies out completely if nature is not
reinforced by art. Sons are often not equal to the vocation of their fathers.

"The poor nobility is of no use to the state." Without wealth, and the virtue and nobility that results from it, these latter qualities all too often languish, cease, and are lost, degenerating into completely different qualities, which trouble and undermine families and sometimes the whole state.[50]

The common people is the source of the nobility.[51] "Nobility's very matter is composed of virtue while wealth is its very cause ..."[52] Its purpose, according to Mayerne, is service to the state. Service to the state itself ennobles. Nobles by descent ought likewise to seek public office since nobility has no other end but to produce an order of men capable of conducting the government of the State.

The merchant is most apt to become noble. The wealth and experience that he accumulates are the best preparation for administrative office. The latter in turn prepares the way for ennoblement. Indeed, the merchant is the most essential element of the state. Trade makes towns and provinces wealthy, makes it possible for the common people to live, and provides an understanding of affairs, especially if it involves foreign commerce. Indeed, trade and marketing are the preoccupation of all levels and segments of society. Nobles have the duty to engage in commerce and to practice the liberal professions. The majority of vocations and enterprises carried on as a result of natural inclination are not inappropriate to nobility and do not entail derogation from it. Idleness alone is a crime. The nobility ought to become educated in law, administration, finance, agriculture, architecture, medicine, surgery, and trade. In short, the nobility ought to carry on bourgeois activities and to become bourgeois.[53]

It follows from this that the practice of arms, the vocation par excellence of the traditional nobility, Mayerne regards as an inferior activity. The properly instructed children of royalty will not regard the practice of arms and war as in themselves desirable and highly prized activities. "The art of war," says Mayerne, "conceived as a profession devoted to conquering and tormenting the world, being undeniably an evil and destructive illness, cannot and ought not to be taken as a principal activity of wise kings, being indeed only accessory in case of necessity."[54] Arms and war are extreme and desperate remedies. They cannot be thus a private profession that is reserved to a class. They are the privilege of the sovereign. As Mousnier notes, "The ideas of Mayerne on this point thus lead to the destruction of the noble class as a hereditary military class, to the annihilation of the gentleman, to the replacement of the noble soldier by the noble of functions ..."[55] As Mayerne envisioned it, the best and leading merchants ought to be able to accede freely to public functions, which are the source of nobility. According to Mousnier, the idea of the equal accession of the whole bourgeoisie to all offices is sketched out by Mayerne.

Annihilated with the idea of the warrior noble is the traditional conception of a society of orders. According to Mayerne, the state ought to reorganize society so as erect the bourgeoisie into the dominant class. The population ought to be divided into five groups: (1) the "agripossessors," (2) men of letters with university degrees, (3) men of trade and commerce, (4) craftsmen and (5) "manoeuvriers."

Everyone, including nobles, will be required to exercise a vocation. At the age of twenty, all young men will be required to register themselves in one of these groups. All the nobles will be able to register in one of the first three groups. Those of the first group will be able to practise the activities of the second and third, but gratuitously. Those of the second and third group may draw a salary or earn money, and without derogation even, if they were noble. Thus, nobles and commoners will be mingled together in classes not based on birth but by function in society. "Indeed, the old nobility would disappear to make room for the bourgeoisie."[56]

Mayerne expects that it is from the first three groups that the functionaries of the state will be drawn. Everyone will be bound to his class during his life but each will be able to advance his children to a higher class. All children will have a common education up to the age of fourteen so as to be able to judge which vocation would best suit them. All are capable of being educated. Everyone will be maintained at a mediocre level of wealth, because both great riches and poverty are dangerous. Politically, Mayerne foresees the establishment of a constitutional monarchy in which sovereignty will lie with the estates-general.

Mousnier rightly considers Mayerne's ideas an anticipation of the political ideas of the Enlightenment. Likewise, he classifies them as a product of the bourgeois milieu out of which Mayerne came. But in a self-contradictory manner, he ultimately dismisses Mayerne's conception as premature or not of its time. He contrasts what he regards as Mayerne's tendency to abstraction with Loyseau who looks at society as a whole such "as it really was."[57]

But can we really dismiss Mayerne as not of his time, while we embrace Loyseau's society of orders as a true reflection of the age? I would argue that Mayerne was of his time as much as Loyseau. Indeed, in my view the ideas of Mayerne are a reflection not only of the limits of middle-class political consciousness but also of the limits of middle-class power at the end of the sixteenth century. They testify to the economic advance of this class, both in peace and war. They are a measure of the degree to which the religious and social conflicts of the period had shaken the traditional conception of society.

Mayerne's notion of a bourgeois social and political order was not an anachronism. It represented a powerful undercurrent in sixteenth-century French society, which was manifest above all in the Protestant revolt of the 1560s, the radical Catholic League, and the upheavals of the 1590s. To be sure, Henri IV ignored Mayerne's work, and Louis XIII's government suppressed it. In its place, the ideas of Charles de Loyseau were to triumph. But the victory of Loyseau itself was not the triumph of a view of society "the way

it really was." Rather, Loyseau's victory represented the triumph of the traditional classes of society over an upstart but still immature enemy. But the
defeat of the middle class ought not to blind us to the fact of its relative ascension
throughout the sixteenth century. That elevation was based on both its enterprise and its contentiousness.

If one looks back at the history of protest movements in the sixteenth century,
it would seem that it was the associations of the towns and peasants of the
plat pays that were the most enduring forms of popular organization. They
were to be found in the Dauphiné, Velay, Agenais, and lower Auvergne in
1548. They played their part in the Vivarais and Dauphiné revolts of 1579
and again in Périgord and Comminges in 1595. Limited in their objectives,
they nevertheless embodied a conscious opposition to noble violence, metro-
politan dominance, and royal fiscal oppression. In the sixteenth century, the
rural league represented the most effective form through which commoners
could protest their exclusion from the society of orders.

In retrospect, we can see that the scale of popular resistance grew larger
through the course of the century. During the first sixty years, protest tended
to be local and intermittent. Nonetheless, the deteriorating economic circumstances of the mass of small producers led to a great multitude of protests,
ranging from subsistence riots to tithe revolt. Moreover, as we have seen,
these movements tended to amplify themselves in the 1540s and to take on
religious overtones.

The outbreak of the religious wars in the 1560s brought these currents
together into a nation-wide movement. Although the Protestants were never
a majority, the ten or fifteen per cent of the population that made up this
movement was composed largely of small producers, including a substantial
number of peasants. Their number was reinforced by the much larger number
of peasants who used the occasion of the Reformation to strike against the tithe.

The successively deeper waves of unrest that marked the popular movements
of the late 1570s, the League, and finally the 1590s were likewise provoked
by ever-mounting levels of economic misery and human despair engendered
by the religious wars. To be sure, the commoners were more acted upon
than actors in this conflict. The wars in the last instance were inspired and
supported by the nobility as a way of maintaining their political and social
predominance within French society. However, the rebellions of the 1590s
mark the point when the offensive of the nobility was brought to an end
by, among other factors, concerted popular protest. Popular rebellion was
not the only reason that the religious wars came to an end. The conciliatory
policies and the bribes Henri of Navarre offered to the nobility played their
part. Nonetheless, it does seem that the wave of popular agitation in the
countryside and revolts in the towns against the League had a good deal to
do with bringing the members of the nobility to their senses.

Notes

PREFACE

1 Solé, *La Révolution en questions*, 85.
2 Cazelles, *Société politique, noblesse et couronne*, 323–9.

INTRODUCTION

1 For the ongoing ascendancy of the nobility at the summit of the state see Harsgor, *Recherches sur le personnel du conseil du roi*; "Maîtres d'un royaume."
2 Du Tillet, *Advertissement*. I have used the edition of 1585 (*Remonstrances ou advertissement*).
3 Du Tillet, *Remonstrances* p. B ii/v.
4 For a discussion of the sixteenth century nobility see Wood, *The Nobility of the Election of Bayeux* and Constant, *La vie quotidienne de la noblesse française aux XVIᵉ-XVIIᵉ siècles*, 125–31.
5 Huppert, *Les Bourgeois gentilshommes*; Bitton, *The French Nobility in Crisis*; Jouanna, *L'Idée de race en France*.
6 Wood has demonstrated that the number of new nobles in fact was too low to pose a serious challenge to the position of the old nobility. Cf. Hickey, *The Coming of French Absolutism*, 151.
7 Crouzet, "Recherches sur la crise de l'aristocratie en France au XVIᵉ siècle; Dewald, *Pont-St-Pierre 1398–1789*, 221–2, 225–7, 237–8, 240.
8 The enduring strength of the nobility emerges from Hickey, *The Coming of French Absolutism*, 156; Major, "Noble Income, Inflation and the Wars of Religion in France"; Bottin, *Seigneurs et paysans dans l'Ouest du pays de Caux*; Charbonnier, *Une autre France*; Souriac, *Le Comté de Comminges*.
9 Bois, *The Crisis of Feudalism*, 360, 381, 389–90.
10 *La France de la fin du XVᵉ siècle*, 3–4.

11 Vaissières, *Gentilshommes campagnardes de l'ancienne France*, 14–26.
12 Of 369 pleas before the Chancellory of the Court in 1542, thirty-three (nine percent) involved attacks of nobles on commoners. In 1556, sixty-two (eleven percent) of 566 pleas involved such assaults. Such percentages are five times higher than the percentage of nobles in the French population. Cf. AN JJ 256ᴬ and 263ᴬ.
13 Porchnev, *Les Soulèvements populaires en France de 1623 à 1648*.
14 Mousnier, *Fureurs paysannes*; Foisil, *La révolte des nu-pieds et les révoltes normandes de 1639*; Bercé, *Histoire des Croquants*; Pillorget, *Les Mouvements insurrectionels de Provence*.
15 Leguai, "Les Révoltes rurales dans le royaume de France"; Chevalier, "Corporations, conflits politiques et paix sociale"; Mollat and Wolff, *Ongles bleus, jacques et ciompi*.
16 Kaplan, *Bread, Politics and Political Economy in the Reign of Louis XV*, 260–1, 345, 353–7 *et passim*; Tilly, *La France conteste, de 1600 à nos jours*.
17 Mousnier's approach can be elicited from "Recherches sur les soulèvements populaires en France avant le Fronde" and in his subsequent writings, including notably *Les Hiérarchies sociales de 1450 à nos jours* and "Les concepts d'"ordres,' d''états,' de 'fidelite' et de 'monarchie absolue' en France."
18 Cf. Goubert, "L'Ancienne société d'ordres: verbiage ou réalité"; Beik, *Absolutism and Society in Seventeenth Century France*, 6–10.
19 Seyssel, *La Monarchie de la France*.
20 Seyssel, *La Monarchie de la France*, 120–1.
21 Ibid., 124.
22 Arriaza, "Mousnier and Barber."
23 Dollinger and Wolff, *Bibliographie d'histoire des villes de France*, Bibliographie de l'histoire de France depuis 1960, BN.

CHAPTER ONE

1 On the largely unsuccessful attempt to control fugitive serfs, see Patault, *Hommes et femmes de corps en Champagne méridionale à la fin du moyen âge*, 273–91.
2 Berland, "Rébellion à main armée de serfs champenoise refugiées à Attichy (Oise)." Cf. Moldavskaia, "Narodnye Dvizhenija I Riformatsiia v Provanse v Pervoi Polovinie XVI V," 206.
3 Dumay, "Les Dernières sires de Pontaillier, seigneurs de Talmay," 178–9. Cf. Boislisle, *Histoire de la maison de Nicolay*, 47–8; Fitch, "Class Struggle in the Countryside," 221; AD Ardèche IJ 124.
4 Harding, *Anatomy of a Power Elite*, 30. The increasingly heavy burden of quartering troops is reflected in the marginal comments to the 1559 edition of the French translation of Thomas More's *Utopia*, 34–45.
5 Hauser, *Ouvriers du temps passé*, 112.

6 Constant, *La Vie quotidienne de la noblesse française*, 247–53.

7 Perraud, *Les Environs de Mâcon*, II, 736–7.

8 Nolin, "Episodes de la 'lutte des classes' à Dijon au XVIe siècle," 270–1.

9 *Livre de Podio ou chroniques d'Etienne Médicis*, I 458–60.

10 Ibid., II, 177–80. Another example of this kind of conflict took place at Laval in 1516. There the parlement ordered that only the canons of St Tugal ought to carry the holy sacrament on Corpus Christi. The clergy of Trinity Church, which was that of the bourgeoisie and the commoners, was thus excluded. The ensuing anger led to an insurrection in which the count of Laval who had supported the canons was forced to flee his chateau. Cf. Couanier de Launay, *Histoire de Laval*, 272–3; Zika, "Hosts, Processions and Pilgrimages," 39–40; James, "Ritual Drama and Social Body in the Late Medieval English Town," 18–9, 24, n. 80.

11 Pasquier, *Requête des consuls et habitants de Vorilhes*.

12 Bellecombe, *Histoire du château*, 102–7.

13 Laplane, *Histoire de Sisteron*, 8–18. For disputes over traditional rights in the forests see Nicholls, "Religion and Popular Movements," 104–5.

14 Perraud, *Les environs de Mâcon*, II, 556.

15 Labouré, *Roanne et le Roannais*, 26.

16 BM Le Puy, MS. 19, f. 223.

17 Segui, *Une Petite place protestante*, 38. Cf. Schnale, "Der Prozess als Widerstandsmittel."

18 Manuscript 19 in the municipal library is entitled *Recueil d'édits royaux et d'arrêts du parlement de Toulouse (1470–1580) ... copie executée sous l'administration de feu M. Henri Vinay, maire du Puy, 1865–1874*, 700 p.

19 Chareyle, "Extension et limites du dimorphisme social et religieux en bas Languedoc."

20 AD Gard FF 48, ff. 66r.–195 v.

21 Cf. Maurette, "Aimargues, vie politique, économique et sociale."

22 Hickey, *The Coming of French Absolutism*, 20–1.

23 On the hostility of the nobility toward the *francs-archers* in the second half of the fifteenth century see Spont, "La milice de francs-archers: 1448–1500," 456, 481; "Le monologue de franc archers de Bagnollet."

24 Vaissières, *Gentilshommes campagnards de l'ancienne France*, 88–90.

25 Bonnault, "La Société française au XVIe siècle," 76.

26 Chevalier, *Les Bonnes villes de France*, 101–28.

27 Bourgueville, *Les Recherches et antiquitez de la province de Neustrie*. I have used the edition of Bourgueville's work published at Caen in 1833; it was originally published in 1588.

28 Bourgueville, *Les Recherches et antiquitez de la province de Neustrie*, 118–19.

29 Menard, *Histoire civile, ecclésiastique et littéraire*, IV, 104–05, appendix, 110.

30 *Livre de Podio ou chroniques d'Étienne Médicis*, I, 374–5.

31 Ibid., I, 377–8. Compare the peasant guerrilla in Provence itself at the same moment against both the French and Imperial forces. See Procacci,

"La Provence à la veille des guerres de religion."

32 Jolibois, *Devastation de l'Albigeois par les compagnies de l'Albigeois*.

33 Menard, *Histoire civile, ecclésiastique et littéraire*, IV, 70, appendix, 80.

34 "Chroniques de Rouen des origines à 1544" 168–9.

35 BN MS Fr. 22458, f. 35.

36 Coudoin, "Recherches sur les métiers de la soierie à Tours," 181.

37 Poinsignon, *Histoire générale de la Champagne et de la Brie*, II, 68.

38 Heller, "Famine, Revolt and Heresy at Meaux."

39 – *The Conquest of Poverty*, 100–3.

40 *Histoire du Lyon et du Lyonnais*, 175–6. Cf. Gontier, "Acteurs et témoins des rebeynes lyonnais à la fin du moyen âge."

41 Hauser, *Ouvriers du temps passé*, 177–234.

42 Nolin, "Episodes de la 'lutte des classes'," 270–5.

43 *Histoire de la Rochelle*, 73–5.

44 Bouges, *Histoire ecclésiastique et civile de Carcassonne*, 290.

45 Despois, *Histoire de l'autorité royale*, 294.

46 Thomé de Maisonneufve, *Histoire de Romans* II, 139–42. See also Chevalier, *Annales de la ville de Romans* X, 82 and Lacroix, *Romans et le Bourg-de-Péage avant 1790*, 43.

47 Raytsas, "Le Program d'insurrection d'Agen en 1514."

48 *Histoire de Rouergue*, 113–4, 191.

49 Hérelle, *La Prise, l'incendie et la ruine de Vitry-en-Perthois*.

50 Hérelle, *Notice sur la création de l'échevinage de Vitry-le-François*.

51 Braudel, *L'Identité de la France*, I, 160–2.

52 Lahondès, *Annales de Pamiers*, I, 379–80.

53 Heller, *The Conquest of Poverty*, 82–85.

54 Mazet, "Etudes sur les statuts, actes des consuls et délibérations de jurade," 481–2.

55 Heller, *The Conquest of Poverty*, 85, 107.

56 AD Haute-Garonne B7, f. 200.

57 *Livre de Podio ou chroniques d'Etienne Médicis*, I, 455.

58 BM, Le Puy MS.19, ff. 186–7, 223, 241–4, 300–1, 304–5, 306, 312, 374–5, 552.

59 Delcambre, "Un inventaire inédit des archives du consulat du Puy."

60 BM, Le Puy, MS.19, ff. 358–96.

61 *Livre de Podio ou chroniques d'Etienne Médicis*, I, 520.

62 Souriac, *Le Comté de Comminges*, 239–40, 246–9, 258, 262; "Mouvements paysans en Comminges au XVIᵉ siècle."

63 Rochon, "Les tiers état aux états provinciaux de Basse Auvergne," 172–3, 176–7.

64 Hickey, *The Coming of French Absolutism*, 21–5.

65 An excellent discussion of the background of the revolt is to be found in the introduction to *La révolte de la Gabelle à Bordeaux en 1548*. Cf. Powis, "Guyenne, 1548."

66 *Histoire de la Rochelle*, 75–6, Massiou, *Histoire de la Saintonge*, III, 426.

67 De Metivier, *Chronique du parlement de Bordeaux*, I, 428.

68 Ibid., 429, 432; Powis, "Guyenne, 1548," 2.

69 Massiou, *Histoire de la Saintonge*, III, 447.

70 Powis, "Guyenne, 1548," 3; *La Révolte de la Gabelle à Bordeaux en 1548*, xxiv-xxv.

71 Soffrain, *Essais, variéties historiques et notices*, I, 178–81.

72 Powis, "Guyenne, 1548," 3.

73 Soffrain, Essais, variéties historiques et notices, I, 178–81.

74 *La Révolte de la Gabelle à Bordeaux en 1548*, 45, Marvaud, *Etudes historiques sur la ville de Cognac*, 277–8.

75 La Boétie, *De la Servitude volontaire*.

76 Audisio, *Les Vaudois de Luberon*.

77 Ibid., 81.

78 Ibid., 331.

79 Ibid.

80 Ibid.

81 Ibid., 361–6.

82 Ibid., 383–5.

83 Ibid., 410. Cf. Moldavskaia, "Narodyne Dvizhenija I Reformatsiia v Provanse v Pervoi Polovinie XVI V," 206–10, who stresses the anti-seigneurial and anti-fiscal nature of Vaudois resistance.

84 Heller, *The Conquest of Poverty*, 191.

85 Ibid., 53–6.

86 AD Gironde B30[bis], f.81, 1B3, f.99.

87 Heller, *The Conquest of Poverty*, 54–5.

88 Ibid., 24–5.

CHAPTER TWO

1 *Documents pour servir à l'histoire des guerres civiles en France*, 126.

2 Souriac, *Le Comte de Comminges*, 319–22.

3 Heller, *The Conquest of Poverty*, 235–40. For discussion of the opposition between revolutionary Protestantism and the society of orders, cf. Goertz, "Das Täufertum-ein Weg in die Moderne," 76–7.

4 Challe, *Histoire des guerres du Calvinisme et de la ligue*, I, 341. For the Catholic "nu-pieds" of Champagne, cf. Serres, *Histoire des choses mémorables avenues en France*, 171–2; for the Catholic riot at Beauvais, cf. Doyen, *Histoire de la ville de Beauvais*, I, 167–71.

5 Palangue, *La Diocèse d'Aix-en-Provence*, 85–6.

6 Haitze, *Histoire de la ville d'Aix*, II, 277–8, 282–3, 292–4, 322–3. Cf. Harding, "The Mobilization of Confraternities Against the Reformation in France."

7 Gimon, *Chroniques de la ville de Salon*, 219–22.

8 Ibid., 313–6.

9 Louvet, *Histoire des troubles de Provence*, I, 152–54; Haitze, *Histoire de la ville d'Aix*, 345–9.

10 The only systematic studies of the urban religious riot – Catholic or Protestant – are Davis, "The Rites of Violence" and Greengrass, "The Anatomy of Religious Riot."

11 Valois, "Les États de Pontoise (août 1561)," 240–1.

12 Mazon, *Notes et documents historiques sur les Huguenots du Vivarais*, I, 234–88.

13 Cubizolles, *Le Noble Chapitre Saint-Julien de Brioude*, 433–5.

14 *Mémoires d'un Calviniste de Millau*, 8, 106, 146, 152–3.

15 *Livre de Podio ou chroniques d'Etienne Médicis*, I, 521–2.

16 *Le Journal de Guillaume et de Michel Le Riche*, 320.

17 Ibid.

18 Baudouin, *Histoire du protestantisme et de la ligue en Bourgogne*, I, 253–4; Belle, *La réforme à Dijon*, 29, 72.

19 Saulx-Tavannes, *Mémoires*, VIII, 253.

20 Cf. Davis, "The Sacred and the Body Social in Sixteenth Century Lyons," 48–9.

21 Thus, James Farr's recent study simply ignores the presence of these workers in analyzing the Protestant and Catholic parties in Dijon. Cf. Farr, "Popular Religious Solidarity in Sixteenth Century Dijon."

22 Gautier, *Précis de l'histoire de la ville de Gap*, 68, 70.

23 Heller, *The Conquest of Poverty*, 247–51.

24 Cf. Le Roy Ladurie, *Les Paysans de Languedoc*, I, 297.

25 Menard, *Histoire civile, ecclésiastique et littéraire*, V, appendix 21–2. For initiatives by private entrepreneurs or the monarchy to stimulate agriculture at this juncture, cf. Bailly, "L'assèchement des étangs de Rochefort-Pujaut," 37; Martin, *Adam de Craponne et son oeuvre*, 18–22, 49–50; *Histoire du commerce de Marseille*, III 437; Dienne, *Histoire du dessèchement des lacs et marais*, 367; La Mare, *Traité de la police*, III, 524; Rebuffi, *Les Édicts et ordonnances des roys de France*, 1489; *Edicts et ordonnances*, ff. sig. Aii v – Aiii r.

26 Menard, *Histoire civile, ecclésiastique et littéraire*, IV, 223.

27 Ibid., IV 232.

28 Ibid., IV 240.

29 Ibid., IV 242.

30 Ibid., V, 8.

31 Vic and Vaissète, *Histoire générale de Languedoc*, XII, 1080–1.

32 Carro, *Histoire de Meaux et du pays Meldois*, 204.

33 AN zz¹ 203, 3 January 1560.

34 Leroy, *Recherches historiques sur le protestantisme*, 18–9.

35 Baudouin, *Histoire du protestantisme et de la ligue en Bourgogne*, I, 257.

36 Vic and Vaissete, *Histoire générale de Languedoc*, XII, 1081.

37 Jeandet, *Mâcon au seizième siècle*, 137.

38 Abord, *Histoire de la réforme et de la ligue*, I, 159–60.

39 Garrison, *Les Protestants du Midi*, 49–51.
40 Pablo, "Contribution à l'étude de l'histoire des institutions militaires huguenotes."
41 Brisson, *Histoire et vrays discours des guerres civilles és pays de Poictou*, n.p.
42 *Mémoires des frères Gay*, 282.
43 Chevalier, *Essai historique sur l'église et la ville de Die*, III, 104, 114, 148–9.
44 *Mémoires des frères Gay*, 282; Mailhet, *Histoire de Die*, 115.
45 Segui, *Une Petite place protestante*, 29–32.
46 Le Roy Ladurie, *Les Paysans de Languedoc*, I, 348–50.
47 For a discussion of rural Protestantism, cf. Heller, *The Conquest of Poverty*, 172, 206, 217; Crouzet, "Le Protestantisme et la ligue à Vitry-le-François et en Perthois." The link between Protestantism and rural industry is suggested by the occupations of non-urban refugees to Geneva. Cf. *Livre des habitants de Genève*, 2 vols, *passim*.
48 *Histoire économique et sociale de la France*, II, 713.
49 BM Le Puy MS.19, ff 300–1, 304–6, 312, 374–5, 502–9, 518–25, 569.
50 *Histoire économique et sociale de la France*, II, 714.
51 Galabert, *Les Guerres protestantes*, 4. The *Histoire économique et sociale de la France* attributes part of these words to the peasants of the Gers to the west of Verdun.
52 Du Tillet, *Remonstrances*, f. sig. C. r.-v.
53 Courteault, *Histoire de Gascogne et de Béarn*, 218.
54 Hémardinguer, "Les Vaudois du Dauphiné."
55 Niçaise, *Epernay et l'abbaye Sainte-Martin*, I, 151.
56 Baudouin, *Histoire du protestantisme et de la ligue en Bourgogne*, I, 464–65.
57 Bourquelet, *Histoire de Provins*, II, 132.
58 Brantôme, *Vies des hommes illustrés et grands captaines*, cited in Challe, *Histoire des guerres du Calvinisme*, II, 292.
59 *Lettre missive d'un gentilhomme*, BN Lb[33] 191, dated Compiègne 1 August 1567.
60 *Response à une lettre escrite à Compiègne*, BN Lb[33] 192.
61 Given the date, the pamphlets likely stem from two nobles involved in the Huguenot conspiracy of Meaux. Cf. Kingdon, *Geneva and the Consolidation of the French Protestant Movement*, 166.
62 Vic and Vaissette, *Histoire générale de Languedoc*, XII, 1081–82.
63 Cf. Huppert, *Les Bourgeois gentilshommes*; Bitton, *The French Nobility in Crisis*; Jouanna, *L'Idée de race en France*; Shalk, *From Valor to Pedigree*.
64 Cf. Major, "Noble Income, Inflation and the Wars of Religion in France"; Bottin, *Seigneurs et paysans*; Charbonnier, *Une Autre France*. For a contrary view see Crouzet, "Recherches sur la crise de l'aristocratie en France."
65 Le Roy Ladurie, *Les Paysans de Languedoc*, I, 465.
66 Vic and Vaissette, *Histoire générale de Languedoc*, XII, 1071.
67 Douais, "Mémoires ou rapports inédits," 353.
68 Ibid., 341. Cf. Roucaute, *Le Pays de Gevaudan au temps de la Ligue*, 93–4, which stresses the role of the lesser nobles in perpetuating the conflict.

69 Challe, *Histoire des guerres du Calvinisme et de la ligue dans l'Auxerrois*, II, 285.

70 Cf. Martin and Jacob, *Histoire de Soissons*, 457.

71 Brisson, *Histoire et vrai discours des guerres civilles és pays de Poictou*, f. sig. kiiii r.-v.

72 *Mémoires de Antoine Batailler*, 42–3.

73 Rossignol, *Monographie communale du département du Tarn*, I, 7–8.

74 Segui, *Un Petite place protestante*, 5.

75 Bourquelet, *Histoire de Provins*, II, 162–64. For later expressions of the idea of the civil wars as a conspiracy of the nobility, cf. Salmon, *Renaissance and Revolt*, 66, 92.

76 St-Jacob, "Mutations économiques et sociales," 31, n. 11.

77 Constant, *Nobles et paysans en Beauce au XVIᵉ siècle*, 291.

78 Tholin, "Documents relatifs aux guerres de religion," 208–9.

79 *Cahiers des doléances du tiers état du pays d'Agenais*, 4–5.

80 Imbert, *Les Grands jours de Poitou*, 129, 135–8, 155, 173. Cf. AN X²ᵇ 1174–80. The seigneurie was strengthened economically by the civil wars. Cf. Jean Jacquart, *La Crise rurale en Ile-de-France*, pp. 214–5.

81 Blauf, *Issoire pendant les guerres de religion*, 166.

82 Longy, *Histoire de la ville d'Issoire*, 234–36; Vaissières, *Une famille, les d'Alègre*, 214–33.

83 Aubenas, *Histoire de Fréjus*, 297–8.

84 Forton, *Nouvelles recherches pour servir à l'histoire de la ville de Beaucaire*, 173–80.

85 Quoted in Greengrass, *France in the Age of Henri IV*, 119.

86 Douais, "Mémoires ou rapports inédits," 345.

87 Bonnault, "La Société française au XVIᵉ siècle," 77.

88 *Histoire de Carcassonne*, 107, 116.

89 Bouges, *Histoire ecclésiastique et civile*, 359–60.

90 Perraud, *Les environs de Mâcon*, I, 259.

91 *The Letters and Papers of Armand de Gontaut*, II, 440.

92 *Les Chroniques de Jean Tarde*, 396.

93 The regional studies that establish this point are cited by Greengrass, *France in the Age of Henri IV*, 123, 136, n. 42.

94 The Swiss bourgeoisie meanwhile reaped immense profits from French war loans. Cf. Körner, *Solidarités financières suisses au XVIᵉ siècle*, 427.

CHAPTER THREE

1 Skinner, *The Foundations*, II, 302–4.

2 *Etats généraux de Pontoise*, art. 4.

3 Kingdon, *Geneva and the Consolidation of the French Protestant Movement*, 153.

4 Skinner, *The Foundations*, II, 235.

5 Quoted in Kingdon, *Geneva and the French Protestant Movement*, 52–3.

6 Ibid., 98, 108.
7 Kingdon, "Calvinism and Democracy."
8 Heller, *The Conquest of Poverty*, 111–41, 165, 198, 228.
9 Quoted in Kingdon, *Geneva and the French Protestant Movement*, 144.
10 Ibid., 106–7.
11 Ibid., 150–2, 166–9.
12 Ibid., 37.
13 Ménard, *Histoire civile, ecclésiastique et litteraire*, V, 88.
14 Ibid. 90.
15 Ibid., 68–9. Cf. Mentzer, *"Disciplina nervus ecclesiae."*
16 Skinner, *The Foundations*, II, 302–38.
17 La Boétie, *De la Servitude volontaire*, pp 66–7.
18 The *Discours* appeared in volume III of Goulart's *Mémoires de l'estat de France sous Charles neufiesme*, first published in 1576 and reprinted in 1577 and 1578. Cf. Kingdon, *Myths about the St. Bartholomew's Day Massacre*, 168–72.
19 *Journal d'un protestant de Millau*, 283.
20 Garrison, *Les Protestants du Midi*, 177–224.
21 Ibid., 206–8.
22 Ibid., 188.
23 *Journal d'un protestant de Millau*, 282.
24 Anquez, *Histoire des assemblées politiques des réformées de France*, 12.
25 Menard, *Histoire civile, ecclésiastique et littéraire*, V, 79, appendix, 88–92.
26 Garrison, *Les Protestants du Midi*, 179–82. Cf. Kingdon, *Myths*, 76–7.
27 Skinner, *The Foundations*, II, 231–3.
28 Menard, *Histoire civile, ecclésiastique et littéraire*, V, 30–1.
29 Trocmé, "Du Gouverneur à l'intendant," II, 617; "Reflexions sur le separatisme rochelais."
30 Holt, *The Duke of Anjou*, 28–33; Kingdon, *Myths*, 62–7.
31 Droz, *Barthélemy Berton*, 116–21.
32 *Histoire de la Rochelle*, 97.
33 Massiou, *Histoire de la Saintonge*, IV, 285–325.
34 *Les Guerres de religion en Languedoc*, 164.
35 *Journal d'un protestant de Millau*, 360–1.
36 Loutchitzky, *Documents inédits*, 69.
37 Ibid., 84–5.
38 Ibid., 93.
39 *Journal d'un protestant de Millau*, 403.
40 Ibid., 408–10.
41 *Histoire de Montauban*, 99–121.
42 Saulx-Tavannes, *Mémoires*, 253.
43 Menard, *Histoire civile, ecclésiastique et littéraire*, V, 251–4.
44 "Diarie de Jacques Merlin," 68–9.
45 Ibid., 69–70.

46 Ibid., 78.
47 Ibid., 74–5, 79, 86; Trocmé, "Du Gouverneur à l'intendant," II, 620–1.

CHAPTER FOUR

1 *Journal d'un protestant de Millau*, 359.
2 Le *Journal de Guillaume et de Michel Le Riche*, 250.
3 Ibid., 254.
4 Louvet, *Histoire et antiquitez du diocèse de Beauvais*, II, 658.
5 Ibid., 660; *Documents pour servir à l'histoire de Beauvais et du Beauvaisis*, 9.
6 Guibert, *La Ligue à Limoges*, 5–6.
7 Carel, *Histoire de la ville de Caen*, 127.
8 De Beauville, *Histoire de la ville de Montdidier*, I, 226.
9 Henry, *La Réforme et la ligue en Champagne*, 64–5.
10 Drouot, *La Première ligue à Bourgogne*, 106.
11 Ibid., 135–48; Clamagéron, *Histoire de l'impôt en France*, II, 262.
12 François, "Noblesse, réforme et gouvernement," 306–7.
13 Foisil, "Harangue et rapport d'Antoine Seguier," 109.
14 Lambert, *Histoire des guerres de religion en Provence*, I, 361–2.
15 Bouché, *Histoire chronologique de Provence*, II, 666.
16 Emmanuelli, *Les Compagnies corses à Aix-en-Provence*, 39–40.
17 Loutchitzky, *Documents inédits*, 103–6.
18 Bouché, *Histoire chronologique de Provence*, II, 667; Denis, *Hyères ancien et moderne*, 75–7.
19 Salmon, "Peasant Revolt in Vivarais"; Le Sourd, *Essai sur les états de Vivarais*, 280–8; Maufront, "Politiques, Ligueurs et Huguenots en Vivarais"; Mazon, *Notes sur les Huguenots en Vivarais*, III, 72–95.
20 Ibid., 10.
21 Quoted in Salmon, "Peasant Revolt in Vivarais," 22.
22 *Histoire de Vivarais*, 121–2; Destezet, "Etat économique et social de sept paroisses rurales"; Souchon, *Etude sur le Haut Vivarais*, I, 52–3.
23 Souchon, *Etude sur le Haut Vivarais*, I, 55–8.
24 Mazon, "Quelques notes historiques sur St. Agrève," 156–9.
25 AD Ardèche Fonds Mazon MS.23, f. 687.
26 Mazon, "Saint Agrève pendant les guerres religieuses," 194. Following the Catholic conquest, the regent of the collège, the son of Judge Reboulet, took refuge at Geneva. Cf. Mours, *Le Haut Vivarais protestante*, 253.
27 Mazon, "Saint Agrève pendant les guerres de religion," 204.
28 Reprinted in Mazon, *Notes sur les Huguenots en Vivarais*, III, 114–20.
29 Ibid., 114.
30 *Histoire de Vivarais*, 127.
31 Le Sourd, *Essai sur les états de Vivarais*, 252.
32 Mazon, *Notes sur les Huguenots en Vivarais*, III, 117.

33 Roman, "La Guerre des paysans en Dauphiné," 24.
34 Cf. Cavard, *La Réforme et les guerres de religion à Vienne*; Le Roy Ladurie, *Le Carnaval de Romans*; Hickey, *The Coming of French Absolutism*.
35 Hickey, *The Coming of French Absolutism*, 39, 41, 51.
36 Ibid., 47–8, 51.
37 Piémond, *Mémoires*, 58–9.
38 Le Roy Ladurie, *Le Carnaval de Romans*, 97–8.
39 Ibid., 100–1.
40 Quoted in Blanc, *La Vie dans la Valentinois*, 99–100, n. 236.
41 Piémond, *Mémoires*, 64.
42 Roman, "La Guerre des paysans en Dauphine," 34.
43 Blanc, *La Vie dans la Valentinois*, 102–3.
44 Piémond, *Mémoires*, 65.
45 Le Roy Ladurie, *Le Carnaval de Romans*, 105.
46 Piémond, *Mémoires*, 66–70.
47 Ibid., 71–2.
48 Le Roy Ladurie, *Le Carnaval de Romans*, 89; Cavard, *La Réforme et les guerres de religion à Vienne*. 220.
49 Quoted in Hickey, *The Coming of French Absolutism*, 58.
50 Quoted in Le Roy Ladurie, *Le Carnaval de Romans*, 85–6.
51 Ibid., 106.
52 Simmler, *La Republique des suisses* (Paris, 1579).
53 Ibid., n.p.
54 Le Roy Ladurie, *Le Carnaval de Romans*, 175–6.
55 Piémond, *Mémoires*, 86.
56 Ibid.
57 Ibid., 88.
58 On the course of the repression see Cavard, *La Réforme et les guerres de religion à Vienne*, 225–39.
59 Le Roy Ladurie, *Le Carnaval de Romans*, 92.
60 Lestrade, *Les Huguenots en Comminges*, 245–6.
61 Prarond, *La Ligue à Abbeville*, I, 175.
62 Bernard, *Les D'Urfé, souvenirs historiques et littéraires de Forez*, 231–8.
63 Loutchitzky, *Documents inédits*, 217–18, 220–5.
64 Le Roy Ladurie, *Les Paysans de Languedoc*, I, 400.
65 Carel, *Histoire de la ville de Caen*, 174–5.
66 Cf. Benedict, "Civil War and Natural Disaster in Northern France," 84–6; Greengrass, "The Later Wars of Religion in the French Midi," 106.
67 Tholin, "Les guerres de religion à Agen," 66–7.
68 Blauf, *Issoire pendant les guerres de Religion*, 157–8, 188–9.
69 *Journal de Louis Charbonneau*, 33–4.
70 Loutchitzky, *Documents inédits*, 202.
71 Ibid., 207.

72 Ibid., 215.

73 Ibid., 204–5.

74 Teissier, *Documents inédits*, 358–60, 371–2, 427–8.

75 Ibid., 459, 482–3, 487–8, 493–5, 511.

76 Ibid., 549.

77 Bernard, *Les D'Urfé*, 245ff.

78 Lambert, *Histoire des guerres de religion en Provence*, II, 46–7.

79 Ibid., II, 56.

CHAPTER FIVE

1 Quoted in Barnavi, *Le Parti de Dieu*, 144.

2 Drouot, *Mayenne et la Bourgogne*, I, 43–55.

3 Harding, "Revolution and Reform in the Holy League."

4 Benedict, *Rouen During the Wars of Religion*, 182.

5 Descimon, *Qui étaient la seize?*, 55.

6 Ibid., 26.

7 Harding, "Revolution and Reform in the Holy League," 400, n. 88. Penmarc'h is an example of another would-be urban republic in Brittany. Cf. *Mémoires du Chanoine Jean Moreau*, 223.

8 Barnavi and Descimon, *La Sainte ligue, le juge et la potence*, 66.

9 Cf. Barnavi, *Le Parti de Dieu*; Salmon, "The Paris Sixteen, 1584–1594."

10 *Histoire d'Angers*, 60–61.

11 Doyen, *Histoire de la ville de Beauvais*, I, 165–77.

12 Guibert, *Documents*, 15–41.

13 Perrière, "Nicolas de Hault."

14 Loutchitzky, *Documents inédits*, 249, 251, 256–8.

15 Ibid., 276–7.

16 Teissier, *Documents inédits*, 283, 292.

17 Fleury, *Cinquante ans de l'histoire*, 292.

18 Richart, *Mémoires sur la ligue dans le Laonais*, 31, 51–4, 116, 134–42.

19 Ibid., 476.

20 *Mémoires de Jean Burel*, II, 290–1, 322.

21 Challe, *Histoire des guerres du Calvinisme*, II, 68–73.

22 *Histoire de Rouergue*, 123–4, 137.

23 Baumgartner, *Radical Reactionaries*, 173–4.

24 Drouot, "Les Conseils provinciaux de la Sainte-Union," 428.

25 Baumgartner, *Radical Reactionaries*, 175.

26 Quoted in Tait, "The King's Lieutenant in Guyenne," 158.

27 Tait, "The King's Lieutenant in Guyenne," 161–2; Tholin, "Documents relatifs aux guerres de religion," 60.

28 Nostradame, *L'Histoire et chronique de Provence*, 921–2; Lambert, *Histoire des guerres de religion en Provence*, II, 56.

29 Gimon, *Chroniques de la ville de Salon*, 308–15.

30 Busquet, *Histoire de Marseille*, 202–4; Harding, "The Mobilization of Confraternities Against the Reformation in France," 94–8.

31 Pocquet, *Histoire de la Bretagne*, 147.

32 "Journal de François Grignart," 90.

33 Floquet, *Histoire du parlement de Normandie*, III, 239–42.

34 Lanvin, *Recherches historiques sur Falaise*, 393–4.

35 Boivin-Champeaux, *Bernay et la ligue*, 25–8.

36 Goulart, *Mémoires de la ligue*, III, 545; Salmon, *Society in Crisis*, 278–9.

37 Fret, *Antiquitez et chroniques percheronnes*, III, 115–6.

38 Grégoire, *La Ligue en Bretagne*, 163.

39 Ibid.; Pocquet, *Histoire de la Bretagne* 107–8.

40 Grégoire, *La Ligue en Bretagne*, 164.

41 Ibid., 145.

42 Quoted in Gregoire, *La Ligue en Bretagne*, 145.

43 "Prise et capitulation du château de Kérouzère," 154.

44 Pocquet, *Histoire de la Bretagne*, 176.

45 Ibid., 179–80.

46 Ibid., 178–9, Morice, *Histoire ecclésiastique et civile de Bretagne*, II, 398–400.

47 Moreau, *Histoire de ce qui s'est passé en Bretagne*," 101.

48 Grégoire, *La Ligue en Bretagne* 168–9.

49 Ibid.

50 Ibid.

51 Barnavi, *Le Parti de Dieu*, 270–2.

52 Ibid., 55–6.

53 Ibid., 145–6.

54 Baumgartner, *Radical Reactionaries*, 92–3.

55 Ibid., 93–4.

56 Ibid., 113.

57 Weill, *Les Théories sur le pouvoir royal en France*, 253.

58 Ibid., 258.

59 Ibid.

60 Challe, *Histoire des guerres du Calvinisme*, II, 66.

61 Henry, *La Réforme et la ligue en Champagne*, 287.

62 Loutchitzky, *Documents inédits*, 267.

63 Bernard, *Les D'Urfé*, 265–6.

64 Baumgartner, *Radical Reactionaries*, 167.

65 *Mémoires et correspondance de Duplessis-Mornay*, IV, 333–4.

66 Ibid., 334.

67 Ibid., 362.

CHAPTER SIX

1 Debuisson, *Provins à travers les siècles*, I, 140.

2 Henry, *La Réforme et la ligue en Champagne,* 219.

3 *Mémoire des choses plus notables advenue,* 43, 46–7.

4 *La Réforme et la ligue en Champagne,* II, 413–14.

5 On Protestants in the villages of the Brie, cf. Telkes, "Les protestants en Brie au dix-septième siècle."

6 Carro, *Histoire de Meaux,* 269.

7 Ibid., 261–2.

8 Ibid., 273.

9 Ibid., 280–1.

10 Vaultier, *Histoire et discours d'une partie des choses faites,* 222.

11 Ibid., 252; "Documents historiques"; "Extraits d'une information sur les ravagés."

12 Estainot, *La Ligue en Normandie,* 240–3.

13 Ibid., 282–3. For popular and elite mentality during the League, cf. Boucher, "Culture des notables et mentalité populaire."

14 Guibert, *Documents,* 53.

15 Blay de Gaix, *Histoire militaire de Bayonne,* I, 314–15.

16 *Journal de Jean Faurin,* 192–3.

17 *Mémoires de Jacques Carorguy,* 136–7.

18 Ibid., 158.

19 Ibid., 160.

20 Henry, *La Réforme et la ligue en Champagne,* 319–20; *Mémoire des choses plus notables,* 149–50.

21 *Mémoires de Jacques Carorguy,* 165.

22 Ibid., 181–2.

23 Ibid., 191.

24 Ibid., 192.

25 Ibid., 200.

26 Ibid., 200–3.

27 *La Réforme et la Ligue,* II, 585.

28 Ibid., 506.

29 Gaillard, "Les Derniers temps de la ligue à Beauvais," 557–8.

30 Ibid., 571–2.

31 Marsy, "Notes sur la ligue en Picardie."

32 *Journal historique de Jehan Patte,* 79.

33 Ibid., 84–93. In the Beauvaisis, the peasantry faced gangs of the poor who attacked at night in quest of grain and goods. Peasants were impelled to arm to protect themselves and their grain. Cf. Doyen, *Histoire de la ville de Beauvais,* I, 201–2.

34 Durand, *Ville d'Amiens,* 248.

35 Drouot, *Mayenne et la Bourgogne,* II, 283–97.

36 Ibid., II, 285.

37 Wilkinson, *A History of the League or Sainte Union,* 181–6.

38 *Registres consulaires de la ville de Villefranche,* III, 119.

39 Perraud, *Les Environs de Mâcon*, II, 503.

40 *Journal de Gabriel Breunot*, III, 84.

41 Ibid., 85–7.

42 Kleinclauz, *Histoire de Lyon*, I, 454–6.

43 Ibid., I, 459; "Fragments du journal de Ponson Bernard."

44 Du Verdier, *Discours sur la réduction de la ville de Lyons*, 8.

45 *Mémoires des frères Gay*, 293–4; Chevalier, Jules, *Essai historique sur l'église et la ville de Die*, II, 314–15; Chevalier, Ulysse, "Annales de la ville de Romans," 184.

46 Guichard, *Souvenirs historiques sur la ville de Digne*, 58–9.

47 Sobolis, *Histoire en forme de journal*, 213.

48 Pietro, *Histoire d'Aigues Mortes*, 241–50.

49 Pillorget, *Les mouvements insurrectionels*, 5. On the mood in Provence in the spring of 1594: "La noblesse qui estoit sur la defensive [contre Esperon] pressoit des fréquentes lettres et depputez le sieur de Lesdiguières d'accourir à leurs secours ... protestans contre luy de la ruyne des serviteurs de sa Majesté par une révolte géneralle plustot suggerée par un désespoir que par faulte d'affection." *Actes et correspondance du connétable de Lesdiguères*, III, 130.

50 Santi, "Un Document municipal sur l'état social du Lauraguais," 510–11.

51 The league of the peasants endured until 1598. Cf. Segui, *Un Petite place protestante*, 139–43.

52 Lestrade, *Les Huguenots en Comminges*, (1900), 29–30.

53 Lestrade, *Les Huguenots en Comminges*, (1910), 245.

54 Ibid., 246.

55 *Une Histoire de la Garonne*, 219.

56 Lestrade, *Les Huguenots en Comminges* (1910), 283–4.

57 Ibid., 280–2.

58 Ibid., 285–6. For the autonomy of the peasant movement cf. Souriac, "Mouvements paysans en Comminges du XVIᵉ siècle," 282.

59 Ibid., 286.

60 Ibid., 286–7.

61 Loutchitzky, *Documents inédits*, 335–6.

62 Ibid.

63 Lestrade, *Les Huguenots en Comminges* (1910), 287–9; Loutchitzky, *Documents inedits*, 335–6.

64 *Mémoires* de Jean Burel, 374.

65 Ibid.

66 Ibid.

67 Ibid.

68 Ibid., 400.

69 Ibid.

70 Le Roy Ladurie, *Les Paysans de Languedoc*, I, 400.

71 Maufront, "Politiques, ligueurs et Huguenots," 29, 32.

72 *Histoire économique et sociale de la France*, I, 837.

73 Bercé, *Histoire des croquants*, 2 vols.

74 Bercé, *Histoire des croquants*, I, 292.

75 Ibid., I, 288. Cf. Tait, "The King's Lieutenant in Guyanne," 213.

76 Cayet, *Chronologie novenaire* 574.

77 Ibid.

78 Ibid., 576.

79 Ibid.

80 Bercé, *Histoire des croquants*, I, 288.

81 Ibid.

82 Cayet, *Chronologie novenaire*.

83 *Les Chroniques de Jean Tarde*, 329. Cf. Bercé, *Histoire des croquants*.

84 *Les Chroniques de Jean Tarde*, 323.

85 Ibid., 326. Cayet estimates the number of peasants present on this occasion to have been thirty-five or forty thousand. Cf. Cayet, *Chronologie novenaire*, 576.

86 Loutchitzky, *Documents inédits*, 340.

87 Salmon, *Society in Crisis*, 282–90.

88 Tait, "The King's Lieutenant in Guyanne," 194–217.

89 Ibid., 199.

90 Ibid., 201–3.

91 Salmon, *Society in Crisis*, 285.

92 Tait, "The King's Lieutenant in Guyanne," 203.

93 Ibid.

94 Salmon, *Society in Crisis*, 210.

95 Boislisle, *Histoire de la maison de Nicolay*, II, 221.

CHAPTER SEVEN

1 Constant, *La Cause des guerres civiles en France*.

2 Ibid., 20–1.

3 L'Alouëte, *Des Affaires d'estat*, 164.

4 Ibid.

5 Jouanna, *L'Idée de race en France au XVIᵉ siècle*, III, 3011. Cf. Devyver, *La sang epurée*.

6 L'Alouëte, *Des Affaires d'estat*, 164.

7 Orleans, *Les Observations de diverses choses*.

8 Ibid., 8. Cf. Boucher *Les Triomphes du tres chretien, tres puissant et invictissime Roy de France, Francois* f. 99v.

9 Flurance Rivault, *Les Estats esquels il est discours du prince*.

10 Ibid., 358–9.

11 Ibid., 361.

12 Ibid.

13 Ibid., 374.
14 Ibid., 376.
15 Ibid., 376–7.
16 Ibid., 381.
17 Charron, *De la Sagesse*, I. I have used the 1970 Genevan reprint of the edition of 1635.
18 Ibid., I, ch. 52, III, ch. 7.
19 Ibid., I, 181–2.
20 Ibid., I, 182.
21 Ibid.
22 Ibid., I, 183.
23 Ibid. Olivier de Serres believed that service in the wars had made agricultural workers proud and arrogant. Cf. Serres, *Théâtre d'agriculture et mesnage de champs*, 39. Barthélemy des Laffemas likewise felt the wars had made workers disrespectful, careless, and prone to combination. Cf. Laffemas, *Reiglement général pour dresser les manufactures et ouvrages en ce royaume*, 12–13. For working class attempts to organize during the wars see Boissonade, *Le socialisme d'état*, 147–50.
24 Ibid., III, 54.
25 Ibid., III, 54–5.
26 Ibid., I, 193–4.
27 Ibid., I, 193.
28 Ibid., I, 172.
29 Ibid., I, 172–3.
30 Schalk, *From Valour to Pedigree*.
31 Ibid., 100–2.
32 *Les Escritures et defenses.* BN LK²661.
33 Ibid., 5.
34 Ibid., 7.
35 Ibid., 11.
36 *Responses et salvations.* BN LK²663.
37 Ibid., 96.
38 Ibid., 96–7.
39 Ibid., 97.
40 Ibid.
41 Le Roy Ladurie, *Le Carnaval de Romans*, 400–1.
42 *Responses et salvations*, 98.
43 Ibid., 31.
44 Ibid., 82.
45 Ibid., 83.
46 Ibid., 4.
47 Ibid., 84.
48 Mayerne, *Le Monarchie aristodemocratique*.

49 Mousnier, "L'Opposition politique bourgeoise," 1–20.
50 Ibid., 6.
51 Ibid., 7.
52 Ibid.
53 Ibid., 8.
54 Ibid., 9.
55 Ibid., 8.
56 Ibid., 9.
57 Ibid., 17.

Bibliography

SOURCES

MANUSCRIPTS

Archives Nationales JJ 256^A
Archives Nationales JJ 263^A
Archives Nationales x^{2b} 1174-80
Archives Nationales zz' 203
Archives départmentales de l'Ardèche 1J 124
Archives départementales de l'Ardèche Fonds
Mazon MS. 23
Archives départementales de la Gard FF 48
Archives départementales de la Gironde B30^{bis}
Archives départementales de la Gironde 1B3
Archives départementales de l'Haute-Garonne B7
Bibliothèque Municipale Le Puy MS.19
Bibliothèque Nationale MS. Fr. 22458

PRIMARY SOURCES

Actes et correspondence du connétable de Lesdiguières. Ed. L.-A. Douglas and
   J. Romans. 3 vols. Grenoble: E. Allier 1878–84.
Bouchet, Jean. *Les Triomphes du très chrétien, très puissant et invictissime Roy de
   France, François premier de ce nom.* Poitiers: Jean and Enguilbert de Marnef
   1550.
Bourgueville, Charles de. *Les Recherches et antiquitez de la province de Neustrie.*
   Caen: V. and J. Le Fèvre 1588; Caen: T. Cholopin 1833.
Brisson, Pierre. *Histoire et vrays discours des guerres civilles és pays de Poictou ...*
   Paris: J. Du Puys 1578.
Cahiers des doléances du tiers état du pays d'Agenais. Paris, 1885.

Cayet, Palma. *Chronologie novenaire contenant l'histoire de la guerre sous le règne du très chrétien roy de France et de Navarre.* In *Nouvelle collection des mémoires pour servir à l'histoire de France,* ed. J.F. Michaud and B. Poujoulat, Vol. XII. Paris: chez l'editeur ... du Code Civil 1836–9.

Charron, Pierre *De la Sagesse, Oeuvres.* 2 vols. Paris: J. Villery 1635; Geneva: Slatkine 1970.

Les Chroniques de Jean Tarde. Ed. Gaston de Gérard. Paris: H. Oudin 1887.

"Chroniques de Rouen des origines à 1544." In *Deux chroniques de Rouen,* ed. A. Heron. Rouen: A Lestringant, Paris: A. Picard 1900.

Constant, Pierre. *La Cause des guerres civiles en France.* Langres: J. Des Preyz 1595.

"Diarie de Jacques Merlin ou recueil des choses les plus mémorables qui se sont passés en ceste ville de La Rochelle de 1589 à 1600." Ed. Charles Dargibeaud. *Archives historiques de la Saintonge et de l'Aunis* 5 (1878): 63–380.

"Documents historiques: pillages des gens de guerre, 1589–1593." *Bulletin de la société de l'histoire de Normandie* 10 (1909): 242–9.

Documents pour servir à l'histoire de Beauvais et du Beauvaisis. Recueil mémorable d'aulcuns cas advenus depuis l'an du salut 1573 tant à Beauvais qu'ailleurs. Ed. Victor Leblond. Paris: H. Champion 1909.

Documents pour servir à l'histoire des guerres civiles en France. Ed. A.D. Liublianskia. Moscow: Academy of Sciences 1962.

Douais, Célestin. "Mémoires ou rapports inédits sur l'état du clergé, de la noblesse, de la justice et du peuple dans le diocèse de Narbonne, de Montpellier et de Castres en 1573." *Mémoires de l'académie des sciences, inscriptions et belles lettres de Toulouse,* 9e série 3(1891): 318–65.

Durand, Georges. *Ville d'Amiens, Inventaire sommaire des archives communales antérieurs à 1790.* III. Série BB. Amiens: Piteux frères 1897.

Du Tillet, Jean. *Advertissement à la noblesse, tant du parti du Roy que des rebelles et conjurez.* Lyons: M. Jove 1558.

– *Remonstrances ou advertissement à la noblesse tant du parti du Roy, que de rebelles.* Paris: A. Rémy 1585.

Du Verdier, Antoine. *Discours sur la réduction de la ville de Lyons à l'obéissance de Henri IV.* Ed. P. M. Gonon. Lyons: Du Moulin, Ronet and Sibuet 1843.

Les escritures et defenses des gents de la noblesse de Dauphiné, le roy y estant, au mois de septembre 1595. BN LK² 661.

Edicts et ordonnances du roy touchant les usures. Rennes 1567.

Etats généraux de Pontoise, Cahiers du tiers estat. Ed. Henri Tartière. Mont-de-Marsan 1867.

"Extraits d'une information sur les ravages causés par les gens de guerre." *Bulletin de la société de l'histoire de Normandie* (1880): 287–94.

Flurance Rivault, David de. *Les Estats esquels il est discours du prince, du noble et du tiers estats, conformément à notre temps.* Lyons: B. Rigaud 1596.

"Fragments du journal de Ponson Bernard, échevin Lyonnais." *Revue du Lyonnais,* nouv. série 31 (1865): 441–2.

Goulart, Simon. *Mémoires de la ligue, 1576–1598.* 6 vols. Amsterdam: Arkstée and Merkus 1758.

– *Mémoires de l'estat de France sous Charles neufiesme.* 3 vols. Meidelbourg: H. Wolf 1578 (1576).

Les Guerres de religion en Languedoc d'après les papiers du baron de Fourquevaux (1562–1574). Ed. C. Douais. Toulouse: E. Privat 1892.

Imbert, Hugues. "Les Grands jours de Poitou: registres criminels (1534, 1567, 1579, 1634)." *Mémoires de la société de statistique, science et arts des Deux-Sevres* 2ᵉ serie 16 (1878).

Journal de Gabriel Breunot. Ed. Joseph Garnier. 3 vols. Dijon: J.E. Rabutot 1864.

"Journal de François Grignart." *Bulletins et mémoires de la société d'émulation des Côtes-du-Nord* 37 (1899): 37–110.

Le Journal de Guillaume et de Michel Le Riche, avocats du roi à Saint-Maixent de 1534 à 1586. Ed. A. D. de la Fontenelle de Vaudoré. Saint-Maixent: Reversé 1843; Geneva, Slatkine 1971.

Journal de Jean Faurin sur les guerres de Castres. Ed. Charles Pradel. (Montpellier: Imprimerie des Chroniques de Languedoc 1878; Marseilles: Lafitte 1981.

Journal de Louis Charbonneau: chronique biterroise – languedocienne concernant l'histoire de la ligue dans le Midi de la France de 1583 à 1587. Ed. A. Germain. Montpellier, 1874.

Journal d'un protestant de Millau. Ed. J.-L. Rigal. Rodez 1911.

Journal historique de Jehan Patte, bourgeois d'Amiens: 1587–1617. Ed. M.J. Garnier. Amiens: Lemeraîné 1873.

La Boétie, Estienne. *De la Servitude volontaire ou Contr'Un.* Ed. Malcolm Smith. Geneva: Droz 1987.

– *Oeuvres complètes.* Ed. Paul Bonnefon. Bordeaux: G. Gounouilhou 1892; Geneva: Slatkine 1967.

Laffemas, Barthélemy des. *Reiglement général pour dresser les manufactures et ouvrages en ce royaume.* Paris: L'Oyselet 1597.

L'Alouete, François. *Des Affaires d'estat, des finances, du prince et de sa noblesse.* Metz: J. d'Arras 1597.

The Letters and Papers of Armand de Gontaut, Baron of Biron (1524–1592). Ed. Sidney Hellman Ehrman. 2 vols. Berkeley: CA: University of California Press 1936.

Lettre missive d'un gentilhomme à un sien compagnon contenant les causes du mescontentement de la noblesse de France, 1567. BN Lb³³ 191.

Livre de Podio ou chroniques d'Etienne Médicis, bourgeois du Puy: 1475–1565. Ed. A. Chaissang. 2 vols. Le Puy: M.P. Marchessou 1869.

Livre des habitants de Genève. Ed. Paul F. Geisendorf. 2 vols. Geneva: Droz 1957–63.

Loutchitzky, Jean. *Documents inédits pour servir à l'histoire de la réforme et de la ligue.* Paris: Sandoz and Fischbacher 1875.

Louvet, Pierre. *Histoire des troubles de Provence.* 2 vols. Sisteron: J.-P. Louvet 1680.

Louvet, Pierre. *Histoire et antiquitez du diocèse de Beauvais.* 2 vols. Beauvais: La Veuve Valet 1631–5.

Mayerne, Louis Turquet de. *La Monarchie aristodemocratique ou le gouvernement composé et meslé des trois formes de légitimes republiques. Dédiée aux états-généraux des provinces confédérées des Pays-Bas.* Paris: J. Berjon 1611.

Mémoire des choses plus notables advenues en la province de Champagne (1585–1598). Ed. Georges Hérelle. Reims: Imprimerie cooperative 1882.

Mémoires de Antoine Batailler sur les guerres civiles à Castres et dans le Languedoc: 1584–86. Ed. Charles Pradel. Paris: A. Picard 1894.

Mémoires de Jacques Carorguy, greffier, 1582–95. Ed. Edmund Bruwaent. Paris: A. Picard 1880.

Mémoires de Jean Burel. Ed. Augustin Chassaing. Rev. ed., 2 vols. Saint-Vidal: Centre d'étude de la Vallée de la Borne 1983.

Mémoires des frères Gay. Ed. Jules Chevalier. Montbéliard: P. Hoffmann 1888.

Mémoires du Chanoine Jean Moreau sur les guerres de la ligue en Bretagne. Ed. Henri Waquet. Quimper: Archives départementales 1960.

Mémoires d'un Calviniste de Millau. Ed. J.L. Rigal. Rodez, 1911.

Mémoires et correspondance de Duplessis-Mornay. Ed. A.-D. de la Fontenelle de Vaudoré and P. R. Auguis. 12 vols. Paris: Treuttel and Würtz 1824–5; Geneva: Slatkine 1969.

Métivier, Jean-Léon. *Chronique du parlement de Bordeaux.* Ed. Arthur de Brezetz et Jules Derit. 2 vols. Bordeaux: Société des Bibliophiles 1886–7.

"Le monologue de francs archers de Bagnollet." In *Nouveau recueil de farces françaises des XVᵉ et XVIᵉ siècles,* ed. Emile Picot and Christophe Nyrop, 47–70. Paris: D. Morgand and Ch. Fatout 1880.

More, Thomas, *La Republique d'Utopie.* Tr. Jean Leblond. Lyons: J. Saugrain 1559.

Moreau, Jean. *Histoire de ce qui s'est passé en Bretagne durant les guerres de la ligue et particulièrement dans le diocèse de Cornovaille.* Ed. Le Bastard de Mesmer. Saint-Brieuc: L. Prud'homme 1857.

Nostradame, César de. *L'Histoire et chronique de Provence.* Lyon: S. Rigaud 1614.

Orleans, Regnault d'. *Les Observations de diverses choses remarqués sur l'éstat, couronne et peuple de France.* Vannes: J. Bourrelier 1597.

Piémond, Eustache. *Mémoires.* Ed. J. Brun-Durand. Valence: Société d'archeol. stat. Drôme 1885; Geneva: Slatkine 1973.

Rebuffi, Pierre. *Les Édicts et ordonnances des roys de France.* Lyons: à la Salamandre 1573.

La Réforme et la ligue en Champagne. Documents. Ed. Georges Hérelle. 2 vols. Paris: H. Champion 1888–92.

Registres consulaires de la ville de Villefranche. Vol. III. Ed. Abel Besançon. Villefranche-sur-Saône, 1915.

Response à une lettre escrite à Compiègne. 1567. BN Lb³³ 192.

Responses et salvations des pieces produites par les gentz du tiers estat de Dauphine. Paris, 1594. BN LK² 663.

La Révolte de la Gabelle à Bordeaux en 1548: textes de Guillaume Paradin et Jean Bouchet. Paris: Atelier Aldo Manuzio 1981.

Saulx-Tavannes, Gaspard de. *Mémoires de Gaspard de Saulx, seigneur de Tavannes*

In *Nouvelle Collection des mémoires pour servir à l'histoire de France depuis le XIIIe siècle jusqu'à la fin du XVIIIe*, ed. J.F. Michaud and J.J.F. Poujoulat, vol. VIII. Paris: chez l'editeur du Code Civil 1836-9.

Serres, Jean de. *Histoire des choses mémorables avenues en France depuis l'an 1547 jusques au commencement de l'an 1597* ... Paris, 1599.

Serres, Olivier de. *Théâtre d'agriculture et mesnage de champs*. Paris: Jammet-Métayer 1600.

Seyssel, Claude de. *La Monarchie de la France*. Ed. Jacques Poujol. Paris: Librairie d'Argences 1961.

Simmler, Josias. *La Republique des suisses*. Paris: J. Du Puys 1579.

Sobolis, Foulquet. *Histoire en forme de journal de ce qui s'est passé en Provence depuis l'an 1562 jusqu'à l'an 1607*. Ed. F. Chavarnac. Aix: A. Makaire 1894.

Teissier, Jean. *Documents inédits pour servir à l'histoire de la réforme et de la ligue à Narbonne*. Narbonne, 1900.

Vaultier, Jean. *Histoire et discours d'une partie des choses faites et passés en ce royaume qui ont eu cours depuis 13 mai 1588 jusqu'au 16 juin 1598. Monuments inédits de l'histoire de France, 1400-1600*. Ed. Adhelm Bernier. Paris, 1834.

SECONDARY SOURCES

Abord, Hippolyte. *Histoire de la réforme et de la ligue dans la ville d'Autun*. 3 vols. Paris: Dumoulin 1855-86.

Anquez, Léone. *Histoire des assemblées politiques des réformées de France: 1573-1622*. Paris: A. Durand 1859.

Arriaza, Armand. "Mousnier and Barber: The Theoretical Underpinnings of the 'Society of Orders' in Early Modern France." *Past and Present* 89 (1980): 39-57.

Aubenas, J.A. *Histoire de Fréjus*. Fréjus: Leydet 1881; Marseille: Lafitte 1974.

Audisio, Gabriel. *Les Vaudois de Luberon: une minorité de Provence, 1460-1560*. Association d'études vaudoises et de Luberon 1986.

Bailly, Robert. "L'assèchement des étangs de Rochefort-Pujaut: XVIe – XVIIe siècles." *Rhodanie* 6 (1983): 36-43.

Barnavi, Elie. *Le Parti de Dieu*. Brussels: Nauwelaerts 1980.

– and Robert Descimon. *La Sainte ligue, le juge et la potence*. Paris: Hachette 1985.

Baudouin, Paul-Médéric. *Histoire du protestantisme et de la ligue en Bourgogne*. 2 vols. Auxerre: Vosgien 1881-4.

Baumgartner, Frederic J. *Radical Reactionaries: The Political Thought of the French Catholic League*. Geneva: Droz 1975.

Beauville, Victor de. *Histoire de la ville de Montdidier*. 2nd ed. 3 vols. Paris: J. Claye 1875.

Beik, William. *Absolutism and Society in Seventeenth Century France*. Cambridge: Cambridge University Press 1985.

Belle, Edmond. *La Réforme à Dijon des origines à la fin de la lieutenance générale de Gaspard de Saulx-Tavannes: 1530-1570*. Paris: Damidot 1911.

Bellecombe, André de. *Histoire du château de la ville et des seigneurs et barons de Montpezat.* Auch: Cocharaux 1898; Marseille: Lafitte 1980.

Benedict, Phillip. "Civil War and Natural Disaster in Northern France." In *The European Crisis of the 1590s: Essays in Comparative History,* ed. Peter Clark, 84–106. London: Allen and Unwin 1985.

– *Rouen During the Wars of Religion.* Cambridge: Cambridge University Press 1981.

Bercé, Yves-Marie. *Histoire des Croquants.* 2 vols. Geneva: Droz 1974.

Berland, J. "Rébellion à main armée de serfs champenoise refugiées à Attichy (Oise)." *Mémoires de la société d'agriculture, commerce, sciences et arts du département de la Marne* 2ᵉ série, 21 (1924–6): 198–249.

Bernard, August Joseph. *Les D'Urfé, souvenirs historique et littéraires de Forez.* Paris: Imprimerie Royale 1839.

Bitton, Davis. *The French Nobility in Crisis, 1560–1640.* Stanford: Stanford University Press 1969.

Blanc, André. *La Vie dans le Valentinois.* Paris: Picard, 1977.

Blauf, Julien. *Issoire pendant les guerres de religion.* Clermont-Ferrand: La Française d'Edition et d'Imprimerie 1977.

Blay de Gaix, Gabriel-François. *Histoire militaire de Bayonne.* 2 vols. Bayonne: Lamaignère 1899.

Bois, Guy. *The Crisis of Feudalism: Economy and Society in Eastern Normandy, c. 1300–1550.* Cambridge: Cambridge University Press 1984.

Boislisle, Arthur Michel de. *Histoire de la maison de Nicolay.* 2 vols. Nogent-le-Routrou: Imprimerie de Gouverneur 1873–5.

Boissonade, Prosper. *Le Socialisme d'état.* Paris: H. Champion 1929; Geneva: Slatkine 1977.

Boivin-Champeaux, Louis. *Bernay et la ligue.* Bernay: Lefèvre 1889.

Bonnault, Claude de. "La société française au XVIᵉ siècle: 1515–1614." *Bulletin des recherches historiques* 62 (1956): 76–87.

Borzeix, Daniel. *Révoltes populaires en Occitanie: moyen âge et ancien régime.* Treignac: Editions "Les Monédières" 1982.

Bottin, Jacques. *Seigneurs et paysans dans l'Ouest du pays de Caux, 1540–1650.* Paris: Le Sycomore 1983.

Bouché, Honoré. *Histoire chronologique de Provence.* 2 vols. Paris: Rollins fils 1736.

Boucher, Jacqueline. "Culture des notables et mentalité populaire dans la propagande qui entraina la chute de Henri III." In *Mouvements populaires et conscience sociale: XVIᵉ–XIXᵉsiècles,* ed. Jean Nicolas, 39–49. Paris: Maloine 1985.

Bourgeon, Jean-Louis. "Pour une histoire, enfin, de la Saint-Barthélemy." *Revue historique* 282 (1989): 83–142.

Bouges, Thomas-Augustin. *Histoire ecclésiastique et civile de Carcassonne.* Paris: Gandouin 1741; Marseille: Lafitte 1978.

Bourquelet, Felix. *Histoire de Provins.* 2 vols. Provins: Lebeau 1839–40; Marseilles: Lafitte 1976.

Braudel, Fernand. *L'Identité de la France.* 3 vols. Paris: Arthaud-Flammarion 1986.

Busquet, Raoul. *Histoire de Marseille*. Paris: Laffont 1978.

Carel, Pierre. *Histoire de la ville de Caen sous Charles IX, Henri III et Henri IV*. Paris: Massif 1886.

Carro, Antoine. *Histoire de Meaux et du pays meldois*. Meaux: Le Blondel 1865.

Cavard, Pierre. *La Réforme et les guerres de religion à Vienne*. Vienne: Blanchard 1960.

Cazelles, Raymond. *Société politique, noblesse et couronne sous Jean Le Bon et Charles V*. Geneva: Droz 1982.

Challe, Ambroise. *Histoire des guerres du Calvinisme et de la ligue dans l'Auxerrois*. 2 vols. Auxerre: Perriquet and Rouillé 1864; Geneva: Slatkine 1978.

Charbonnier, Pierre. *Une Autre France. La seigneurie en Basse-Auvergne du XIVe au XVIe siècle*. 2 vols. Clermont-Ferrand: Institut d'Études du Massif Central 1980.

Chareyle, Philippe. "Extension et limites du dimorphisme social et religieux en bas Languedoc: Aimargues, 1584–1635." Mémoire de maîtrise, Université de Montpellier, 1981.

Chevalier, Bernard. *Les bonnes villes de France du XIVe au XVIe siècle*. Paris: Aubien 1982.

– "Corporations, conflits politiques et paix sociale en France aux XIVe et XVe siècles." *Revue historique* 268 (1982): 17–44.

Chevalier, Jules. *Essai historique sur l'église et la ville de Die*. 4 vols. Valence: Bourron 1909.

Chevalier, Ulysse. "Annales de la ville de Romans." *Bulletin de la société d'archéologie et de statistique de la Drôme* 10–11 (1876–7).

Clamagéron, Jean-Jules. *Histoire de l'impôt en France*. 2 vols. Paris: Guillaumin 1867–76.

Constant, Jean-Marie. *La Vie quotidienne de la noblesse française aux XVIe-XVIIe siècles*. Paris: Hachette 1985.

– *Nobles et paysans en Beauce au XVIe siècle*. Lille: Service de Reproduction des Thèses 1981.

– "La noblesse seconde et la Ligue." *Bulletin de la société d'histoire moderne* 87 (1988): 11–20.

Courteault, Paul. *Histoire de Gascogne et de Béarn*. Paris: Boivin and Cie 1938.

Couanier de Launay, Stephen. *Histoire de Laval*. Laval: Godbart 1856.

Coudoin, André. "Recherches sur les métiers de la soierie à Tours dans la première moitié du seizième siècle." PhD Thesis, University of Tours, 1976.

Crouzet, Denis. "La violence au temps des troubles de religion (vers 1525–vers 1610)," *Histoire, économie, société* 8 (1989): 507–25.

– "Recherches sur la crise de l'aristocratie en France au XVIe siècle: les dettes de la maison de Nevers." *Histoire, économie, société* 1 (1982): 7–50.

Crouzet, René. "Le protestantisme et la ligue à Vitry-le-François et en Perthois." *Revue historique* 52 (1927): 1–40.

Cubizolles, Pierre. *Le Noble Chapitre Saint-Julien de Brioude*. Brioude: Institution Saint-Julien 1980.

Dartique-Peyrou, Charles. *La Vicomté de Béarn sous le règne d'Henri d'Albert: 1517–1555*. Paris: Les Belles Lettres 1934.

Davis, Natalie Zemon. *Fiction in the Archives: Pardon Tales and Their Tellers in Sixteenth Century France*. Stanford: CA: Stanford University Press 1987.

– "The Rites of Violence." In *Society and Culture in Early Modern France*, 152–87. Stanford: CA: Stanford University Press 1975.

– "The Sacred and the Body Social in Sixteenth Century Lyons." *Past and Present* 90 (1981): 40–70.

Debuisson, René. *Provins à travers les siècles*. 2 vols. Coulommiers-Paris: Brodard 1920–34.

Delcambre, Etienne. "Un Inventaire inédit des archives du consulat du Puy." *Bull. hist. du Puy* 14 (1929): 8.

Denis, Alphonse. *Hyères ancien et moderne*. Hyères: Souchon 1910; Marseille: Lafitte 1975.

Descimon, Robert. *Qui étaient la seize?* Paris: Klincksieck 1983.

Despois, L. *Histoire de l'autorité royale dans le comté de Nivernais*. Paris, 1912.

Destezet, Christian Foriel. "Etat économique et social de sept paroisses rurales du Haut-Vivarais d'après un registre d'estimes de 1464." In *Fédération historique du Languedoc Méditerrannéan et du Roussillon XLIVe Congrès. Privas 22–23 Mai 1971: Vivarais et Languedoc*, 175–82. Montpellier, 1972.

Devyver, André. *La Sang epurée: la naissance du sentiment et de l'idée de "race" dans la noblesse française: 1566–1726*. 2 vols. Brussels, n.d.

Dewald, Jonathan. *Pont-St-Pierre 1398–1789: Lordship, Community and Capitalism in Early Modern France*. Berkeley: University of California Press 1987.

Dienne, Edouard de. *Histoire du dessèchement des lacs et marais en France avant 1789*. Paris: H. Champion 1891.

Dollinger, Philippe and Philippe Wolff. *Bibliographie d'histoire des villes de France*. Paris: Klincksiek 1967.

Doyen, C.L. *Histoire de la ville de Beauvais depuis le quatorzième siècle*. 2 vols. Beauvais: Moisaud 1842.

Drouot, Henri. "Les conseils provinciaux de la Saint-Union: 1589–1595." *Annales du Midi* 65 (1953): 415–33.

– *Mayenne et la Bourgogne: étude sur la ligue, 1587–1595*. 2 vols. Paris: Picard 1937.

– *La Première ligue à Bourgogne et les débuts de Mayenne*. Dijon: Bernigaud and Privat 1937.

Droz, Eugénie. *Barthélemy Berton: 1563–1573*. Geneva: Droz 1960.

Dumay, Gabriel. "Les dernières sires de Pontaillier, seigneurs de Talmay (1471–1636)." *Mémoires de la société Bourguignonne de géographie et d'histoire* 28 (1912): 1–244.

Emmanuelli, René. *Les Compagnies corses à Aix-en-Provence*. Paris: Picard 1953.

Estainot, Robert d'. *La Ligue en Normandie: 1588–94*. Rouen: Lebrument 1862.

Farr, James R. *Hands of Honour: Artisans and their World in Dijon, 1550–1650*. Ithaca: NY: Cornell University Press 1988.

- "Popular Religious Solidarity in Sixteenth Century Dijon." *French Historical Studies* 14 (1985): 192–214.
Fitch, Nancy Elizabeth. "Class Struggle in the Countryside. Social Change and Politics in Central France, 1200–1914." PhD Thesis, University of California, Los Angeles, 1985.
Fleury, Edouard. *Cinquante ans de l'histoire de Notre Dame de Laon.* Laon: Padiez 1875.
Floquet, Amable-Pierre. *Histoire du parlement de Normandie.* 7 vols. Rouen: E. Frère 1840–2.
Foisil, Madeleine. "Harangue et rapport d'Antoine Seguier, commissaire pour le roi en Basse-Normandie (1579–80)." *Annales de Normandie* 28 (1976): 25–40.
- *La Révolte des nu-pieds et les révoltes normandes de 1639.* Paris: PUF 1970.
Forton, Chevalier de. *Nouvelles recherches pour servir à l'histoire de la ville de Beaucaire.* Avignon: Séguin 1836: Marseille: Lafitte 1979.
Fourqueron, Gilles. "La république Malouine mythe ou realite?" *Annales de la société d'histoire et d'archéologie de l'arrondisement de Saint-Malo* (1987): 281–302.
- *La France de la fin du XVᵉ siècle.* Ed. Bernard Chevalier and Philippe Contamine. Paris: CNRS 1985.
François, Michel. "Noblesse, réforme et gouvernement du royaume de France dans le deuxième moitié du XVIᵉ siècle." In *Actes du colloque L'amiral de Coligny et son temps: Paris, 24–28 Octobre 1972,* 301–12. Paris: Société de l'histoire du protestantisme français 1974.
Fret, Louis-Joseph. *Antiquitez et chroniques percheronnes.* 3 vols. Mortagne: Glaçon 1838–40.
Gaillard, J. "Les Derniers temps de la ligue à Beauvais." *Mémoires de la société académique d'archéologie, sciences et arts du département de l'Oise* 17 (1898–1900): 544–92.
Galabert, F.A. *Les Guerres protestantes autour de Verdun-sur-Garonne: 1560–1580.* Fribourg: Imprimerie de l'Oeuvre de Saint-Paul 1898.
Garrison, Janine. *Les Protestants du Midi: 1559–98.* Toulouse: Privat 1980.
Gautier, Théodore. *Précis de l'histoire de la ville de Gap.* Gap: Allier 1844.
Gimon, Louis. *Chroniques de la ville de Salon depuis ses origines jusqu'en 1792.* Aix: Remondet-Aubin 1882.
Goertz, Hans Jürgen. "Das Täufertum-ein Weg in die Moderne." In *Zwingli und Europa,* ed. Peter Blickle et al., 165–81. Zurich: Vandenhoeck and Ruprecht 1985.
Gontier, Nicole. "Acteurs et témoins des rebeynes lyonnais à la fin du moyen age." In *Révolte et société: Actes du IVᵉ colloque d'histoire au présent, Paris, mai 1988,* ed. Fabienne Gambelle et Michel Trebitsel, 34–42. Paris: Publications de la Sorbonne 1989.
Goubert, Pierre. "L'Ancienne société d'ordres: verbiage ou réalité." In *Colloque Franco-Suisse d'histoire économique,* 35–40. Geneva: Librairie de l'Université 1969.
Greengrass, Mark. "The Anatomy of Religious Riot in Toulouse in May, 1562." *Journal of Ecclesiastical History* 34 (1983): 367–91.

– *France in the Age of Henri IV: The Struggle for Stability*. London: Longman 1984.
– "The Later Wars of Religion in the French Midi." In *The European Crisis of the 1590s: Essays in Comparative History*, ed. Peter Clark, 106–35. London: Allen and Unwin 1985.

Grégoire, Louis. *La Ligue en Bretagne*. Paris and Nantes: Dumoulin 1856.

Guibert, Louis. *Documents, analyses de pièces, extraits et notes relatifs à l'histoire municipale des deux villes de Limoges*. 2 vols. Limoges: Plainemaison 1897–1902.
– *La ligue à Limoges*. Limoges: Ducourtieux 1884.

Guichard, Firmin. *Souvenirs historiques sur la ville de Digne et ses environs*. Digne: Guichard 1847; Marseille: Lafitte 1973.

Guinodie, Raymond. *Histoire de Libourne et des autres villes et bourgs de son arrondissement*. 3 vols. Libourne: L'Auteur 1876; Marseille: Lafitte 1979.

Haitze, Pierre-Joseph. *Histoire de la ville d'Aix*. 6 vols. Aix: Makaire 1880–92.

Harding, Robert R. *Anatomy of a Power Elite: The Provincial Governors of Renaissance France*. New Haven, CT: Yale University Press 1978.
– "The Mobilization of Confraternities Against the Reformation in France." *Sixteenth Century Journal* 10 (1980): 85–107.
– "Revolution and Reform in the Holy League: Angers, Rennes, Nantes." *Journal of Modern History* 53 (1981): 379–416.

Harsgor, Mikhail. "Maîtres d'un royaume: le groupe dirigeant français à la fin du XVᵉ siècle." In *La France de la fin du XVᵉ siècle*, ed. Bernard Chevalier et Philippe Contamine, 135–46. Paris: CNRS 1985.
– *Recherches sur le personnel du conseil du roi sous Charles VIII et Louis XII*. 4 vols. Lille: Service de Reproduction des Thèses 1980.

Hauser, Henri. *Ouvriers du temps passé: XVᵉ–XVIᵉ siècles*. Paris: Alcan 1899; Geneva: Slatkine 1982.

Heller, Henry. *The Conquest of Poverty: The Calvinist Revolt in Sixteenth Century France*. Leiden: Brill 1986.
– "Famine, Revolt and Heresy at Meaux: 1521–25." *Archiv für Reformationsgeschichte* 68 (1977): 133–57.

Hémardinguer, J.-J. "Les vaudois du Dauphiné de la resistance à l'insurrection d'après des documents inédits." *Boletino de la società di studi valdesi* 103 (1958): 53–63.

Henry, Edouard-Georges. *La Réforme et la ligue en Champagne*. Saint-Nicolas: Trenel 1867.

Hérelle, Georges. *Notice sur la création de l'échevinage de Vitry-le-François d'après des documents inédits*. Vitry-le-François: L. Bitsch 1882.
– *La Prise, l'incendie et la ruine de Vitry-en-Perthois: 24 juillet, 1544*. Vitry-le-François: L. Bitsch 1922.

Hickey, Daniel. *The Coming of French Absolutism: The Struggle for Tax Reform in the Province of Dauphiné: 1540–1640*. Toronto: University of Toronto Press 1986.

Histoire d'Angers. Ed. François Lebrun. Toulouse: Privat 1975.

Histoire de Carcassonne. Ed. Jean Guillaine and Daniel Fabre. Toulouse: Privat 1984.

Une Histoire de la Garonne. Ed. Janine Garrison and Marc Ferro. Paris: Ramsay 1982.

Histoire de la Rochelle. Ed. Marcel Delafosse. Toulouse: Privat 1986.

Histoire de Montauban. Ed. Daniel Ligou. Toulouse: Privat 1984.

Histoire de Rouergue. Ed. Henri Enjalbert. Toulouse: Privat 1979.

Histoire de Vivarais. Ed. Gérard Cholvy. Toulouse: Privat 1988.

Histoire du commerce de Marseilles. Vol. III, *de 1480 à 1594*, ed. Gaston Rambert. Paris: Plon 1951.

Histoire du Lyon et du Lyonnais. Ed. André Latreille. Toulouse: Privat 1975.

Histoire économique et sociale de la France. Tome I: de 1450 à 1660. Ed. E. Le Roy Ladurie and Michel Morineau, vol. 2. Paris: PUF 1977.

Holt, Mack P. *The Duke of Anjou and the Politique Struggle During the Wars of Religion*. Cambridge: Cambridge University Press 1986.

Huppert, George. *Les Bourgeois gentilshommes: an essay in the definition of elites in Renaissance France*. Chicago, IL: University of Chicago Press 1977.

Jacquart, Jean. *La crise rurale en Ile-de-France: 1550–1670*. Paris: A. Colin 1974.

James, Mervyn. "Ritual Drama and Social Body in the Late Medieval English Town." *Past and Present* 98 (1983): 3–29.

Jeandet, Abel. *Mâcon au seizième siècle*. Mâcon, 1892.

Jouanna, Arlette. *L'Idée de race en France au XVIe siècle et au début du XVIIe siècle*. 3 vols. Montpellier: Chez l'auteur 1981.

Jolibois, Emile. *Devastation de l'Albigeois par les compagnies de l'Albigeois*. Albi: E. Desrue 1837.

Kaiser, Wolfgang. "Sozialgefüge und Fraktionskämfe in Marseille während der Burgerkriege." *Francia* 14 (1986): 181–207.

Kaplan, Steven. *Bread, Politics and Political Economy in the Reign of Louis XV*. The Hague: Martinus Nijhoff 1976.

Kettering, Sharon. "Clientage during the French Wars of Religion." *Sixteenth Century Journal* 20 (1989): 221–39.

Kingdon, Robert M. "Calvinism and Democracy: Some Political Implications of Debates on French Reformed Government, 1562–1572." *American Historical Review* 69 (1964): 393–401.

– *Geneva and the Consolidation of the French Protestant Movement: 1564–1572*. Geneva: Droz 1967.

– *Myths about the St. Bartholomew's Day Massacre: 1572–1576*. Cambridge: MA: Harvard University Press 1988.

Kleinclauz, Arthur. *Histoire de Lyon*. 3 vols. Lyons: P. Masson 1939–52; Marseilles: Lafitte 1978.

Körner, Martin H. *Solidarités financières suisses au XVIe siècle*. Paris–Lucerne: Payot 1980.

Labouré, Maurice. *Roanne et le Roannais: Etudes historiques*. Lyons: Presses de Courrier républicain 1957.

Lacroix, André. *Romans et le Bourg-de-Péage avant 1790*. Valence: J. Ceas 1897; Marseille: Lafitte 1978.

Lahondès, Jules de. *Annales de Pamiers*. 2 vols. Toulouse: Privat 1882-4; Marseille, 1979.

La Mare, Nicolas de. *Traité de la police*. 4 vols. Paris: Cot 1705-38.

Lambert, Gustave. *Histoire des guerres de religion en Provence*. 2 vols. Toulon: Laurent 1870.

Lanvin, P.G. *Recherches historiques sur Falaise*. Falaise, 1814.

Laplane, Edouard de. *Histoire de Sisteron*. Digne: Guichard 1843; Marseille: Lafitte 1974.

Leguai, André. "Les révoltes rurales dans le royaume de France du milieu du XIVᵉ siècle à la fin du XVᵉ." *Le Moyen Age* 88 (1982): 49-76.

Leroy, Gabriel. *Recherches historiques sur le protestantisme dans le Melunais*. Meaux: Le Blondel 1874.

Le Roy Ladurie, Emmanuel. *Le Carnaval de Romans*. Paris: Gallimard 1979.

– *Les Paysans de Languedoc*. 2 vols. Paris: SEVPEN 1966.

Le Sourd, Albert. *Essai sur les états de Vivarais depuis leurs origines*. Paris: Société générale d'imprimerie et d'édition 1926.

Lestrade, Jean. *Les Huguenots en Comminges*. Paris: H. Champion 1900.

– *Les Huguenots en Comminges*. Paris: H. Champion 1910.

Longy, Albert. *Histoire de la ville d'Issoire*. Clermont-Ferrand: Mont-Louis 1890; Marseille: Lafitte 1975.

Mailhet, André. *Histoire de Die*. Paris: Buttner-Thierry 1897.

Major, J. Russell. "Noble Income, Inflation and the Wars of Religion in France." *American Historical Review* 86 (1981): 21-48.

– *Representative Government in Modern France*. New Haven, CT: Yale University Press 1980.

Marsy, Comte A. C.-A. de. "Notes sur la ligue en Picardie d'après une correspondance du duc de Mayenne." *La Picardie* 7 (1884): 254-68.

Martin, Felix. *Adam de Craponne et son oeuvre*. Paris: Dunod 1874.

Martin, Henri and Paul L. Jacob. *Histoire de Soissons depuis les temps les plus reculés jusqu'à nos jours d'après les sources originales*. Soissons: Arnould 1837; Marseilles: Lafitte 1977.

Marvaud, Francis. *Etudes historiques sur la ville de Cognac*. Niort: Clouzot 1870; Marseilles: Lafitte 1977.

Massiou, D. *Histoire politique, civile et religieuse de la Saintonge*. 2nd ed. 6 vols. Saintes: Charnier 1846.

Maufront, Nicole. "Politiques, ligueurs et Huguenots en Vivarais pendant le dernier quart du XVIᵉ siècle." *Revue du Vivarais* 49 (1943): 5-38.

Maurette, A. "Aimargues, vie politique, économique et sociale de la fin du XIIIᵉ siècle à la fin du XIVᵉ siècle." Mémoire de maîtrise, Université de Montpellier, 1971.

Mazet, Fernand de. "Etudes sur les statuts, actes des consuls et délibérations de jurade de la commune et jurisdiction de Villeneuve d'Agen." *Revue de l'Agenais* 25 (1898): 478–88.

Mazon, Albin. *Notes et documents sur les Huguenots du Vivarais.* 3 vols. Privas: Imprimerie Centrale de l'Ardèche 1901–9.

– "Quelques notes historiques sur St. Agrève avant les guerres de religion." *Revue du Vivarais* 9 (1901): 152–63.

– "Saint Agrève pendant les guerres religieuses." *Revue du Vivarais* 9 (1904): 193–207.

Menard, Léon. *Histoire civile, ecclésiastique et littéraire de la ville de Nîmes.* 7 vols. Paris: Chaubert 1744–58.

Mentzer, Raymond A. "*Disciplina nervus ecclesiae*: The Calvinist Reform of Morals at Nîmes." *Sixteenth Century Journal* 18 (1987): 89–115.

Moldavskaia, M.A. "Narodnye Dvizhenija I Reformatsiia v Provanse v Pervoi Polovinie XVI V." *Srednie Veka* 48 (1985): 195–213.

Mollat, Michel and Philippe Wolff. *Ongles blues, jacques et ciompi, les révolutions populaires en Europe aux XIVe et XVe siècles.* Paris: Calmann-Lévy 1970.

Morice, Pierre Hyacinthe. *Histoire ecclésiastique et civile de Bretagne.* 2 vols. Paris: Delaguette 1750–6.

Mours, Samuel. *Le Haut Vivarais protestante.* Alboussière (Ardèche): Trait d'Union 1935.

Mousnier, Roland. "Les concepts d'"ordres,' d'"états,' de 'fidelité' et de 'monarchie absolue' en France de la fin du XVe siècle à la fin du XVIIIe." *Revue historique* 247 (1972): 289–312.

– *Fureurs paysannes: les paysans dans les révoltes du XVIIe siècle.* Paris: Calmann-Lévy 1967.

– *Les Hiérarchies sociales de 1450 à nos jours.* Paris: PUF 1969.

– "L'opposition politique bourgeoise à la fin du XVIe siècle et au début du XVIIe siècle." *Revue historique* 213 (1955): 1–20.

– "Recherches sur les soulèvements populaires en France avant le Fronde." *Revue d'histoire moderne et contemporaine* 5 (1958): 81–132.

Neuschel, Kristen B. "Noble Households in the Sixteenth Century: Material Settings and Human Communities." *French Historical Studies* 15 (1988): 595–622.

– *Word of Honour: Interpreting Noble Culture in Sixteenth Century France.* Ithaca NY: Cornell University Press 1989.

Niçaise, Auguste. *Epernay et l'abbaye Sainte-Martin.* 2 vols. Châlons-sur-Marne: Le Roy 1869.

Nicholls, David. "Religion and Popular Movements in Normandy during the French Religious Wars." In *Religion and Rural Revolt*, ed. Janos Bak and Gerhard Beneke, 104–22. Manchester: Manchester University Press 1984.

Nolin, E. "Episodes de la 'lutte des classes' à Dijon au XVIe siècle." *Annales de Bourgogne* 36 (1964): 270–5.

Pablo, Jean de. "Contribution à l'étude de l'histoire des institutions militaires huguenotes: l'armée huguenote entre 1562 et 1573." *Archiv für reformationsgeschichte* 48 (1957): 192–215.

Palangue, Jean-Rémy. *Le diocèse d'Aix-en-Provence*. Paris: Beauchesne 1975.

Pasquier, Félix. *Requête des consuls et habitants de Vorilhes à Henri d'Albret, comte de Foix, roi de Navarre: texte inédite en langue romane de 1535*. Foix: de Barthe 1882.

Patault, Anne-Marie "Hommes et femmes de corps en champagne méridionale à la fin du moyen âge. In *Annales de l'est publiées par l'univeristé de Nancy* II, mémoire no. 58 (1978).

Perraud, François. *Les Environs de Mâcon*. 2 vols. Mâcon: Protat 1912; Marseille: Lafitte 1979.

Perrière, H. de la. "Nicolas de Hault, Maire de Troyes, 1588–92." *Mémoires de la société d'agriculture, sciences et arts du département de l'Aube* 89 (1925): 13–118.

Pietro, F. Em. di. *Histoire d'Aigues Mortes*. Paris: Furne and Perrotin 1849; Marseilles: Lafitte 1979.

Pillorget, René. *Les mouvements insurrectionels de Provence entre 1596 et 1715*. Paris: A. Pedore 1975.

Pocquet, Barthélemy. *Histoire de la Bretagne. La Bretagne Province*. Rennes: J. Plihon and L. Hommay 1913.

Poinsignon, Auguste-Maurice. *Histoire générale de la Champagne et de la Brie*. 2nd ed. 3 vols. Châlons-sur-Marne: Martin 1896–8.

Porchnev, Boris. *Les Soulèvements populaires en France de 1623 à 1648*. Paris: SEVPEN 1963.

Powis, Jonathan. "Guyenne, 1548: The Crown, the Province and Social Order." *European Studies Review* 12 (1982): 1–15.

Prarond, Ernest. *La Ligue à Abbeville: 1576–1594*. 3 vols. Paris: Dumoulin 1868–73.

– "Prise et capitulation du château de Kerouzère, novembre, 1590." *Bulletin de la société archéologique du Finistère* 20 (1893): 152–73.

Procacci, Giovanni. "La Provence à la veille des guerres de religion, 1535–1545." *Revue d'histoire moderne et contemporaire* 5 (1958): 245–51.

Raytsas, Vladimir I. "Le program d'insurrection d'Agen en 1514." *Annales du Midi* 153 (1981): 255–77.

Richart, Antoine. *Mémoires sur la ligue dans le Laonais*. Laon: Tous les libraries 1869.

Richet, Denis. "Les barricades de Paris, le 12 mai 1588." *Annales: ESC* 45 (1990): 383–91.

Rochon, Gilbert. "Les tiers état aux états provinciaux de Basse Auvergne aux XVIᵉ et XVIIIᵉ siècles: bonnes villes et plat pays." *Bulletin philologique et historique (jusqu'à 1715) du comité des travaux historiques* (1930–1): 165–89.

Roman, Joseph. "La guerre des paysans en Dauphine, 1597–80." *Bulletin de la société d'archéologie et de statistique de la Drôme* 40 (1877): 22–50, 149–71.

Rossignol, Elie A. *Monographie communale du département du Tarn, première partie. Vol I: Arrondissement de Gaillac*. Toulouse: Delboy 1864.

Roucaute, Jean. *Le Pays de Gevaudan au temps de la Ligue*. Paris: A. Picard 1900.

St-Jacob, Pierre de. "Mutations économiques et sociales dans les campagnes bourguignons à la fin du XVIᵉ siècle." *Etudes rurales* 1 (1961): 34–49.

Salmon, J. H. "The Paris Sixteen, 1584-1594: The Social Analysis of a Revolutionary Movement." *Journal of Modern History* 44 (1972): 540–76.

– "Peasant Revolt in Vivarais, 1575–80." *French Historical Studies* 2 (1979): 1–28.

– *Renaissance and Revolt: Essays in the Intellectual and Social History of Early Modern France.* Cambridge: Cambridge University Press 1987.

– *Society in Crisis: France in the Sixteenth Century.* New York, NY: St Martin's Press 1975.

Santi, L. de. "Un document municipal sur l'état social du Lauraguais après les guerres de religion: 1595–1601." *Revue des Pyrennées* 24 (1912): 503–14.

Schnale, Wolfgang. "Der Prozess als Widerstandsmittel. Uberlegungen zu Formen der Konflictsbewaltigung am Beispiel der Feudalkonflikte im Frankreich des Ancien Regime." *Zeitschrift für historisches Forschung* 18 (1986): 386–424.

Shalk, Ellery. *From Valor to Pedigree: Ideas of Nobility in France in the Sixteenth and Seventeenth Century.* Princeton, NJ: Princeton University Press 1986.

Segui, Emile. *Une Petite place protestante pendant les guerres de religion, 1562–1629: Faugères en Biterrois.* Nîmes: Larguier 1933.

Skinner, Quentin. *The Foundations of Modern Political Thought.* 2 vols. Cambridge: Cambridge University Press 1978.

Solé, Jacques. *La Révolution en questions.* Paris: Seuil 1988.

Souchon, Cécile. *Etude sur le Haut Vivarais d'après des registres d'estimes de 1464.* 2 vols. Paris, Thèse de l'école de Chartes, 1970.

Souffrain, Jean-Baptiste Alex. *Essais, variéties historiques et notices sur la ville de Libourne et ses environs.* 2 vols. Bordeaux: Brossier 1806.

Souriac, René. *Le Comte de Comminges au milieu du XVIᵉ siècle.* Paris: CNRS 1978.

– "Mouvements paysans en Comminges au XVIᵉ siècle." In *Mouvements populaires et conscience sociale: XVIᵉ – XIXᵉ siècles,* ed. Jean Nicolas, 276–81. Paris: Maloine 1985.

Spont, Albert. "La milice de francs-archers: 1448–1500." *Revue des questions historiques* 31 (1897): 441–89.

Tait, Richard. "The King's Lieutenant in Guyenne, 1580–1610. A Study in the Relations Between the Crown and the Great Nobility." PhD Thesis, Oxford University, 1977.

Telkes, Eva. "Les protestants en Brie au dix-septième siècle." Mémoire de maîtrise, Paris-Sorbonne, 1970-1.

Tholin, Georges. "Documents relatifs aux guerres de religion tirées des archives municipales d'Agen, juillet 1558 – décembre 1595." *Archives historiques de la Gironde* 29 (1894).

– "Les guerres de religion à Agen." *Revue de l'Agenais* 18 (1891).

Thomé de Maisonneufve, Paul. *Histoire de Romans.* 2 vols. Romans: Rambaud 1937-42.

Tilly, Charles. *La France conteste, de 1600 à nos jours.* Paris: Fayard 1986.

Trocmé, Etienne. "Du gouverneur à l'intendant: l'autonomie rochelaise de

Charles IX à Louis XIII." In *Recueil de travaux offert à M. Clovis Brunel*, vol. II, 616–32. Paris, 1955.

– "Reflexions sur le separatisme rochelais: 1568–1628." *Bulletin de la société de l'histoire du protestantisme française* 122 (1976): 203–10.

Tuetey, Alexandre. *Inventaire analytique des livres de couleur et des bannières de Châtelet de Paris*. Histoire générale de Paris. 2 vols. Paris: Archives Nationales 1899–1907.

Vaissières, Pierre de. *Une Famille, les d'Alègre*. Paris: Emile-Paul 1914.

– *Gentilshommes campagnardes de l'ancienne France*. Paris: Perrin 1904; Geneva: Slatkine 1975.

Valois, Noël. "Les états de Pontoise (août 1561)." *Revue d'histoire de l'église de France* 29 (1943): 237–56.

Vic, Claude de and Joseph Vaissète. *Histoire générale de Languedoc*. 15 vols. Toulouse: Privat 1872–92.

Weill, Georges. *Les Théories sur le pouvoir royal en France pendant les guerres de religion*. Paris: Hachette 1891.

Wilkinson, Maurice A. *History of the League or Sainte Union, 1576–1595*. Glasgow: Jackson Wylie 1929.

Wood, James, B. *The Nobility of the Election of Bayeux: 1463–1666*. Princeton, NJ: Princeton University Press 1980.

Zika, Charles. "Hosts, Processions and Pilgrimages: Controlling the Sacred in Fifteenth Century Germany." *Past and Present* 118 (1988): 25–64.

Index